THE
MALE
SURVIVOR

NATIONAL UNIVERSITY
LIBRARY

THE
MALE
SURVIVOR

The
Impact
of
Sexual
Abuse

Matthew Parynik Mendel

Foreword by Kathleen Coulborn Faller

 SAGE Publications
International Educational and Professional Publisher
Thousand Oaks   London   New Delhi

Copyright © 1995 by Sage Publications, Inc.

All rights reserved. No part of this book may be reproduced or utilized in any form or by any means, electronic or mechanical, including photocopying, recording, or by any information storage and retrieval system, without permission in writing from the publisher.

For information address:

 SAGE Publications, Inc.
2455 Teller Road
Thousand Oaks, California 91320

SAGE Publications Ltd.
6 Bonhill Street
London EC2A 4PU
United Kingdom

SAGE Publications India Pvt. Ltd.
M-32 Market
Greater Kailash I
New Delhi 110 048 India

Printed in the United States of America

Library of Congress Cataloging-in-Publication Data

Mendel, Matthew Parynik.
  The male survivor: the impact of sexual abuse / Matthew Parynik Mendel.
    p.   cm.
  Includes bibliographical references (pp. 217–229) and index.
  ISBN 0-8039-5441-7. — ISBN 0-8039-5442-5 (pbk.)
    1. Adult child sexual abuse victims—United States—Case studies.
  2. Male sexual abuse victims—United States—Case studies.   3. Child
  sexual abuse—United States—Case studies.   I. Title.
  HV6570.7.M46   1995
  362.7′64′0973—dc20   94-31778

95 96 97 98 99 10 9 8 7 6 5 4 3 2 1

Sage Production Editor: Astrid Virding

The Male Survivor *is dedicated to the men who participated in my study, and to male survivors of childhood sexual abuse everywhere.*

Contents

Foreword

In the early 20th century child sexual abuse was considered a very rare occurrence, and most accusations were thought to derive from the child's wish to have sex with an adult, rather than from actual abuse. In the 1950s and 1960s, a small number of case studies about incest involving fathers and daughters appeared, but often the writers blamed the victim or the mother rather than the father for the abuse.

In 1974, federal legislation was passed that led to mandatory reporting of suspected child maltreatment by professionals involved with children. Although initially most of the cases identified involved physical maltreatment, as time passed increasing numbers of sexual abuse cases were reported. Thus, in 1976, only 6,000 cases of sexual abuse were referred to protective services agencies in the United States, 3% of maltreatment reports. In 1986, however, 132,000 cases were identified, almost 16% of reports, a 22-fold increase over a 10-year period (American Association for the Protection of Children, 1988). This trend continues so that in 1992 almost 500,000 sexual abuse cases were reported, these making up 17% of maltreatment cases (McCurdy & Daro, 1993).

Concurrent with these system changes were the activities of the feminist movement, which brought attention to the plight of sexually victimized girls. Moreover, researchers began to undertake studies of college students and community-based populations of adults, asking them about sexual victimization as children.

These efforts focused primarily on female victims and found the overwhelming majority of offenders to be men. Only about 20% of victims reported to protective service agencies were boys (American Association for the Protection of Children, 1988), and many prevalence studies did not survey males (e.g., Russell, 1983; Wyatt, 1985). When men were included, although study findings vary greatly, the rates of victimization for men were about half (3%-31%) of those for women (6%-62%) (Peters, Wyatt, & Finkelhor, 1986). Moreover, when men described their sexual contact with adults as children, they often reported less trauma than women (Finkelhor, 1979) and might not characterize the experience as abusive, especially if the offender was a female (Risin & Koss, 1987).

In the past 5 or 6 years, however, clinicians have begun to recognize that these findings may be misleading. The increasing knowledge and publicity about sexual abuse has caused men victimized as children to seek treatment.

What is being learned about the population of male survivors suggests that the impact of sexual abuse upon them can be severe and pervasive. Such observations are reflected in the small number of books and articles about male survivors (e.g., Bolton, Norris, & MacEachron, 1989; Grubman-Black, 1990; Hunter, 1990a, 1990b, 1990c; Lew, 1988; Sanders, 1991; Thomas, 1989). These works are instructive for the clinician but somewhat parochial, being based primarily on the individual writer's experience. Moreover, there have been almost no efforts to collect information systematically about male survivors.

Matt Mendel's work represents a significant contribution to our knowledge about sexual abuse of boys and about men who were so harmed by child sexual abuse that they have sought treatment. It is the first national study of male survivors and therefore is really a pioneering effort. The results of the study are sobering. The extent of sexual abuse these men endured is dismaying, in terms of types of sexual activity and number and gender of perpetrators. The reported impact on their sexuality and other aspects of functioning destroys myths about the invulnerability of male victims. These men needed and continue to need extensive treatment. This book is not just about the numbers, however. Included as well are case histories of men who were interviewed intensively. These vignettes add depth to our appreciation of the impact of sexual abuse on boys and men.

This is a landmark study that will lead us into the 21st century in our endeavor to understand and address the phenomenon of sexual abuse.

Kathleen Coulborn Faller, Ph.D.
The University of Michigan

Preface

This book includes an original study of male survivors of childhood sexual abuse, based on questionnaire responses of 124 men and semi-structured clinical interviews with 9 of those men. The first five chapters of this work are intended to provide a context within which the study may be read. The introductory chapter presents a brief history of the topic of sexual abuse and describes the "lens" through which this topic will be examined. Chapter 2 explores factors that stand in the way of recognizing male sexual abuse. Chapter 3 surveys the literature on the prevalence, incidence, and descriptive characteristics of male sexual abuse. Chapter 4 reviews major conceptual frameworks regarding the long-term impact of sexual abuse. Chapter 5 reviews the literature on the short- and long-term impact of sexual abuse on boys.

Presentation of the study itself begins with Chapter 6, which describes the methodology. Chapter 7 presents the men who participated in the study and describes their demographic characteristics, psychiatric histories, current psychosocial functioning, and the characteristics of the abuse they experienced. Chapter 8 examines the relationship between these abuse characteristics and adult psychosocial functioning, and suggests avenues for future research. Chapter 9 focuses on the interview portion of this study as it examines aspects of abuse and recovery of particular salience to male survivors and explores implications of these findings for treatment.

There are two purposes for this book. The first is "clinical." I hope to reduce the stigma and isolation that male survivors of childhood sexual abuse experience. The depth and intensity of the stigma surrounding abuse have often been noted.

A consistent finding in clinical as well as research interventions with incest survivors is that, for several reasons, there is enormous difficulty around disclosure. These reasons include the incest taboo itself, threats directed at the victim should he or she tell, and the utilization of dissociation and denial as defenses against the overwhelming and disorganizing experience of abuse. As a result of the efforts of researchers, clinicians, and survivors who have called attention to the experience of female survivors, I believe that the stigmatization associated with sexual abuse has been somewhat reduced. As more publicity is afforded the topic of sexual abuse, ever-increasing numbers of women recognize their experiences as less rare than they had once believed. As long as the experience of the male survivor is virtually unexplored, the taboo against disclosure will remain as fierce as ever. A primary goal of this work is, therefore, to contribute to an atmosphere in which more men are able to join their female counterparts and embark on the road to recovery. Thankfully, this process appears to be gaining momentum. Over the years I have been involved in this research, the sexual victimization of boys has received increasing attention, both in academic circles and in the popular media.

The second purpose is to add to the state of knowledge about male survivors of child sexual abuse. It should be noted from the outset that this work is specifically about the impact of *childhood* sexual abuse upon males. Research on the sexual assault of adult males is cited but not systematically reviewed. It is hoped that the present study, with its multimethod format of questionnaire and semi-structured clinical interview, will contribute to the understanding of male survivors.

Conceptual frameworks regarding the long-term sequelae of childhood sexual abuse are examined in order to determine to what extent they are appropriate to male experience and to what extent these models must be modified to accommodate male experience. Modifications and revisions of these frameworks are proposed. Especially little is known about the impact of various characteristics of sexual abuse upon males. Browne and Finkelhor (1986) and Conte and Schuerman (1987) have addressed these issues with respect to female victims, but to date there have been no systematic studies of long-term variations in outcome depending on differences in factors related to the abuse for male victims. A central focus of the study contained in the second portion of this book is therefore upon within-group comparisons to assess the effects of such variables as relationship to perpetrator, victim's age at time of abuse, duration and severity of abuse, number of abusers, the existence of physical abuse along with the sexual abuse, and the use of alcohol or other drugs by the perpetrator.

Interspersed throughout this book are the "life-stories" of six men. The histories presented here represent distillations of lengthy clinical interviews, the focus of which was upon the impact of abuse on the lives of these men. How do men who were sexually victimized during childhood experience their abuse? How do they understand its impact on various aspects of their lives? How have they dealt with their abuse and worked to overcome it? These pages chronicle the particulars of the abuse and other aspects of the respondents' lives fairly briefly, and emphasize the various sequelae of the abuse. It should be noted that a particular life-story is not intended to correlate specifically with the chapter it follows or precedes. Rather, the stories are intended to illustrate and bring to life typical experiences of male survivors of childhood sexual abuse. Prominent themes that emerged from these interviews are discussed in Chapter 9. Details of the interview procedure are provided in Chapter 6. Nine men were interviewed. These six histories were selected in order to depict a wide range of abuse histories. The sample of nine men, however, did not include anyone who was solely abused by someone outside of his family. Therefore, all of the histories involve intrafamilial abuse. One of the six men, "Ben," experienced "emotional incest" (Love, 1990) rather than overt or covert *sexual* activity. Three of the 124 men in the total sample explicitly identified themselves as survivors of ritual abuse. One of these men, "Ned," enclosed a brief piece of prose describing his childhood experience. I have included a verbatim transcript. (The topic of ritual child abuse is not explored here. I believe it to be an extremely important area that demands increased study.) All names and other identifying information have been changed in order to protect the confidentiality of the participants.

This book would not have been possible without the support of a number of people and organizations. This volume, and the study included herein, grew out of my doctoral dissertation at the University of Michigan. For their advice, encouragement, and constructive criticism, I would like to thank the members of my dissertation committee, Eric Bermann, Ph.D., Chair; Sallie R. Churchill, Ph.D.; Kathleen Coulborn Faller, Ph.D.; and Christopher Peterson, Ph.D. Generous financial support was provided by the following organizations: Horace H. Rackham School of Graduate Studies; the Interdisciplinary Training Program in Child Abuse and Neglect; the Department of Psychology, and the Center for the Child and the Family, at the University of Michigan; and the Society for the Psychological Study of Social Issues, Division Nine of the American Psychological Association. I received invaluable assistance with data analysis from Ken Guire of the Center for Statistical Consultation and Research at the University of Michigan and Anthony J. Asciutto, M.P.H., M.A., currently of Harvard Community Health Plan. For their help in transforming this work from a dissertation into a book, I would like to thank the reviewers of this volume, Kathleen Coulborn Faller, Ph.D., Larry Morris, Ph.D., and Jon Conte, Ph.D., Consulting Editor; and C. Terry Hendrix, Senior Editor at Sage Publications; Kristin Bergstad, Copy Editor; Astrid Virding, Senior Production Editor; Dale Grenfell and Tricia Bennett, Editorial Assistants; and Marjorie Rigg, Indexer. I would also like to thank my parents, Arthur and Sara Mendel, for their inspiration, encouragement, and support. Thank you, S. P. Mendel, for helping me relax, and finally, a heartfelt thanks to my wife, Cynthia, without whom I could not have survived the research process, for all of her insight, assistance, advice, patience, and love.

1 Examining the Lens

Masculinity and Child Sexual Abuse

The past 15 years have witnessed an explosion of interest in the topic of sexual abuse (Bolton, Morris, & MacEachron, 1989; Conte, 1982; Finkelhor, 1984) and a proliferation of conceptual frameworks aimed at explicating its impact on its victims. The vast majority of writings in this area, however, have been based upon female experience. As Faller (1989) writes with regard to intrafamilial sexual abuse, "historically, girl victims of incest by father figures have been the primary focus of inquiry and concern" (p. 281). With few exceptions, only in the past half-decade have serious efforts been made to evaluate the prevalence and incidence of male child sexual abuse or to assess its impact. Similarly, conceptual frameworks are, by and large, predicated upon clinical and research interventions with female survivors. The present work explores the phenomenon of sexual maltreatment of male children in an effort to redress this imbalance.

Male survivors of child sexual abuse constitute an extremely under-identified, underserved, and, all too often, misunderstood population. The lack of recognition of this phenomenon is, I believe, determined largely by a constellation of societal myths or beliefs regarding what it means to be male and by complementary myths or beliefs regarding what

1

it means to be female. Before turning to these specific notions, I should briefly like to discuss postmodernist theories, which provide a backdrop and a sort of litmus test for my thinking on this topic.

Postmodernism and the Male Survivor

As I understand this challenging, subtle, and intricate philosophy, postmodernism and constructivist theories of epistemology assert that "objective reality" or "absolute truth" do not exist; instead, one must constantly bear in mind the perspectives, assumptions, and subjectivity of the observer. "Without context, there is no meaning" (Hare-Mustin & Maracek, 1990, p. 1). "We do not discover reality, we invent it. Our experience does not directly reflect what is out there but is a selecting, ordering, and organizing of it" (Hare-Mustin & Maracek, 1990, p. 27). The eye of the beholder inevitably influences the nature of the thing beheld. Thus, as Hare-Mustin and Maracek (1990) state in their discussion of postmodernism and gender, "differences between women and men, by and large, are made; that is, gender is not a natural category based on essential differences between the sexes. . . . Gender is an invention of human societies, a feat of imagination and industry" (pp. 3-4). In other words, the notions we hold of "masculinity" and "femininity" are not inherent, innate, or immutable; they are, instead, socioculturally derived. I believe this fact to be critical to any attempt at understanding males' experience of sexual abuse: A central, and uniquely male, aspect of their reaction to sexual abuse is their struggle to understand, overcome, and integrate into their selves experiences antithetical to our cultural notions of maleness.

A second tenet of postmodernist theory is that information is power. Those who control the means of production and dissemination of information possess enormous power in that their subjective understandings of reality become diffused across society. Thus the assumptions, preconceptions, and mythology of the dominant culture tend to become the "reality" of the society that includes that dominant culture. Within the context of gender, a mythology that benefits males tends to hold sway. When one looks specifically at abused males, however, the issue becomes much more complicated than this simplistic rendering would indicate. Is a male struggling to overcome the impact of his childhood abuse truly aided by the notion that men are competent, strong, and able to protect themselves? by the belief that men inevitably want sex? or by the idea that an adolescent boy who interacts sexually with an adult female is to be envied?

A final caveat before turning to a review of attitudes and beliefs regarding sexual abuse: The term *society* is used with great frequency in the present work and in other writings that explore the sociocultural context of abuse. Phrases such as *societal beliefs* and *societal constructions* are ubiquitous. It seems to me that "society" often becomes externalized and reified, as if it could be detached from its constituents. We, as researchers, are society. We, as clinicians, are society. We, as survivors, are society. We, as supporters, are society. We, as perpetrators, are society. Thus, an astute writer or therapist may note the negative impact upon a male survivor of the societal myth that men are able to protect themselves. The greatest tragedy of such myths, however, is that the survivor himself, as a component of his society, is likely to subscribe to them. He does not simply fear the condemnation or scorn of those around him, thus bearing the burden of the secret of his abuse. Instead, he lives with the belief in his own failing as a man due to his "inability" to live up to the vaunted standard of the "ideal man."

Similarly, as clinicians, it is incumbent upon us to examine our own assumptions and beliefs regarding sexual abuse. I believe that a significant proportion of responsibility for the underreporting of male sexual abuse must be placed on the doorsteps of professionals. Until very recently— and, unfortunately, to some extent even today—professionals have subscribed implicitly or explicitly to a fundamental misconception in the area of sexual abuse: "Abuse doesn't happen to boys." As postmodernist or constructivist theories of epistemology imply, we tend to see what we expect to see or are open to seeing. Just as reporting (and prevalence estimates) of female sexual abuse rose precipitously following the recognition of its existence, there needs to be a parallel reframing of the abuse issue in order to enable men to come forward with their abuse histories.

It is of equal importance that professionals rethink their assumptions regarding abuse in order to recognize that men are, in fact, coming forward, albeit with disguised or masked presentations of their abuse histories. Professionals, including therapists, school personnel, and those in the criminal justice system, tend not to recognize sexual abuse in boys. This, I believe, is largely due to a schema of sexual abuse that primarily encompasses female victims. There is an allied notion, similarly based on societal (mis)conceptions of masculinity, in which males are more readily recognized as victimizers than as victims. The identification of past abuse history—for the minority of men fortunate enough to have such experience acknowledged at all—often comes about only subsequent to identification of current perpetrator status. The latter category resonates with our mythology regarding men and is, therefore, accommodated, whereas the former is overlooked because of its dissonance. We are primed and ready to recognize male perpetrators but turn a blind eye to male victims. All of us who are in a position to recognize male abuse survivors as such and thus assist them in their process of recovery must examine our belief system and expand our notions of abuse in order to incorporate their experience (see Kasl [1990] for a similar argument).

Recognition of Sexual Abuse:
A Brief History

The 20th century has seen a series of shifts in attitudes and beliefs regarding incest and sexual abuse. For much of the century, the existence of these phenomena has been denied or severely minimized. Weinberg (1955), for example, estimated the incidence of incest to be one in a million. More recently, the *Comprehensive Textbook of Psychiatry* (Freedman, Kaplan, & Sadock, 1975) made the same estimate. One source of this denial was Sigmund Freud's rejection of his initial theory of the etiology of psychopathology. In his early works (Breuer & Freud, 1893-1895/1955; Freud, 1896/1962), Freud described female patients' recollections in therapy of childhood incestuous interactions with their fathers or other adult men. His first understanding of such events was straightforward: These women were recalling repressed traumatic memories of actual early-life events. Such events, the anxiety they evoked, and the consequent necessity to repress them, resulted in later psychopathology. As is true of many other aspects of his theories, Freud was far ahead of his time in his initial formulation, anticipating later theorists by 70 or so years. Freud reversed his field, however, asserting that his patients' recollections were not of actual events, but rather represented childhood libidinal fantasies (Freud, 1905/1953). There has been much speculation regarding the reasons for the change in Freud's thinking from his early "seduction" theory to his later positing of the Oedipus complex. These theories will not be reviewed here (see, for example, Masson [1984], Miller [1980/1984], and Rush [1980] for discussions of this shift and its causes).

Suffice it to say that Freud's rejection of his early theory has had profound effects upon the treatment of incest survivors (Finkelhor, 1984; Herman, 1981; Masson, 1984). Through his development of the psychoanalytic method of free association, he created a means by which survivors could access repressed memories of childhood events. Because the theory of the Oedipus complex has guided so much of psychoanalysis and psychoanalytic therapy, however, such recollections were often assumed to be derivative of childhood wishes rather than memories of actual events. As discussed earlier, a basic tenet of postmodernism is that what we observe is influenced by what we think. Psychoanalytic therapists throughout much of this century have, therefore, been likely to misconstrue indications of actual, rather than fantasied, childhood sexual interaction. An early supervisor of mine, a woman of about 60 with a classic psychoanalytic bent, noted with wonder the abundance of cases at our clinic that included a history of sexual abuse. She stated that she had never had such a case in her own career as a therapist. It is possible, of course, that she had simply never come across such a case (or that incest survivors gravitated away from her due to her approach). I think it more likely, however, given the prevalence of sexual abuse, that the lens through which she viewed her clientele led her to overlook indications of sexual abuse. Ronald Krug (1989), a psychoanalytic therapist, discussed eight clinical cases in which adult males reported incest experiences with their mothers. Krug acknowledged that he initially disbelieved these reports, assuming them to be fantasies rather than accurate memories.

Recently, the argument has been made that things have gone too far, that our earlier blindness has been replaced with credulity. The concept of "false memories" has been forwarded (see Loftus [1993] for a review of this topic), and allegations of childhood sexual abuse have been likened to the Salem Witch Trials (Gardner, 1991). There can be no doubt that instances of false allegations have occurred; the trauma and pain resulting to the unjustly accused should not be underestimated. I believe it also to be beyond doubt, however, that sexual abuse remains more of an underidentified than an overreported phenomenon. Studies of the prevalence of childhood sexual abuse of boys, for example, which are reviewed in

Chapter 3, suggest that between one in six and one in eight boys experience sexual maltreatment. Estimates based on case reports, in contrast, are in the one-in-a-thousand range.

One study that appears effectively to refute claims that many or most "repressed" memories of abuse are actually false, is that of Linda Williams (1992). She interviewed adult women who, during their childhoods, had reported sexual abuse and had been taken to a hospital emergency room for treatment and collection of forensic evidence. Details of the abuse were recorded at that time as part of a National Institutes of Mental Health study. Seventeen years later, Williams contacted these women and found that an astounding 38% did not recall the abuse! (More than half of these women reported a different instance of sexual abuse.) In other words, even in cases where the maltreatment was severe enough to result in a hospital referral, more than a third of the survivors had repressed the memories. Similarly, Briere and Conte (1993) found that 59% of individuals in treatment for sexual abuse had experienced periods in their lives during which they did not recall the abuse. A further implication of the Williams (1992) and the Briere and Conte (1993) studies is that even recent prevalence estimates may understate the true incidence of sexual abuse, because adult survivors may indicate that no maltreatment occurred. Herman and Schatzow (1987) conducted a study of women in group therapy who recalled childhood incest, often after a long period of repression, and concluded that "the presumption that most patients' report of childhood sexual abuse can be ascribed to fantasy no longer appears tenable" (p. 11). Of the women in their study, 74% were able to obtain confirmation of the sexual abuse from another source (the perpetrator, other family members, physical evidence such as diaries or photographs, or discovery that another child had been abused by the same perpetrator). An additional 9% reported evidence strongly indicative of siblings having been sexually abused, but did not inquire about this directly. The majority of those who did not obtain any corroborating evidence made no effort to do so. Only 6% attempted to have their recollections confirmed and were unable to do so. Herman and Schatzow's study strongly supports the position that false memories represent a relatively small portion of claims of childhood sexual abuse.

I believe that the underrecognition of childhood sexual abuse is especially pronounced for males, who appear to be far less likely than females to identify, acknowledge, or report their abuse experiences (see Chapters

2 and 3 for a discussion of these issues). There is little to be gained from false claims of sexual abuse. This is particularly true for men, who experience profound shame and stigma regarding their experiences of victimization. I found all of the men interviewed for this study to be credible. I accept as true their statements regarding their experiences and believe that they were, in fact, sexually mistreated. Moreover—although I believe that sexual abuse, like any issue, should be examined with appropriate skepticism—in light of the gross underestimation of the prevalence of male sexual victimization, I view efforts to cast doubt on the experiences of male survivors to be a regressive and regrettable development.

The status of male sexual abuse now, in its clamoring for recognition, is like the status of sexual abuse more generally throughout much of this century. The consensus once was that childhood sexual abuse barely existed. Incest was particularly underidentified and sexual offenders were thought typically to be strangers to their victims. Gradually, however, the facts of incest and child sexual abuse forced themselves upon the awareness of the public and of professionals. The present research, and others like it aimed at increasing awareness of the sexual maltreatment of boys, stands on the shoulders of a number of landmark works. Writers such as Susan Forward (1978), Karen Meiselman (1979), David Finkelhor (1979), and Judith Herman (1981) argued persuasively that incest and child sexual abuse are pervasive, common problems with long-lasting negative effects on those subjected to it. Feminist scholars brought attention to the imbalances of power within the family as well as within the greater society and the role of such power imbalances in the abuse of women (Brownmiller, 1975; Millett, 1969; Russell, 1986). Another significant force in the burgeoning recognition of child sexual abuse was the work of Kempe and his colleagues (Kempe, Silverman, Steele, Droegemiller, & Silver, 1962) on battered children. Though their initial focus was upon physical rather than sexual maltreatment, these physicians brought to the public eye the extent of harm and malevolence that occurs within what had been considered the sanctity of the home. This research did much to set the stage for the later recognition of incest.

By the mid-1970s child sexual abuse had begun "to appear on the agenda of mental health and child welfare professionals" (Finkelhor, 1986, p. 10). Clinical and research interventions with young victims and adult survivors of child sexual abuse proliferated. In the 1980s, several models of the long-term impact of abuse appeared (Finkelhor & Browne, 1985; Gelinas, 1983; Herman, 1981). Virtually all writings in the area, however, were exclusively on female victimization. The perspective of the helping professions had progressed from blind to one-eyed with respect to sexual abuse. It was as if a qualifier had been affixed to the recognition of sexual abuse: "OK, it exists, but it only happens to little girls." The primary exceptions were case studies, which did little to correct the notion that the sexual abuse of boys was extremely rare (see, for example, Awad [1976], Dixon, Arnold, & Calestro [1978], and Shengold [1980]). Sarrell and Masters (1982) make an astute point regarding how research is influenced by what we *do not* ask. They note that the

> failure of the health care professions to recognize the possibility that a man can be sexually assaulted has influenced research on the subject; there has been none. Two of the original Kinsey investigators were asked if they were aware of any male sexual-assault victims in the Kinsey research population. They confirmed that there were none they knew of but also stated that they had never asked any man if he had been sexually assaulted. Other authorities in the field of sex research were contacted, none of whom have ever included such a question in their surveys. (p. 129)

Recently, the state of abuse research has evolved further, and male survivors have begun to receive greater recognition. In addition to case-report studies of male victims, a number of books have been published on the topic of male sexual abuse in the past few years (Bolton et al., 1989; Grubman-Black, 1990; Hunter, 1990a, 1990b; Lew, 1990b). Violato and Genuis (1993) provide a brief but thorough review of issues in research on male child sexual abuse. However, the preconception that sexual abuse is something that happens only to little girls maintains, I believe, a rather tenacious hold on the implicit perspective of those within the field. Male survivors continue to feel underrecognized and underserved. Although it is likely that females are, in fact, abused more frequently than males even after the underreporting of male abuse is taken into account, the sexual maltreatment of boys is clearly not a rare phenomenon. Current estimates range as high as one in five to one in seven males (Finkelhor, Hotaling, Lewis, & Smith, 1990; Fromuth & Burkhart, 1987, 1989). The overwhelming focus of the sexual abuse field upon females does not serve male survivors well. Similarly, the seemingly innocuous pattern of referring to victims/survivors as "she" and perpetrators/offenders as "he," which appears to be almost universal in writings in this area, invalidates the experience of the male survivor. The next chapter looks in greater depth at the sources of the underrecognition of male victims.

Ron's Story

Ron is a 38-year-old single heterosexual chiropractor. He is the second of five children, with one brother and three sisters. Ron's parents separated when he was 6 years old. He was frequently physically abused by his father, who was an alcoholic. When Ron was 10, his mother became bedridden with cancer, which she died of when he was 13 years old. Upon her diagnosis, he was placed in an orphanage, where he remained until her death, at which point he was adopted.

Ron was sexually abused by his adoptive father, Glen. The abuse included fondling and oral sex and took place several times per week over a 3- or 4-year period. In addition, Ron was forcibly undressed by a female stranger at age six. As is characteristic of the men interviewed, however, this extrafamilial incident was not seen as a significant event. Ron's emphasis during our interview was on the ongoing sexual relationship with his adoptive father. Glen was the first man to show any affection for Ron. Initially, he felt loved for the first time in his life. This was his "dream in life, all (he) had ever wanted." Glen was everything he admired and aspired to be: outgoing, smart, and likable. He imitated Glen and realizes now that he was desperately searching for a male role model, because he did not identify with his alcoholic, abusive father. He had been very independent and self-reliant from an early age, but longed for a father. With the development of the father-son relationship with Glen, he felt that the "sky was the limit."

The sexual abuse shattered that hope for Ron. As he put it, "All my dreams were stopped." He rebelled against everything Glen promoted. He became withdrawn, avoided sports and the arts, and started to do poorly in school. Ron now has minimal contact with his adoptive father, visiting about once every other year, and occasionally talking with him by telephone. He spoke with him briefly about the abuse, and said that Glen stated that he hated himself for what he did. With the help of therapy and supportive friends, he feels ready to discuss the abuse with Glen in greater depth. His hope is that the two of them can return to where they started, a time when, he believes, Glen loved him for himself, rather than due to his physical attractiveness. He stated that all he has ever wanted is to be close with someone. Despite the enormous impact Ron feels the abuse has had upon his life, Glen remains a largely positive figure for Ron. He was "the father I would have liked to have had." Foremost in his mind, Glen is the person who gave him the love and affection he had never received in his own home, and who provided him with a role model after whom he could pattern himself.

Ron has been in therapy for 2 years, with an additional year spent in a group for male incest survivors. He feels that until recently he has denied his past, but that with the help of therapy he is becoming able to find an identity that incorporates this past. He noted that as a child, he found the sexual interactions with Glen to be very distressing and confusing, but that he did not label them as abusive until he began therapy. He reports considerable amnesia about these events, and indicated that he can only clearly recall a few incidents, though he knows the abuse to have continued over a 3- to 4-year period.

He feels that his childhood sexual interactions have had a profound impact upon his life. As he put it, had the sexual abuse not occurred, he would have been a totally different person. He has had a tremendous amount of shame and embarrassment about the abuse and, until recently, felt almost incapable of discussing it. Until college, he did not disclose the abuse to anyone. Each person he has told has responded positively and supportively and he now feels increasingly comfortable discussing it. He likened disclosure of the abuse to the experience of a gay person "coming out of the closet." He "stuffed" all of his feelings because of the necessity of keeping his "shameful" secret hidden. Until recent years, he reports being "emotionally deceptive," acting as if things were fine inside but remaining guarded about his true emotions. Recently, with the help of therapy, he has begun to feel better about himself and to recognize that his problems are largely due to something that has been done to him, which removes much of the guilt and self-blame that have plagued him.

Much of Ron's focus in our interview was on boundaries. A critical dynamic in his abuse was the violation of appropriate boundaries and the consequent confusion between affection and sex. He sees much of his current struggle as an attempt to maintain boundaries between himself and others, while at the same time meeting his needs for emotional and physical gratification. He reports a tendency to be very passive in relationships and not to express his needs. He stated that he never initiates sex, but simply responds to others' initiative. He thinks that he is often manipulated emotionally within relationships due to this passivity, and views this dynamic as a repetition of his passivity and manipulation vis-à-vis his adoptive father. He desperately longs for more closeness with women, but doesn't feel able to be sufficiently open with them about his feelings and vulnerability.

At this point in his life, Ron thinks that his abuse history has its most deleterious impact upon his sexuality. He stated that his victimization "devalued sex. . . . (As a result,) sex is not a wonderful thing to do with someone; it just seems strange." He views his relationship with Glen as his first experience with emotional closeness and sees it as having been ruined by the intrusion of sex. He continues to long for intimacy and to perceive sex as an intrusion upon that quest. He has several close friendships with women and resents the sense that they inevitably become interested in him sexually.

His feelings about men have also been strongly affected by his abuse. He indicated that he is often scared by men, especially by older men, and stated that as a teenager he generally associated with younger boys. A part of him wants to be a "traditional male," by which he means strong and assertive. He feels uncomfortable around that sort of men, however. Ron has had few close friendships with men, feeling more at ease around women. Both men and women often think that he's gay, which he attributes to his gentle nature and the fact that he doesn't pressure women to have sex. He generally feels more comfortable with gay men than with straight men. As was the case with respect to women, he reported that a number of the men with whom he has developed friendships were interested in him sexually. He wants so desperately to be close to people that he finds it difficult to tell these men that he is straight.

Ron sees his career as a chiropractor as an adaptive outcome of his abuse. He views himself as providing for others what he wishes had been provided him—warm, healthy, physical contact in the context of safe boundaries. He hopes that his practice will eventually evolve into more general counseling. He began practicing massage/chiropractic therapy following time spent in dance therapy and in a dance troupe, each of which provided the sort of safe physical contact he sought. Ron believes that the abuse has had some positive effects upon him. It has made him more sensitive to the victimization of others. He described himself as passionately and actively feminist, antiracist, and antihomophobic. He said that he "can't tolerate it when people put gays down or see women as objects because (he) was treated as an object (him)self."

I asked Ron how he thought things would be different for him if he had not been physically abused prior to his sexual abuse. He sees the former as priming him for the latter. Without the physical abuse, and with a more positive relationship with his parents, he thinks he would not have let Glen touch him. "I would have known the boundaries, I would have been stronger, not so starved for attention . . . I would have recognized the difference between sex and affection and not allowed the sexual abuse to occur." He indicated that he had never received anything from his father, while from his mother he received only her dependence and emotional distress.

Finally, Ron wished to express his theory of the transmission of abuse. He said that men can't express their pain and grief and that they see themselves as the oppressors rather than the oppressed in society. Therefore, they identify themselves as oppressors and end up as perpetrators. He sees men as lashing out in anger because they cannot express their pain. Women see themselves as victims and end up being victimized again. One of the aspects of his own life that he has struggled to understand is his sense of repeated victimization, of being manipulated in relationships and providing for others' needs rather than his own. He thinks that this may be due to other factors in his life, such as his mother's earlier dependence on him or the terror associated with the physical abuse.

2 The Underidentification
of Male Sexual Abuse

Recognition of sexual molestation in a child is dependent upon the individual's inherent willingness to entertain the possibility that the condition may exist.

Sgroi, 1975, p. 18

The various beliefs that impede recognition of the full scope of the sexual abuse of males may be divided into two categories. The first category comprises notions of masculinity that make it difficult to recognize males as victims. These culturally derived ideas influence men not to see the sexual interactions in their childhood as abusive and/or to refrain from reporting these incidents. They are also held, implicitly or explicitly, by society at large and by helping professionals. Subscription to these beliefs distorts the perspective of professionals in the field of child abuse, thus making them less likely to recognize sexual abuse of boys even when confronted with evidence of such maltreatment. The second category consists of analogous beliefs about femininity that obscure female perpetration. Both male victims and the society of which they are a part tend to deny or minimize female perpetration and to view abuse as an inevitably male phenomenon.

Each of these notions, as is true of stereotypes more generally, contains within it a kernel of truth. Thus, it would appear on the basis of prevalence and incidence studies of victims and perpetrators (Finkelhor, 1979; Finkelhor et al., 1990) that girls are, in fact, sexually abused more frequently than boys and that men perpetrate sexual abuse more frequently than women. Belief in the male abuser-female victim pattern of sexual abuse has become paradigmatic within the field, however, thus obscuring recognition of boy victims and female perpetrators. As was the case with female victims some 15 to 20 years ago (Finkelhor, 1984), increased attention to boy victims has recently resulted in higher reporting rates. It will be necessary for professionals in the area of child abuse to continue to update their beliefs regarding child abuse in order to recognize the full extent of the sexual abuse of males.

The first portion of this chapter examines beliefs that contribute to the underreporting of male sexual abuse. The second part of the chapter examines the often-related notions that stand as obstacles in the way of recognition of female perpetration. Sexual abuse of children of either gender often fails to be reported or recognized. The same factors that prevent disclosure in female victims—the fear of reprisal; the wish to keep the family together or not to be blamed for its dissolution, in cases of intrafamilial abuse; amnesia or dissociation in response to the abuse; the fact that warmth, attention, and affection may also be received from the perpetrator; and so forth—have similar impact upon male victims. These factors have been amply reviewed. What follows is an analysis of factors with particular influence upon male victims.

Underrecognition of Males as Victims

Several researchers have discussed aspects of male socialization that contribute to the underreporting of their experiences of sexual victimization (Dimock, 1988; Faller, 1989; Finkelhor, 1984; Groth, 1979a, 1979b; Lew, 1990b; Nasjleti, 1980; Neilsen, 1983; Sepler, 1990; Struve,

1990; Vander Mey, 1988). A number of studies of abused males have found that the vast majority had never before told anyone about their abuse experiences and that boys were more reluctant to report sexual abuse than were girls (Finkelhor, 1984; Fritz, Stoll, & Wagner, 1981; Johnson & Shrier, 1985; Knopp, 1986; Landis, 1956; Myers, 1989; Nasjleti, 1980; Neilsen, 1983; Porter, 1986; Rogers & Terry, 1984; Swift, 1979). Myers (1989), for example, described 14 adult men whom he had seen clinically, each of whom had been sexually abused in childhood and/or sexually assaulted in adulthood. None of the 14 had disclosed the victimization at the time of its occurrence, and only 4 had told anyone about it prior to the disclosure in therapy.

Several recurrent themes appear in research into male socialization and its impact on reporting of sexual abuse in childhood. These themes are summarized in Table 2.1. First, males are socialized to be, and to experience themselves as, powerful, active, and competent, rather than as passive, helpless, or victimized (see Franklin [1984], Ingham [1984], Maccoby & Jacklin [1974], and Pleck [1981] for general discussions of male socialization). Therefore, the experience of victimization is highly dissonant and threatening to males. Confronting and acknowledging sexual abuse poses a major threat to a male's sense of masculinity. A male victim may assume that he is "less of a man" due to his inability to protect himself and to his experience in a helpless, victimized role. Men may equate being abused with being weak, homosexual, or female (Dimock, 1988; Nasjleti, 1980; Pleck, 1981; Vander Mey, 1988). Lew (1990b) writes that, "If men aren't to be victims, then victims aren't men" (p. 63). As Robert Bly (1990) writes: "Men are taught over and over when they are boys that a wound that hurts is shameful. A wound that stops you from continuing is a girlish wound. He who is truly a man keeps walking, dragging his guts behind" (p. 42). Dimock (1988) notes that males "have been socialized from early childhood to hide physical and emotional vulnerability" (p. 204). He sees this factor as the primary source of the underreporting of male abuse. Struve (1990) emphasizes the capacity to protect oneself as a critical aspect of male self-image and suggests that the inability to do so is among the most traumatic aspects of the victimization experience for males. In what he terms the male ethic of self-reliance, Finkelhor (1984) states that males are socialized to act tough and invulnerable, to be "big boys" and not to reveal doubts, fears, and weaknesses. Even if the abuse is recognized as such by the victim, it is still inordinately

Table 2.1 Masculinity and the Underrecognition of Males as Victims

Male socialization as powerful, active, competent, rather than
    passive, helpless, and victimized

Male avoidance of recognizing weakness or helplessness in oneself

Belief in males' indiscriminate and constant sexual willingness:
    Corollary that sexual interaction with older females is benign
    or positive

Males' primarily cognitive (as opposed to affective) orientation

The stigma of homosexuality and belief that sexual abuse may signify
    that the victim is gay

Fear-based denial or distortion of male victimization by
    predominately male disseminators of information

difficult for him to tell others because of the perceived stigma and feared negative response such disclosure would evoke (Nasjleti, 1980). Nasjleti argues that the belief that boys are strong and responsible leads male victims not to report because they fear they will be blamed or disbelieved.

Second, the male victim is likely to act in such a way so as to avoid seeing himself as a helpless victim. Sepler (1990) asserts that treatment interventions aimed at helping male survivors recognize that the abuse was not their fault and that they were helpless to do anything about it represent an unfortunate carryover from work with female survivors. She argues that perceiving oneself as helpless, as lacking in control, or as a victim is a male's greatest fear. It is largely to escape this self-image that the male victim acts out aggressively or perpetrates abusive acts upon others. In other words, men gravitate toward aggression and activity to avoid an enormously painful state of victimization and helplessness. Only when a man is secure in his competence and power can he hope to integrate or accept his abuse.

An additional set of beliefs regarding male sexuality comprise a third factor in the underrecognition by males of their own victimization and the consequent underreporting of such abuse. These beliefs revolve around a notion that males are, or should be, eternally sexually willing and eager, at least with female partners (Finkelhor, 1984; Gerber, 1990; Lew, 1990b). If this axiom is true, then sexual interaction cannot be abusive and the male must have, in fact, sought it out or at least welcomed it. A related issue is that boys and adolescent males are no different than anyone else in our society in misconstruing sexual interaction with older females as something other than abuse (Fromuth & Burkhart, 1987, 1989; Johnson & Shrier, 1985, 1987; Risin & Koss, 1987; Vander Mey, 1988). (This issue will be discussed in greater depth below, in the section on underrecognition of female perpetrators.) As Fromuth and Burkhart (1987) write, "male sexual socialization encourages men to define sexual experiences as desirable as long as there is no homosexual involvement" (p. 252). These beliefs are compounded by male avoidance of self-perception as victim (Sepler, 1990), as discussed above. Males, in Sepler's view, are likely to welcome the notion that they were in fact willing participants in the sexual activity, because this belief saves them from the trauma of seeing themselves as helpless.

Sarrel and Masters (1982), in a study of males sexually molested by females, attempt to dispel the myth that men cannot become aroused or obtain and sustain an erection amidst force and coercion. The corollary to this myth is that if arousal occurs then the interaction could not have constituted abuse. They state that erections can be forced (see also Finkelhor, 1984, p. 182; Groth, 1979b) and compared this phenomenon with women who report lubrication and orgasms during rape. Sarrel and Masters found that concern surrounding the arousal added enormously to the trauma of the men in their study. These men felt guilty about their response and worried that their arousal indicated that the events were not in fact abusive. A common worry among the men in their study was a sense that "a normal man would have been impotent" at such a time, and their arousal, therefore, indicated that they must be abnormal or homosexual (p. 127).

Gerber (1990) focused on the role of arousal and pleasure in influencing male victims not to perceive themselves as victims or to report their abuse. If sexual arousal occurs or pleasure is obtained, then the victim assumes that he must have actually wanted the sexual interaction. Although this dynamic is common to male and female victim alike, Gerber argues that it is more prominent for males because of the societal belief in male sexual appetite and because of the fact that "for males . . ., unlike females, their arousal is markedly visible" (p. 173). In his experience working with male survivors, Gerber reports that perpetrators often comment on the size of the victim's erection. To the victim, this contraindicates abuse. Gerber refers to this phenomenon as "the myth of complicity" (p. 173). It would appear that this myth exists in various gradations. All males are likely to subscribe to it to some degree, but those abused by females and those for whom the sexual interaction involved arousal or pleasure are likely to assume their complicity more fully.

Hunter (1993) proposes a fourth aspect of male socialization that may obscure recognition of abuse. He asserts that because of their primarily cognitive (as opposed to affective) orientation, men have less access to nonverbal memories. They are less likely than women to tune in to the sensations, feelings, and fleeting images that may lead toward the recovery of repressed childhood trauma.

Homosexual involvement and the stigma of homophobia constitute a fifth factor in the underreporting of male sexual abuse. It appears to be almost universal for male survivors of childhood sexual abuse to have doubts and fears regarding their sexual orientation. In short, they wonder if the abuse means that they are gay (Dimock, 1988; Faller, 1989; Finkelhor, 1984; Lew, 1990b; Nasjleti, 1980; Struve, 1990). This concern does not appear to be limited to those abused by men, but instead crops up in most male survivors. Nasjleti (1980) proposes that the concern over homosexuality is intrinsic to the abuse experience because male socialization includes a denial of helplessness, with passivity equated with homosexuality. In other words, being cast in a role of submission or helplessness may inevitably evoke such doubts. For males abused by men, there appears to be an additional fear that they were chosen on the basis of some indication that they were in fact gay (Dimock, 1988; Lew, 1990b); their concerns over homosexuality are exacerbated to the extent that they assume complicity in the abuse or obtained pleasure or arousal from the sexual interaction. Males abused by women are also prone to doubts regarding sexual orientation. Sexual interaction with older females is treated by our culture as something desirable and enviable (see the section on the cinematic treatment of this phenomenon, below). What does it mean, then, if a boy instead finds such an experience harrowing, painful, and traumatic? One possibility, in his mind, is that he may be gay and did not enjoy the event as a result. Because of the homophobia endemic to our culture a male victim may refrain from disclosure for fear that he will be seen as a homosexual (Nasjleti, 1980; Struve, 1990).

Susan Brownmiller (1975), in her work on the sociocultural bases of rape, suggests a sixth source of the denial or minimization of the sexual victimization of males. She reasons that confronting such abuse is overly threatening to men, who are in charge of the production and dissemination of information. Therefore, instances of male victimization are suppressed, denied, or distorted to appear as if they instead represented abuse of females. Brownmiller cites two examples of this phenomenon. In a chapter entitled "The Myth of the Heroic Rapist," which documents the idealization of rapists in history, she notes that Dean Allen Corll, a serial rapist and murderer, is virtually unknown. Corll, unlike the infamous Richard Speck, Jack the Ripper, and The Boston Strangler, turned to males rather than females for his crimes. Brownmiller argues that Corll has been forgotten for this reason. "What heterosexual man . . . [Brownmiller asks] could safely identify with Corll without at the height of his fantasy slipping a little and becoming for one dread instant that cringing, whimpering naked lad manacled wrist and foot to the makeshift wooden torture board?" (p. 293). Brownmiller also describes the transformation of Gilles De Rais, the real-life Bluebeard, in popular history. Although De Rais raped and murdered between 40 and 100 male children, his legend has metamorphosed into that of "a devilish rake who killed seven wives" (p. 292).

It is easier to recognize a male perpetrator than a male victim. This simple proposition has, I believe, profound ramifications for abused men, for the psychotherapeutic community, and for the field of criminal justice. The cultural stereotype of men as active, violent, and aggressive rather than passive, helpless, or victimized makes it easy to recognize behaviors that fit the former pattern and difficult to perceive the latter. Moreover, if we expect abused boys or male survivors of child sexual abuse to behave just like their female counterparts, we will miss a lot of abused males. The victimization of males is, unfortunately, only likely to come to light through their later sexual offenses, if at all (Ramsey-Klawsnik, 1990b; Sepler, 1990).

Holly Ramsey-Klawsnik (1990b) conducted an archival study of all the child sexual abuse cases that had gone through the Commonwealth of Massachusetts's Department of Protective Services from 1984 to 1989. She found that "girls were four times more likely than boys to be referred based solely on the presence of psycho-social indicators of possible sexual abuse" (p. 1). Reinhart (1987) obtained similar results in his study. In other words, when professionals see a girl in distress, they consider the possibility of sexual victimization. I would argue that boy victims, by contrast, are often seen "simply" as oppositional-defiant, hyperactive, attention-deficient, conduct-disordered, or as some other sort of disruptive behavioral problem. The possibility that sexual maltreatment may contribute to their presentation is inadequately considered. Unlike girls, boys are frequently referred on the basis of initiating sexual activity with other children (Ramsey-Klawsnik, 1990b). A number of studies have indicated that boys are only likely to be identified as incest victims if a sister is first identified (Finkelhor, 1984; Pierce & Pierce, 1985; Vander Mey & Neff, 1982). In short, males tend not to be recognized as victims; it is only when their behavior fits more comfortably into our schemas regarding masculinity that interventions proceed. I am not, of course, suggesting that interventions not ensue when one person aggresses against another, sexually or otherwise; rather, I would argue that fewer such interventions would be necessary if the frame could be enlarged so as to include males as victims.

Fran Sepler (1990) provides a compelling argument for the necessity of expanding the purview of victimology to embrace male as well as female victims. She states that, just "as individuals who cared passionately about the plight of female victims were forced to break through oppressive and stereotypical thinking, suffering derisive and sometimes cruel treatment and bearing the scorn of the majority, the same must now be done for male victims" (p. 73). She reviews the development of victim advocacy from the feminist movement and its focus on (female) rape victims and argues that as a result of this focus, "victimization, and the symptoms and responses to victimization, have been largely defined from the perspective of the adult female rape victim" (p. 75). Sepler calls this process the "feminization of victimization." A parallel process, which I would term the "masculinization of oppression," has also occurred. As Sepler writes, "violence, the central ideological core of rape crisis thinking about rape, came to be viewed as an exclusive province of male culture" (pp. 74-75). With the rape of adult females by adult males as prototype, interpersonal sexual violence came to be seen as exclusively unidirectional, with male as oppressor and female as victim.

Underrecognition of Females as Perpetrators

Just as we see males as abusers rather than as abused, we see females as victims rather than victimizers. In each case, our beliefs about these gender roles blinds us to disconfirming (and discomfiting) examples.

Table 2.2 The Underrecognition of Females as Perpetrators

Self-fulfilling assumption that female perpetration is rare or nonexistent

Denial of female sexuality and aggression

Belief that sexual interaction with older females is benign or positive

Greater leeway given to females than males in their physical interactions
with children

Greater tendency for female perpetration to be intrafamilial

Greater tendency for female perpetration to be covert and subtle

Assumption that female perpetrators act under the initiation or
coercion of male perpetrators

"Overextension" of feminist explanations of child sexual abuse as
stemming from male violence and power differentials between
the sexes

Politically based avoidance of acknowledgment of female perpetration

---

There is no doubt, of course, that males do abuse. It also appears that
males do, in fact, perpetrate sexual offenses more frequently than do
females. The extent of this discrepancy has been called into question,
however (Fritz et al., 1981; Groth, 1979a; Johnson & Shrier, 1987;
Justice & Justice, 1979; Kasl, 1990; Olson, 1990; Ramsey-Klawsnik,
1990a). What is argued here is that preconceptions distort the lens
through which observers of the human condition perceive the question
of abuse. Foremost among these preconceptions are those of males as
abusers, oppressors, and perpetrators, and females as "more sinned
against than sinning." Exaggerated assumptions as to the extremity of this
dichotomy make it all too easy to miss examples that do not fit the pattern.
Beliefs about women that obscure female perpetration (and, thus, a
portion of male victimization) are summarized in Table 2.2.

   Just as the existence of abuse in general and, later, that of boys, was
once denied, so too the presence and prevalence of female perpetrators
appears to have been grossly underestimated. Until very recently, research
on child sexual abuse found perpetrators to be almost uniformly male.
Even when the attention of the field began to turn to abused boys, findings

of female perpetration continued to be relatively rare. Numerous recent studies, however, have found female perpetration rates of more than 40% in samples of abused males (Fritz et al., 1981; Fromuth & Burkhart, 1987, 1989; Johnson & Shrier, 1987; Olson, 1990; Risin & Koss, 1987; Seidner & Calhoun, 1984). It is especially significant that self-report studies find much higher proportions of female perpetration than do studies that rely on reported cases of abuse. This suggests that sexual interactions between women and children are much more common than data from case reports would indicate; it appears that a lower proportion of female perpetration than male perpetration is reported or recognized.

Some of the most compelling evidence for the underidentification of female perpetration comes via the methodology of studies of child sexual abuse. Several authors (e.g., Finkelhor, 1984; Fromuth & Burkhart, 1987, 1989; Kasl, 1990) note the importance of asking interview respondents about "childhood sexual interactions" rather than about "abuse" per se. The former phrasing will yield higher rates of positive response, because individuals often do not see such interactions as abusive. This would appear to be a more severe problem with respect to female perpetrators. A number of researchers have speculated that males are less likely to report abuse by females because they do not consider such sexual interaction to be abusive (Fromuth & Burkhart, 1987, 1989; Johnson & Shrier 1987; Vander Mey, 1988). Johnson and Shrier (1987) report that 11 of the 25 sexually abused adolescent males in their study had been abused by females. In an earlier study (Johnson & Shrier, 1985), zero respondents indicated sexual abuse by females. The main difference between the two studies was that in the earlier study, Johnson and Shrier (1985) asked the adolescents whether they had "ever been raped, sexually abused, or forced to engage in a sexual act" (p. 650), whereas in the 1987 study they inquired into their sexual experiences more generally. During the interviews in the earlier study, several of the adolescents described sexual interaction with adult females (despite indicating that they had not been sexually abused), which led Johnson and Shrier to conduct their second study.

These studies notwithstanding, the perspective of the field has remained focused upon sexual abuse as a phenomenon perpetrated by males. This is conveyed both implicitly, through the ubiquitous use of *he* to refer to perpetrators,[1] and explicitly. Even writers knowledgeable and experienced with regard to male survivors assert flatly that the "vast majority of offenders are male" (Briere, 1989, p. 156). John Briere, one of the finest researchers in this area, cites as evidence for this assertion four studies, those of Finkelhor (1979), Runtz (1987), Russell (1983), and Wyatt (1985). Of these, however, all but Finkelhor's dealt specifically and exclusively with female survivors. Female-female abuse appears to be a very rare (or, with the skepticism appropriately exercised with regard to prevalence estimates, at least a very rarely reported) phenomenon. Thus, to look primarily to studies of female survivors in an attempt to estimate male-female ratios among perpetrators inevitably underestimates the rate of female perpetration.

Since the late 1970s a number of researchers have pondered the low incidence of reported cases of female perpetration and suspected that this was an underidentified phenomenon. Moreover, the notion that nonrecognition of abuse by women compounds the nonrecognition of abuse of boys was also first suggested more than a decade ago. Justice and Justice (1979), Groth (1979a), and Plummer (1981) each speculated that the actual rate of female perpetration was far higher than prevalence estimates would indicate. In a recently published volume on abused males Hunter (1990b), Kasl (1990), Sepler (1990), and Mathews, Matthews, and Speltz (1990) each discussed the topic of female perpetration and analyzed reasons for its underidentification. I believe that the persistence of the notion that abusers are almost uniformly male reflects a cultural bias that stands in the way of recognizing female perpetration and of identifying sexual interaction between adult females and juvenile males as abusive (see Justice & Justice [1979] and Kasl [1990] for similar arguments).

The most comprehensive examination of this issue is provided by Craig Allen (1990) in a chapter entitled "Women as Perpetrators of Child Sexual Abuse: Recognition Barriers." He argues that a number of beliefs "intertwine to produce barriers that prevent the recognition of female child sexual abuse" (p. 109) and identifies three main barriers: overestimation of the strength of the incest taboo; overextension of feminist explanations of child sexual abuse; and overgeneralization of the observation that female child sexual abuse is rare.

In the first barrier, the notion that a woman could sexually abuse a child was considered preposterous and, in those rare cases in which it occurred, indicative of severe mental illness on the part of the woman. These beliefs, argues Allen, "have contributed to substantial bias on the part of professionals against the possibility that females could sexually abuse children" (p. 110). Friedman (1988) noted that professionals tend to see things within gender-specific schemas, observing sexual misbehavior in fathers while ignoring that of mothers. Similarly, Kempe and Helfer (1980) state that with respect to sexually abusive mothers, "intervention is very difficult because mothers are given an enormous leeway in their actions, while fathers and brothers are not" (p. 207).

The second barrier to recognition proposed by Allen (1990) is the overextension of feminist explanations of child sexual abuse. He accepts the reasoning of such researchers as Herman (1981) and Finkelhor and Russell (1984) that "male dominance, differential socialization, and sexual exploitation in fact may help to explain a substantial portion of child sexual abuse" (Allen, 1990, p. 111). He argues, however, that seeing sexual abuse solely in these terms leads inevitably to a minimization of female perpetration. He calls Finkelhor and Russell to task for what he sees as their effort to review the data "solely to demonstrate that child sexual abuse is primarily perpetrated by males" (p. 113). Finkelhor and Russell (1984) had concluded that females constitute a small percentage of perpetrators and that the vast majority are male. As Bolton et al. (1989) have noted, however, they dismiss studies that find high proportions of female perpetrators or argue that the results of these studies must be due to unusual, and ungeneralizable, samples. Allen asserts that Finkelhor and Russell's conclusions are not based on a dispassionate analysis of the data. Instead, he argues that they are determined to confirm their theory that "sexual abuse should . . . be described as a problem of *masculine socialization*" (Finkelhor & Russell, 1984, p. 12, emphasis in original).

I agree with Allen that the issue of male and female rates of perpetration of child sexual abuse is fundamentally an empirical rather than a theoretical issue. Finkelhor and Russell go beyond simply concluding that available data indicate that female perpetration is rare; they insinuate that those questioning this notion have ulterior motives for doing so:

> We believe that some workers and researchers are ideologically uncomfortable with the idea of a male preponderance and thus have been quick to rush to the possibility that it might not be true. . . . But reality cannot be twisted to suit any particular ideological or political need. The solution to the widespread and destructive problem of child sexual abuse can be found only if we face the truth about it. (Finkelhor & Russell, 1984, pp. 184-185)

I agree with this sentiment. The "truth" that Finkelhor and Russell allude to, however, appears to be that female perpetration is far more common than once was assumed. Reality must, indeed, be twisted in order to avoid recognizing the implications of the numerous studies that have demonstrated this since Finkelhor and Russell wrote the passage quoted above. I believe it strains credulity to suggest that the studies of Condy, Templer, Brown, and Veaco (1987), Fritz et al. (1981), Fromuth and Burkhart (1987, 1989), Johnson and Shrier (1987), Olson (1990), Petrovich and Templer (1984), Pierce and Pierce (1985), Ramsey-Klawsnik (1990a), and Risin and Koss (1987) are all invalid due to ulterior motives on the part of their authors. The data in these studies lead persuasively to the conclusion that female perpetration, although probably less common than male perpetration, is a far more frequent phenomenon than earlier, primarily case-report-based studies indicated.

Allen's third barrier to recognition of female perpetration is the overgeneralization of the empirical observation that female child sexual abuse is rare. Essentially, his argument here is that the belief that female child sexual abuse is rare has become a self-fulfilling prophecy. This works in two ways: Researchers and clinicians fail to explore or inquire into abuse by females; and "the beliefs and attitudes these professionals [hold] against the occurrence of female child sexual abuse may have actually prepared them to *not* see it" (Allen, 1990, p. 115, emphasis in original). This is consistent with postmodernist theory, as outlined in the previous chapter. We notice that which we are conditioned to or prepared to notice. "Theoretical, cultural, or idiosyncratic beliefs, which state that female sexual abuse does not occur, may, in fact, prevent professionals from observing it" (Allen, 1990, p. 116). It appears that professional oblivion to mothers as perpetrators may gradually be subsiding. For example, the 1993 Fifth Annual National Conference on Male Survivors included three separate workshops on mother-son incest.

Ramsey-Klawsnik (1990a) and Banning (1989) both argue that "the incidence of female sexual perpetration has been underestimated due to our disbelief that this can occur" (Ramsey-Klawsnik, 1990a, p. 6). Allen (1990) and Ramsey-Klawsnik (1990a) cite examples of judges ordering child abuse charges to be dropped against mothers, despite overwhelming evidence (including, in both cases, the mother's admission!) of the existence of the abuse. The reasoning was that, "women don't do those kinds of things. . . . Besides, the children need their mother" (Allen, 1990,

p. 117). In Ramsey-Klawsnik's (1990a) study, the abuse perpetrated by females was severe and extensive, as will be described below. Despite this fact, only one case resulted in prosecution of an offending female. She writes that "there was a strong reluctance on the part of decision-makers to believe the allegations of female sex offending" (p. 4). Allen argues that the belief that women do not sexually abuse children acts at several points to derail the process that would lead ultimately to recognition of the abuse: "Informants may be less likely to report occurrences of female sexual abuse of children, investigators less diligent in conducting inquiries, attorneys less likely to prosecute, and judges more likely to dismiss or reduce charges" (p. 117). I would add that this belief manifests itself first in the victim him- or herself, who is less likely to view the sexual interaction as abusive and/or to report it.

A number of researchers have discussed additional reasons for the underidentification of female perpetration (Groth, 1979a; Kasl, 1990; Mathews et al., 1987, 1990; Plummer, 1981; Sepler, 1990). Several of these reasons are mirror images of those that make male perpetration so easy to perceive and male victimization so seemingly incongruous. There appears to be a denial or minimization of female sexuality and capacity for aggression, and these attributes are discouraged in the socialization of the female child (Banning, 1989; Kasl, 1990; Maccoby & Jacklin, 1974; Masters, Johnson, & Kolodny, 1985; Mathews et al., 1990; Ramsey-Klawsnik, 1990a). Behaviors that run counter to the accepted image of femininity are suppressed or denied (Kasl, 1990). Abuse—particularly sexual abuse—does not fit the cultural construction of femininity.

Groth (1979a) proposes that another source of the underestimation of female perpetration is that abuse by women is more likely to be intra- rather than extrafamilial and thus less likely to come to the attention of authorities. Research on sexual abuse in day-care settings (Finkelhor, 1988) suggests that this pattern, too, may be less pronounced than earlier research would indicate. Moreover, the increased attention that incest has received in the past decade suggests that this factor alone cannot account for much of societal obliviousness to female perpetration.

Groth (1979a) and Kasl (1990) speculate that abuse by women is not recognized because the specific nature of the abuse is different than that committed by males. According to these writers, the former is more covert and subtle, often consisting of caressing, fondling, inappropriate bathing, seductive and exhibitionistic behavior, and so forth, rather than the acts

of penetration and violence thought to be characteristic of male perpetration. Researchers examining the particular acts performed by male and
by female perpetrators have, in fact, found less severe acts to have been
committed by females (Finkelhor, 1979; Fromuth & Burkhart, 1987,
1989; Risin & Koss, 1987).

As with other findings, however, this pattern may not be as extreme or
dichotomous as first appeared. Petrovich and Templer (1984), who found
a high incidence of female-perpetrated sexual abuse in a sample of adult
male rapists, noted that the specific acts perpetrated were very severe.
Out of a total of 73 cases of sexual abuse of a boy or adolescent male
by an older female, 60 involved vaginal or anal sex, with 38 including
oral sex (see Condy et al. [1987] for similar results). Ramsey-Klawsnik
(1990b), in her archival study of Massachusetts sexual abuse cases, found
severe acts of sexual abuse and torture to have been committed by male
and female alike, and did not find distinctions along gender lines in the
severity of acts committed. Female perpetrators in her study engaged in
oral-genital contact in 60% of cases, vaginal intercourse in 29%, rape
with objects in 27%, sadistic sexual activity (defined as "burning, beating,
biting or pinching breasts or genitals, or tying the child during acts of
sexual assault," p. 4) in 56%. She writes that, "these findings refute the
myth that sexual offending by females is gentle, and often exhibited in
the form of personal care which crosses appropriate boundaries" (Ramsey-
Klawsnik, 1990a, p. 6). It may be difficult to generalize from her study
to victims outside of the Protective Services system. Nonetheless, her
findings suggest that the notion of female perpetrators acting predominantly in a delicate and gentle, albeit inappropriate or overstimulating,
fashion may be as much a cultural artifact as a reflection of the actual
nature of such abuse.

Several researchers have examined the phenomenon of female perpetration and noted a high incidence of abuse in concert with or under the
initiation and/or coercion of a male perpetrator (Faller, 1987; Mathews,
1987; Mathews et al., 1990; McCarty, 1986; Wolfe, 1987). In many of
the cases reviewed by these authors, women who perpetrate sexual abuse
against children are themselves physically, emotionally, and/or psycho-
logically abused by their husbands or boyfriends. They may allow and
participate in the abuse of their children because they are scared of a male
partner or in order to sustain the relationship with a man upon whom
they are dependent. Wolfe (1987), for example, found that in 6 of 12

cases of female sexual abuse the female perpetrator was accompanied or coerced by a male. Mathews (1987; Mathews et al., 1990) developed a typology of female perpetrators that includes "male-coerced" and "male-accompanied" as two of the categories. McCarty (1986) also found a high incidence of abuse with a male accomplice. Faller (1987) concludes that in polyincestuous abuse, "women are typically not the initiators, but . . . are persuaded, coerced, or otherwise drawn into sexual abuse by men" (p. 274). As these authors note, this pattern is quite distinct from that of male perpetrators, who typically act alone. The impact upon a child of being sexually abused by two parents or caretakers is also likely to be particularly traumatic.

As with other assumptions about female perpetration, the paradigm of women acting under the duress or coercion of male perpetrators may in part reflect cultural assumptions of female victimization. That is, the schema of females as victims may predispose observers to see women in this light. A husband and wife equally involved in the maltreatment of their child may be perceived very differently, with the woman seen as a victimized, dependent follower, and the man as an active, aggressive initiator. Thus, two of Wolfe's (1987) six examples of female perpetrators accompanied or coerced by men were women who acknowledge that they initiated the abuse, but indicate that they did so in order to enhance their male partner's interest in them. Cultural stereotypes should be borne in mind when assessing such cases. Would a man who claims to have initiated the sexual abuse of his child in order to attract his girlfriend's affection be seen as a relatively innocent accomplice, much less a victim? This caveat is not meant to suggest that women do not abuse children under the instigation or pressure of male partners. The evidence that a significant proportion of female perpetration occurs as a result of male coercion or initiative appears compelling.

Societal attitudes toward sexual interaction between adult or adolescent females and younger boys play a pivotal role in the underidentification of sexual abuse of this sort. Neither society as a whole, nor the survivor component of it, frame such interactions as abuse. They are instead often glorified or seen as a sort of "initiation" of the fortunate boy into manhood. In a study of societal attitudes regarding sexual abuse, Finkelhor (1984) surveyed 521 parents in the Boston area. He gave respondents a series of vignettes that they were asked to rate on a scale from 1 to 10, with 1 being "definitely not sexual abuse" and 10 being "definitely sexual abuse." The conditions in the vignettes were experimentally manipulated so that factor analytic techniques could be applied indicating the extent to which respondents emphasized such factors as type of abuse, age of victim, age of perpetrator, and relationship between perpetrator and victim in arriving at their rank-orderings of sexual abuse. Among the findings of this study was that "the relationships [between perpetrator and victim] considered as the least abusive were those involving women as perpetrators. . . . Male perpetrator-female victim combinations are considered the most abusive, and female perpetrator-female victim combinations the least abusive" (p. 116). It should be noted that other factors, including type of abuse, were held constant while one variable was manipulated. Therefore, the judgment that female perpetration is less abusive than male perpetration was not due to females exercising less severity or coercion in their abusive acts.

The belief that sexual interactions between older females and juvenile males does not constitute abuse is, I believe, an implicit assumption of professionals, laypeople, and survivors alike. As noted above, Finkelhor's (1984) study of societal attitudes toward sexual abuse found that people considered sexual interaction with female perpetrators to be the least abusive. The point was brought home to me quite powerfully during one of my first experiences lecturing on child sexual abuse. I referred to the fact that the incidence of sexual abuse of boys was severely underestimated and quickly ran through some types of sexual abuse that males experience. When I mentioned female teachers or baby-sitters having sex with early adolescent boys, a voice rang out from the back of the class: "lucky dog!" The class was convulsed with laughter. I think that this response represents a norm rather than an exception and that the initial reaction of most people is that such an experience can hardly be considered abusive. Instead, it is seen as a fortunate initiation into adult sexuality that any red-blooded male would desire. As Bolton et al. (1989) write:

> Age discrepant heterosexual contact with young females is viewed with disdain at best and [as] sexual abuse at the worst. The same situation involving a young male may be seen as an early introduction to sexual prowess and "manhood." Not only does this negate any possible anxiety on the part of the young male, it may go so far as to find him being the victim of jealousy from age-mates and older males. (p. 17)

This would appear to be an enormous factor in the underreporting of sexual abuse of boys. One does not report sexual abuse when one sees instead a "lucky dog." Woods and Dean (1984), in a study of adult male survivors, found that 52% of those abused by males perceived the interactions negatively, compared to 30% of those victimized by females. Of those abused by females, 50% viewed their experience as positive, whereas only 16% of those whose perpetrators were male saw it positively. The fact that such experience is not seen as abusive, however, does not indicate that it is not traumatic, either in the short or the long term (Freeman-Longo, 1986; Fromuth & Burkhart, 1989; Koss & Dinero, 1988; Risin & Koss, 1987). Fromuth and Burkhart's (1989) survey of 253 sexually abused male college students, among whom females constituted 78% of the perpetrators, found that there were significant negative consequences associated with childhood sexual experiences with older females, despite the fact that such experiences were not considered abusive (see also Sarrell & Masters [1982] for a discussion of the negative sequelae of sexual abuse of males by adult females).

The underidentification of female perpetration has a political source as well. Charlotte Kasl (1990), in a chapter entitled "Female Perpetrators of Sexual Abuse: A Feminist View," provides an excellent discussion of the political dangers and controversies that identification of this phenomenon entail. She notes that when first presenting her findings, she was told by a few women that "we should not be talking about female perpetrators because it lets men 'off the hook' and they will use the information to obscure the extent of male-perpetrated sexual abuse" (p. 259). I received similar feedback upon initiating this research. Jim Struve (1990), in a chapter entitled "Dancing With the Patriarchy," in the same volume, expresses similar concerns. He writes that, "as the movement to identify and treat male survivors grows, one danger is that such a focus may shift attention away from women's victimization" (p. 39).

I believe that the concerns expressed by Kasl and by Struve are valid and important. In a society in which males hold disproportionate power, it is critical to ensure that male issues not supersede or obscure those of females. Because the abuse of females does, in fact, appear to be a more common phenomenon than that of males, it is especially important that we not lose sight of their plight. Nonetheless, I believe that there is a more immediate danger: that the experience of male survivors will be denied and invalidated. A man who has been sexually abused is no less a victim by virtue of the fact that those in his "class" may be more likely to perpetrate than to be victimized.[2] For this reason I believe it is essential to devote more attention to the phenomena of male victimization and female perpetration. Kasl (1990) succinctly explains her reasons for exploring sexual abuse by females: "We need to explore female perpetrators of abuse because they exist. Without knowledge and understanding, we cannot help perpetrators and their victims to heal. . . . By focusing on the infrequency of female perpetrators cited in numerous studies, we overlook both the victimizers and the victims" (p. 262).

Cinematic Views of Sexual Activity
Between Women and Boys

Perhaps the clearest image of the societal sense of sexual interaction between women and boys emerges from a review of motion pictures dealing with this issue. In a manner similar to Brownmiller's (1975) review of the cinematic treatment of rape, James Trivelpiece (1990) undertook a review of films that include instances of rape, incestuous abuse, or molestation of males. What is most striking in his review is the fact that in watching these films, such events are simply not recognized as abusive. The cognitive schema for sexual abuse of males is woefully underdeveloped. We observe interactions that, if the genders were reversed, would clearly constitute sexual abuse, and see something very different. Kasl (1990) makes the same observation, noting that when she saw *The Last Picture Show,* "in which a woman probably in her thirties has sex with a teenage boy, it never occurred to [her] that this was a form of sexual exploitation" (p. 263).

Trivelpiece discusses an exhaustive list of films that he divides into the following categories: sexual initiation, molestation, incest, and rape. The fourth category, rape, refers to sexual assault upon adult males; because the present work is about childhood sexual abuse, I will limit my review of his discussion to films involving sexual interactions with boys rather than with men. His list of sexual initiation films, in which sexual interaction between a boy and an older female is portrayed as a positive initiation rather than as abusive, include *The Last Picture Show; Summer of 42; The First Time; The Chapman Report; Class; Private Lessons; Weird Science;*

and *The Tin Drum*. I had seen several of these films and had the same reaction as Charlotte Kasl: It had never occurred to me to consider such interactions abusive. Films that portray the molestation of boys include *JoJo Dancer, Your Life is Calling; Tommy; My Life as a Dog; Fanny and Alexander; Satyricon; Rage;* and *A Chorus Line*. My initial reaction to reading this list was to ponder where abuse had occurred, but upon reflection the victimization was generally far from subtle. Trivelpiece points out that in several of these films, molestation is presented as a humorous event. Again, had the same events occurred with young girls, the abusive quality would have been quite clear.

Incest between mothers, stepmothers, or grandmothers and boys is presented as a neutral or even positive experience in films. Trivelpiece identifies four such films: *Murmur of the Heart; Midnight Cowboy; Mishima: A Life in Four Chapters;* and *Little Big Man*. Trivelpiece writes that, "as with real-life male survivors who enter therapy, there is no recognition in the films that the sexual act was abusive" (p. 53). As is also the case in real life, "the films portray the victims later in life as troubled individuals, but give no indication that their abusive childhood sexual experiences may be related to their dysfunction as adults" (p. 53). Trivelpiece points out the vast difference between societal—or, at least, cinematic—attitudes toward mother-son and father-daughter incest. *Murmur of the Heart,* which is about mother-son incest, was described by Limbacher (1983) as "a delightful no holds barred sex film by Louis Malle, in which mother sleeps with son and loves it." Keyser (1975), another reviewer writing about sexuality in the cinema, writes that "the act is presented as a positive, indeed lovely and touching moment in his life, a stage in a natural cycle" (both examples cited in Trivelpiece [1990, p. 50]). It is difficult to imagine father-daughter incest portrayed in this light. Indeed, Trivelpiece examines films dealing with the sexual abuse of females and contrasts the sensitivity with which the victims in such films (e.g., *Nuts* and *The Color Purple*) are treated with the emotional callousness and outright obliviousness that characterizes cinematic depiction of male victimization.

Probably the most famous depiction of the sexual victimization of a male is the rape that occurs in the film *Deliverance*. Although it involves an adult male victim and is, therefore, outside the focus of this work, I believe that the handling of this event is quite telling. Though the rape is the central incident of the story and fuels the two murders that follow, it is never discussed beyond two oblique references to "what happened to Bobby." The victim, Bobby, explicitly states that he does not want others to know what happened to him. So, the incident, like the rapist himself, is buried. This burial seems to be a suitable metaphor for the handling of male sexual victimization in cinema and in the society of which it is a part.

To summarize, I believe that cultural notions about femininity and masculinity represent systematic biases against recognition of sexual abuse of boys and perpetration by females. As Ramsey-Klawsnik (1990b) writes, "the high rate of female perpetration of boys . . . likely contributes to the under-identification of male victims. Sexually abused children in our society are underserved. However, it appears that sexually abused boys are even more highly underserved than girls" (p. 2). Ramsey-Klawsnik (personal communication, summer 1991) speculates that the nonrecognition of female perpetration and the underidentification of male victimization are two sides of one coin; that is, turning a blind eye to female perpetration is a major source of the underestimation of the prevalence of sexual abuse of males. Societal views on the phenomenon of child sexual abuse have progressed from outright denial, to a recognition that little girls are victimized, to a nascent understanding that little boys, too, are vulnerable. A caveat appears to be applied, however, that such abuse as exists is perpetrated by men. Recognizing that sexual abuse is done by those with power, regardless of gender, to those without power, regardless of gender, is, I believe, the next important step for research into child sexual abuse to take.[3]

Notes

1. To my knowledge, the only previous consideration of this issue was in an editors' note prefacing a book entitled *The Incest Perpetrator* (Horton, Johnson, Roundy, & Williams, 1990, p. 15). The editors acknowledge the hardship caused by the lack of gender-neutral pronouns. Their solution, however, is to maintain and perpetuate the stereotype of the female victim and male perpetrator: "victims will commonly be referred to in the feminine gender, and perpetrators, or offenders, in the masculine gender."

2. Another, related, issue that will be addressed in Chapter 9 is the question of what it is like for males to be victimized but to receive a simultaneous message that they are in fact members of an "oppressor class" (Struve, 1990, p. 36).

3. Once one's perspective on abuse has been broadened so as to encompass the possibilities of male victimization and female perpetration, examples emerge from all corners. For example, a recent Take Back The Night rally at the Michigan State Capitol in

Lansing (June 1991) included a discussion of partner battering within Lesbian relationships. One speaker noted that society has a hard time seeing women as aggressors, rather than only as victims. "Just because you have two women in a relationship doesn't mean it won't be violent. People think it's men being violent against women, but sometimes a woman can be the aggressor." Another speaker stated that there has been little research into Lesbian battering, partly because society and the Lesbian community do not want to deal with the issue. A third argued that "part of the problem is [that] Lesbians want to believe that relationships with women are safe, and men are violent" (Robinson, 1991; quoted by permission from *The State News*).

David's Story

David is a 38-year-old homosexual. He has one younger sister. He is dying of AIDS and is likely to have approximately one year left to live.[1] He is currently very weak and has difficulty walking, and therefore rarely leaves his home. David was physically and sexually abused by his mother during childhood. The physical abuse was extreme and sadistic. It included frequent beatings, punching, kicking, and objects thrown at him. He described his mother making him stand against a wall while she threw knives at him. At other times she crushed cigarettes out in his mouth, impulsively slammed his face into his dinner plate, beat him with various objects, held his hand over burners, and slapped him across the face repeatedly until he would cry. Most of these actions were experienced as coming out of the blue rather than in response to anything he had done. He described his childhood as akin to that depicted in *Mommy Dearest*. He stated that his mother was an alcoholic and had wild mood swings that were entirely unpredictable. From an early age, his mother told him that she was unable to have children, that he was adopted, and that he would be returned to the adoption agency. He recalls searching for the adoption papers at around age five.

The sexual abuse began at age four or five and continued until about age 12. It began with his mother inviting him into the bathtub with her and showing parts of her body to him. Later, she would reach into his pants, ostensibly to check if his underwear was too tight. She constantly demanded that he take his shirt off, and would threaten that if he didn't take his shirt off, she would go topless. David stated that his mother often "dragged" him and his sister with her to join her drinking partners and would put them in front of the TV while she would kiss or dance with other men. Often she would spend the night out with other men. He reported that his father was a "wimp" who never confronted her and conveyed the message to David never to talk about what went on in their home. There was no physical or sexual abuse by the father, but an absence of support or assistance.

Like a number of the men with whom I have spoken about their participation in this study, David indicated that he found it to be very helpful. He said that it made him confront feelings that he tends to push out of his mind. He said that his abuse was bottled up inside of him and this brought some of it out, along with powerful feelings of hatred. He said that he has almost never reflected on these experiences, and that even in intimate relationships he has avoided talking about his childhood. He never told anyone about the abuse when he was a child, because he was convinced no one would believe him and because of the indoctrination that one should never tell. He said that everyone saw his mother as "a gem," and he was sure no one would believe her capable of such atrocities. He told his first girlfriend, in high school, about the abuse. She did not believe him, which reinforced his reticence about the events.

David feels that the most pronounced impact of his abuse is the wall that he has erected between himself and others. The necessity of keeping the abuse a secret is one source of this barrier. Even those with whom he feels closest have commented that they "could never really get inside (him)." The abusive events themselves have also trained him to keep his distance from others and to maintain a guarded, wary quality. He said that, "I wouldn't let anyone break the shell I had around myself. I wouldn't let others close. I wouldn't allow anyone to touch me." He indicated that he would even reflexively raise his arm in self-defense if anyone tried to touch him. He has attempted to explain to partners in intimate relationships why he has so much difficulty allowing people to be close, by indicating how hard it is to undo years of saying "stay away."

He said that others feel that this is unfair to them, that they should not have to pay the price of what was done to him in childhood.

It is understandably difficult for David to distinguish the effects of the physical and the sexual abuse. He speculates that if only the physical abuse had occurred, he would find sexual relationships more tolerable. He said that he desperately wants to touch and to be touched, but is "deathly afraid" of it. Had only the sexual abuse, and not the physical abuse, occurred, he thinks that he would not have such a deep and abiding hatred of his mother. He said that all of his life he has tried to understand "why?" Over and over, he has asked her, in his mind, "How could you treat your child like that?"

David describes himself as growing up with no self-worth whatsoever. He feels that he was cheated out of a childhood and of normal relationships with both parents. In addition to the abuse and the unavailability of his father, he stated that it was always drilled into him that he should sacrifice his interests and needs for those of others. He constantly protected his sister from his mother's abuse and resents the fact that she has now rejected him, first due to his homosexuality and then because of his disease. Following graduation from high school, he worked for years to help his father in his business, sacrificing his own education and career pursuits in the process. He worked without pay and recognizes that he was essentially his father's slave. He was never encouraged to develop hobbies or leisure-time pursuits by his parents, whom he describes as "wet rags" on his interests. The sense of being cheated out of a normal life is a powerful dynamic for David.

David has held only menial jobs and feels that he has wasted much of his life. He never applied himself in school or attempted to learn new skills. He drank an enormous amount from around age 18 until he quit about one year ago. He stated that his drinking reached the point where he was imbibing three fifths of alcohol a day, a quantity he recognizes may sound unbelievable. He feels that he "lived for the booze" and destroyed what dreams he had with it. He lived in tremendous denial, telling himself he had no problem. He finally entered an in-patient treatment program in 1986 and began Alcoholics Anonymous about one year ago. He has not had a drink in the past year and quit a long-term nicotine addiction a few months ago. He sees a strong possibility of a causal connection between childhood events and his later alcoholism, but hesitates to attribute his drinking to his mother's influence. He said that, "it would be easy to say, 'yeah,' I was influenced by my mom, but why not take the example of my dad and not drink? I think it had a big part to play in my addiction, but I can't say for sure. It's easy to blame others and that's a cop out." He is uncertain about the impact of the abuse itself upon his drinking.

David is now in a good relationship of 3 years' standing. The first 2 years of this relationship were dominated by their mutual alcoholism and included terrible physical fights, with each nearly killing the other. He and his partner entered AA together one year ago. Since that time, he "could not have been happier with the relationship." The sense of having been cheated out of things takes on particular salience for David in light of his terminal illness. He feels that he had finally begun to put his life in order, quitting alcohol and cigarettes, and developing a positive, healthy relationship. All of this was accomplished with the help of Alcoholics Anonymous and of the therapy he began when hospitalized in 1986 due to his alcohol abuse. The therapy has helped him to recognize the impact of his childhood abuse, and he feels that had he not contracted AIDS, he would return to school and obtain new skills. Currently David feels very alone and isolated, with only his partner and a very few friends to speak with about his pain.

Note

1. David died about 6 months after our interview.

3 Prevalence and Descriptive Characteristics

A Review of the Literature

The first step in improving the lot of sexually victimized boys and, hopefully, reducing the incidence of abuse, is to arrive at a better understanding of the phenomenon. As the last chapter indicates, the sexual abuse of boys is an extremely understudied as well as underreported area. Nonetheless, during the 1980s and early 1990s a number of studies were conducted that aimed at estimating the prevalence of male sexual abuse, assessing the proportion of male victims within populations of sexually abused children, and examining characteristic features of the abuse. This chapter reviews these studies and notes common patterns in their findings.

Prevalence

Among the conclusions of the previous chapter is that the sexual victimization of males is likely to be even more severely underreported than is sexual abuse generally. For all of the reasons discussed above—the male ethic of self-reliance; the stigma of homosexuality; the notion that sexual interaction with older females is not abusive; the victim's sense that his experience is extremely rare; the tendency toward self-blame and responsibility; the feared disbelief or unresponsiveness of parents and professionals; and so forth—boys are unlikely to report their victimization and others in the community are unlikely to suspect or recognize the sexual abuse of boys. As might be expected, the attempt to estimate the prevalence of this phenomenon has been fraught with peril. As Vander Mey (1988) writes:

> At this time, estimates of prevalence and incidence must be used with caution. Barriers to accepting males as victims, the silence surrounding the victimization of males, and the possibility that at least the incestuous abuse of males may go undiscovered in the absence of sister victims preclude confidence in these estimates. (p. 62)

Estimates of childhood victimization of males have ranged from 2.5% or 3% (Bell, Weinberg, & Hammersmith, 1981a, 1981b; Kercher & McShane, 1983; Murphy, 1987) to 33% (Landis, 1956). Much of this variation stems from discrepancies in the methodology employed in the various studies, including differences across the populations sampled and utilization of differing definitions of what constitutes abuse. Therefore, before turning to the studies themselves, let us briefly consider methodological and definitional issues in such studies.

METHODOLOGICAL AND DEFINITIONAL ISSUES

The purpose of prevalence studies is, of course, to arrive at as accurate an estimate as possible of the true rate of a given phenomenon—in this case, the childhood sexual abuse of males—in an overall population. Reliance upon official figures, which reflect only reported cases, yields but a fraction of the actual extent of victimization. Several researchers have noted that official rates are especially likely to understate the actual prevalence of abuse of boys (e.g., Urquiza & Keating, 1990; Vander Mey, 1988). In addition to the various sources of the underidentification of male sexual abuse, official figures come primarily from the child protective services system. Boys appear more likely to be abused outside of the home and thus outside of the purview of protective services, which focuses its attention on abuse within parental and caretaker situations (Faller, 1989; Finkelhor, 1979, 1984; Rogers & Terry, 1984; Russell & Finkelhor, 1984). Finkelhor (1984), for example, noted that a very conservative population estimate of abuse of boys—2.5% (Bell et al., 1981a, 1981b)—would still produce 46,000 new cases of sexual abuse per year, but there were, in fact, only 7,600 reported cases in 1981.

In order to obtain an estimate of the rate of child sexual abuse, researchers survey a certain number of people, using this sample as a means of estimating the rate of abuse in the population from which the sample is taken. The choice of sample has profound implications for the eventual estimate, however. Extremely high rates of childhood sexual activity have been found in certain populations. Simari and Baskin (1982) found that 46% of homosexual men had experienced incest in their childhood, but if the definition of incest is expanded to include extended family, that percentage rises to 64%. McCormack, Burgess, and Janus (1986) found that 38% of adolescent male runaways had been sexually victimized. Ann Heiss-Shulte (personal communication, spring 1991) estimates that two out of three male juvenile delinquents in a Michigan residential facility have been sexually abused. Serrill (1974) and Carlson (cited in Kasl, 1990) have found sexual abuse histories in 75% and 91%, respectively, in studies of adult male sex offenders. Groth (1979b) interviewed 348 men convicted of sexual assault. Of these, 106 or 31% reported "sexual trauma" before the age of 15.[1] It appears likely, however, that this understates the true rate of sexual abuse in this population because the criteria used to define sexual trauma—"sexual activity witnessed or experienced *which was emotionally upsetting or disturbing*" (p. 11, emphasis mine)—will tend to overlook many of these men's childhood sexual experiences, particularly those involving older females, which are often not construed as upsetting or disturbing. Petrovich and Templer (1984) looked at sexual victimization in the backgrounds of convicted rapists and found an extremely high prevalence of female-perpetrated sexual abuse. (They did not report the frequency of male-perpetrated sexual abuse.) Of the 83 men they interviewed, 49 (59%) reported sexual abuse by a female perpetrator before the age of 16. These 49 men reported sexual interaction with a total of 73 older females.

Clearly, attempting to estimate the prevalence of sexual abuse in the population as a whole from any of these samples would yield inaccurately high rates. Fortunately, no one is suggesting making such a leap. It is common practice, however, to use undergraduate samples and similar questions may be raised regarding the appropriateness of generalizing from undergraduates to the broader population. Most of the large studies of sexually abused males used undergraduate samples (Finkelhor, 1979; Fritz et al., 1981; Fromuth & Burkhart, 1987, 1989; Landis, 1956; Risin & Koss, 1987; Seidner & Calhoun, 1984; Urquiza, 1988). Criticism of undergraduate samples include underrepresentation of ethnic minorities and individuals with lower socioeconomic status (SES). Finkelhor (1979) and Herman (1981) have noted that, at least in the case of females, lower SES individuals appear more likely to be sexually victimized.

Wyatt and Peters (1986a), in their assessment of methodological considerations in prevalence research, found the method of data collection to be a very important factor. Face-to-face interview studies tended to yield higher prevalence estimates than self-administered questionnaires. Fromuth and Burkhart (1987) addressed this issue with regard to male victims and found the method of data collection to be less important than the definition of abuse in explaining the variation in prevalence estimates. Each of the large college samples (Finkelhor, 1979; Fritz et al., 1981; Fromuth & Burkhart, 1987, 1989; Landis, 1956; Risin & Koss, 1987; Seidner & Calhoun, 1984) used self-administered questionnaires. Some of the lowest estimates of the prevalence of sexual abuse among males have come via this method, as well as some of the highest. Telephone surveys have been conducted by Cameron et al. (1986), Finkelhor et al. (1990), and Murphy (1987) and yielded prevalence estimates ranging from 3% to 16% among males. To date, no study of the prevalence of sexual victimization among males has relied upon face-to-face interviews, although Finkelhor (1981) conducted such interviews as part of his study. In short, no consistent pattern has emerged regarding the impact of method of data collection upon prevalence estimates for male victims. Face-to-face interviews would be an important contribution in this area.

DEFINING ABUSE

Another important methodological consideration is the definition of abuse. Fromuth and Burkhart (1987) have emphasized the importance of phrasing interview questions to ask about "sexual interactions" rather than about "sexual abuse," because the former wording is likely to tap respondents who may not consider their childhood incidents to be abusive. This appears to be of particular concern with males, who are extremely likely to view such interactions as neutral or positive, especially in the case of female perpetrators. Fromuth and Burkhart (1987) focused on such definitional issues. In their survey study of male undergraduates, they found that 20% to 24% of respondents reported childhood sexual activity. When the criterion for abuse was instead events *defined* by the respondent as abuse, this percentage dropped dramatically, to 4%. Similarly, Murphy (1987, 1989) conducted two prevalence studies. The first (1987) used a criterion of "adult perpetrator using physical or psychological force on a person under the age of 18 to engage in unwanted sexual contact." The second study (1989) used a less restrictive definition of abuse. The prevalence of abuse in the two studies rose from 3% to 11%, though each study excluded adolescent perpetrators. A survey conducted by the *Los Angeles Times* (Finkelhor et al., 1990) is likely to have underestimated the prevalence of male victimization by asking only about experiences that the respondent considers to have been sexually abusive.

A variety of definitions of sexual abuse have been used in prevalence studies. Age limits have been variously set at 13, 16, or 18 years. Fritz et al. (1981) looked only at preadolescent boy victims and adult perpetrators, excluding both adolescent perpetrators and adolescent victims from consideration. Similarly, the general population study by Cameron et al. (1986) looked only at adult perpetrators. Another important difference across studies is the type of abuse included. Several studies include only contact offenses, or what Urquiza (1988; Urquiza & Keating, 1990) calls direct abuse, although most of the recent studies also include noncontact or indirect forms of abuse, such as exhibitionism or exposure to pornography. Fromuth and Burkhart (1987) and Bolton et al. (1989) provide more detailed discussions of definitional and methodological issues in research on male victims, whereas Wyatt and Peters (1986a, 1986b) offer comprehensive considerations of these issues with respect to child sexual abuse more generally.

PREVALENCE ESTIMATES

In recent years, some consensus has been obtained in terms of criteria of abuse. Many large studies (Finkelhor, 1979; Fromuth & Burkhart, 1987, 1989; Murphy, 1989; Risin & Koss, 1987; Urquiza, 1988) use multiple definitions of abuse. Any sexual interaction between a preadolescent child and adult is considered abusive, regardless of whether overt force is used. Although age criteria beyond this vary, several studies have used criteria similar to those first proposed by Finkelhor (1979): sexual interactions when the subject is younger than 13 with a perpetrator at least 5 years older, or sexual interactions when the subject is between 13 and 16 with a perpetrator at least 10 years older. Several recent studies (Bruckner & Johnson, 1988; Finkelhor, 1984; Fromuth & Burkhart, 1987, 1989; Risin & Koss, 1987; Urquiza, 1988; Urquiza & Keating, 1990) have also included, or advocated including, sexual interaction with same-age or similar-age peers if elements of force or coercion exist.

These studies have yielded a wide range of prevalence estimates, which are presented in Table 3.1. Surveys of college students estimate the prevalence of sexual abuse of boys to be 8.7% (Finkelhor, 1979); 4.8% (Fritz et al., 1981); 24% and 20% for two different college samples (Fromuth & Burkhart, 1987, 1989); 33% (Landis, 1956); 7.3% (Risin & Koss, 1987); 5% (Seidner & Calhoun, 1984); and 32% (Urquiza [1988], consisting of 17.3% who reported "direct" abuse and 14.6% who reported "indirect" abuse). With the exception of the Seidner and Calhoun study, those with the lowest rates had the most restricted criteria for abuse. Fritz et al. included only physical contact of an "overtly sexual nature" and did not include adolescent perpetrators. Risin and Koss included only victims younger than 14 years of age at the time of victimization.

Nonundergraduate samples have yielded the following estimates of the prevalence of sexual abuse of male children: 4.9% of homosexuals and 2.5% of heterosexuals in San Francisco (Bell et al., 1981a, 1981b); 6% of a sample of fathers in Boston (Finkelhor, 1981); 3% of a sample of drivers in Texas (Kercher & McShane, 1983); 8% of British boys (Baker, 1985); 3% and 11% of males in Minneapolis, depending on criteria for sexual abuse (Murphy, 1987, 1989); 16% of men in a random probability sample in Denver, Louisville, Omaha, Los Angeles, and Washington, D.C. (Cameron et al., 1986); and 16% of men in a national sample conducted by the *Los Angeles Times* poll (Finkelhor et al., 1990). Cameron et al.'s study looks only at interactions with adults, whereas Finkelhor et al.'s survey asks specifically about incidents that the respondent considered to have been sexually abusive, a criterion that excludes much sexual interaction between boys and older females.

Table 3.1 Prevalence of Sexual Abuse Among Males

Sample Source	Study	Prevalence	Comments
General Population	Baker (1985)	8%	British sample
	Cameron et al. (1986)	16%	National; excludes adolescent perpetrators
	Finkelhor et al. (1990)	16%	National; only counts sexual acts construed as abusive
	Kercher & McShane (1983)	3%	Drivers in Texas
	Murphy (1987, 1989)	3%, 11%	First study considered only "unwanted contact involving force"; both studies exclude adolescent perpetrators
Undergraduates	Finkelhor (1979)	8.7%	
	Fritz et al. (1981)	4.8%	Excludes adolescent perpetrators; Only counts physical contact
	Fromuth & Burkhart (1987)	20%, 24%	
	Landis (1956)	33%	
	Risin & Koss (1987)	7.3%	Victims under age 14 only
	Seidner & Calhoun (1984)	5%	
	Urquiza (1988)	32%	17% "direct (contact) abuse" 15% "indirect abuse"
Other Specific Populations	Bell et al. (1981a, 1981b)	4.9% 2.5%	Homosexuals in San Francisco Heterosexuals in San Francisco
	Carlson (in Kasl, 1990)	90%	Adult male sex offenders
	Condy et al. (1987)	16% 46%	Male college students Male prisoners; both studies include female perpetrators only
	Finkelhor (1981)	6%	Fathers in Boston
	Groth (1979b)	33%	Adult male sex offenders
	Johnson (1988)	49%	Boy perpetrators of sexual abuse (ages 4 to 13)
	Johnson & Shrier (1987)	2.5%	General intake at adolescent medicine clinic
	McCormack et al. (1986)	38%	Adolescent runaways
	Petrovich & Templer (1984)	59%	Adult male sex offenders; female perpetrators only
	Simari & Baskin (1982)		Homosexual men
		46%	Immediate family incest
		54%	Immediate/extended family incest
	Swett et al. (1990)	13%	Adult outpatient psychiatric clinic; included only pressured or forced sexual contact

Official data on the frequency of male sexual victimization is typically reported in terms of incidence rather than prevalence. The distinction between these two constructs is that *prevalence* refers to the proportion of a given population that has experienced a certain phenomenon (in this case, the percentage of males who have experienced childhood sexual abuse), whereas *incidence* refers to the rate at which the phenomenon occurs during a given time period (e.g., the number of confirmed cases of boy victims of sexual abuse during 1994).

The primary sources of official data on the incidence of male victimization are the U.S. Department of Health and Human Services' National Incidence Studies (NIS), published in 1981 and 1988, and annual reports analyzed by the American Humane Association (AHA), the most recent of which was published in 1987. The NIS-II (National Center on Child Abuse and Neglect [NCCAN], 1988) found incidence rates of 0.9 males per 1,000 and 3.5 females per 1,000. Using slightly less stringent criteria for defining sexual abuse, NIS-II arrived at a second set of estimates: 1.1 boy victims and 3.9 girl victims per 1,000 children of that sex in the population. These rates are lower than one might expect given the prevalence data reviewed above. There are at least two reasons for this. First, the NIS database consists solely of cases that come to the attention of child protective services or other professionals. Therefore, unreported instances of sexual abuse and instances of sexual activity that are not construed as abusive were not included in the NIS estimates. For the reasons discussed in the previous chapter this is likely to deflate estimates of male victimization especially severely. Second, the NIS counts only cases involving adult caretakers. Abuse by strangers, adolescents, and adults not in caretaking roles is excluded from consideration.

One pattern that may be discerned from the prevalence studies cited above is that the most recent large studies in each category—Fromuth and Burkhart's (1987, 1989) and Urquiza's (1988) among the college samples and Cameron et al.'s (1986) and Finkelhor et al.'s (1990) among the general population surveys—have yielded the highest estimates. I would speculate that the increased attention on sexual abuse in general and the growing recognition of male victimization in particular have served to provide permission to men to access and disclose memories related to childhood sexual victimization. It is not, of course, possible to determine which estimate comes closest to the true prevalence of male sexual abuse in our society, but somewhere in the range of one in five to one in eight men appears to be a reasonable approximation.

PROPORTION OF MALE TO FEMALE SEXUAL ABUSE VICTIMS

In addition to adducing estimates of the prevalence of sexual abuse of boys in the general population, several researchers have examined the proportion of boy victims within the total population of sexually abused children. The majority of these studies rely on reported abuse—that is, sexual activity that comes to the attention of a hospital or child protective services. For the reasons outlined above, such estimates are likely to understate the actual proportion of male victims. Data analyzed by the American Humane Association (American Association for the Protection of Children, 1987) indicate that 22.8% of "sexually abused or exploited" children are male. NIS-II (NCCAN, 1988) found that girls were sexually abused almost four times as often as males. The proportion of boy victims within reported sexual abuse cases have consistently been in the 10% to 25% range (De Francis, 1969; DeJong, Emmett, & Hervada, 1982; Ellerstein & Canavan, 1980; Jaffe, Dynneson, & Ten Bensel, 1975; Pierce & Pierce, 1985; Reinhart, 1987; Rogers & Terry, 1984; Spencer & Dunklee, 1986). Finkelhor's (1984) review of the literature found that studies report between 2 and 10 female victims per male victim (i.e., male victims would constitute between approximately 10% and 33% of the total victim population).

Faller (1989) argues that the AHA figure is an underestimate, due to the underreporting of male sexual victimization. Rogers and Terry (1984) and Finkelhor (1984) have also speculated that the true ratio of male to female victims was much higher due to males' tendency not to report. Finkelhor noted that hospital and protective services studies yield lower male to female ratios among abuse victims than do police and general population surveys. He asserts that the former two categories underestimate the abuse of boys because of their primary focus on caretakers and boys' greater likelihood of victimization outside of the home. Finkelhor (1984) and Neilsen (1983) have each noted that estimates of caseloads in treatment programs range from about 25% to about 35% male. An informal survey conducted by the *Virginia Child Protection Newsletter* (Grayson, 1989) of clinicians working in the area of sexual abuse found estimates of boy victims to be as high as 50%. Findings regarding the ratio of boy to girl victims are presented in Table 3.2.

Looking beneath these numbers reveals evidence to support the hypothesis that the actual ratio of male to female victims is much higher

Table 3.2 Percentage of Male Victims in Sexual Abuse Populations

Study	Proportion of Males	Comments
American Association for the Protection of Children (1987)	23%	Cases reported to Child Protective Services (CPS)
De Francis (1969)	9%-13%	CPS cases
DeJong et al. (1982)	17%	Hospital-based study
Ellerstein & Canavan (1980)	11%	Hospital-based study
Finkelhor (1984)	10%-33%	Literature review
Jaffe et al. (1975)	12%	Police sexual offense complaints
Neilsen (1983)	25%-35%	Estimates of caseloads in treatment programs
NIS-II (1988)	22%	Reported cases
Pierce & Pierce (1985)	12%	Child abuse hot line
Ramsey-Klawsnik (1990b)	39%	Referrals to CPS
	45%	Confirmed cases of sexual abuse
Reinhart (1987)	16%	Referrals for sexual abuse evaluation
Rogers & Terry (1984)	25%	Hospital-based study
Spencer & Dunklee (1986)	9%	Hospital-based study
Grayson (1989)	25%-50%	Interviews with clinicians

than official figures indicate. It appears that the sexual abuse of boys is a far more severely underreported, underrecognized phenomenon than is the sexual abuse of girls. Groth (1979a, p. 149) cites an ingenious study of Michigan schoolchildren from Grades 4 to 9 (Tobias & Gordon, 1977). Approximately equal numbers of male and female children surveyed indicated sexual activity with an older child or adult (46% of the total who indicated such activity were male). A review of police records for that year in the same area, however, indicated that male victims constituted only 17% of the total abuse cases, a percentage consistent with the findings of reported cases. In other words, a much lower proportion of boys who experienced sexual activity with older individuals came to the attention of authorities.

Spencer and Dunklee's study (1986), which found one of the lowest proportions of male victims (9%), nonetheless revealed an interesting pattern. These researchers cited the numbers and percentages of male victims for each year that they examined hospital records. In 1979, there was one referral for a male victim; in 1980, 10; in 1981, 33; in 1982, 39; and in 1983, 61. This increase did not simply represent an increase in overall abuse referrals. The percentage of male victims went from less than 1% in 1979 to 14% in 1984, rising each year. Spencer and Dunklee conclude that this increase reflects the new and growing awareness of the phenomenon of male sexual victimization.

Ramsey-Klawsnik (1990b) conducted a compelling archival study. She reviewed Massachusetts Child Protective Services' files from 1984 through 1989 for all sexual abuse cases involving victims aged 12 or younger. She found that boys constituted 39% of the total referrals. Sexual abuse cases involving boys, however, were confirmed at a higher rate than were those involving girls (82% for boys vs. 64% for girls). Therefore, boys constitute 45% of the confirmed cases. In her review of these data, Ramsey-Klawsnik also noted that boys had been abused more severely than had girls. Finally, girls were four times more likely than boys to be referred due to suspicions based on behavioral indicators. She concluded that these findings were related: In order for the abuse of a male to be recognized, it must be blatant and severe. People don't notice subtle signs of sexual victimization in boys and report suspected abuse; when a boy acts out, the possibility that his behavior may be due to sexual maltreatment is not considered. Boys only reach protective services when their abuse is obvious and indisputable, thus accounting for the high rate of confirmation once a referral has been made.

Pierce and Pierce (1985) reached some similar conclusions regarding differential professional response to male and female victims. In their study of calls to a child abuse hot line, they were able to assess 205 sexual abuse cases, 25 of which involved male victims. They found that boys were much more severely abused than were girls. Perpetrators engaged in oral intercourse with the males in 52% of the cases compared to 17% of the females and in masturbation with 40% of the males compared to 21% of the females. Ninety-two percent of the males were subjected to three or more kinds of sexual activity compared to 48% of the females. Astoundingly, despite the greater severity of the abuse, "after the incident was known to the agency, only 4% of the male victims, compared to 20% of the female victims, were removed from their homes" (p. 193).

These findings suggest that the reported ratios of male to female victims, as well as the prevalence of male victimization, be regarded with considerable caution. Although the actual rate of female victimization is most likely higher than that of males, the differences are probably not nearly so great as has generally been thought. Reported rates reflect the fact that boys do not often disclose about their abuse. These rates also indicate the tendency of parents, teachers, and helping professionals not to suspect or recognize male victimization.

Descriptive Characteristics

As more studies are conducted on the topic of the sexual abuse of males, an increasing amount becomes known about the characteristic features of such abuse. This section reviews the literature on the following characteristics of male sexual child abuse: age at time of abuse; type and severity of abuse; gender of perpetrator; relationship between perpetrator and victim; and number of perpetrators.

AGE AT TIME OF ABUSE

Several studies have compared the ages of boy and girl victims, with mixed results. Boy victims have been found to be younger than girl victims (American Humane Association [AHA], cited in Finkelhor, 1984; DeJong et al., 1982; Pierce & Pierce, 1985; Rogers & Terry, 1984), approximately the same age as girl victims (Ellerstein & Canavan, 1980; Finkelhor et al., 1990), or slightly older than girl victims (Faller, 1989; Finkelhor, 1979). The average age of boy victims has ranged from 5.9 years (Ramsey-Klawsnik, 1990b) to 11.2 years old (Finkelhor, 1979). Almost all studies have found mean age at time of onset of abuse to be between 7 and 10 years old (DeJong et al., 1982; Ellerstein & Canavan, 1980;[2] Finkelhor et al., 1990; Pierce & Pierce, 1985; Risin & Koss, 1987; Spencer & Dunklee, 1986). Two exceptions are Faller's (1989) and Ramsey-Klawsnik's (1990b) studies, both of which are based largely on protective services cases. These studies found mean ages of 6.3 and 5.9, respectively, for boy victims.

David Finkelhor has thoroughly explored the issue of age at time of victimization. His survey of college students in 1979 found that male victims were slightly older than their female counterparts, with mean ages of 11.2 and 10.2 years, respectively. In 1981 Finkelhor reviewed the literature on victims' age by gender and indicated that boy victims are roughly the same age as girl victims, with mean ages for each group falling in the 10 to 13 range. In 1984, Finkelhor returned to the topic once again.

He offered a response to data by the American Humane Association, which had indicated that male victims were much younger than female victims, with mean ages of 8.46 years and 12.40 years, respectively. Finkelhor argued that this finding was because age was assessed in terms of age at time of report rather than age at onset of abuse. He saw the discrepancy between boys' and girls' ages as an outgrowth of the former being abused outside of the home more frequently than the latter. Because in-home abuse is likely to continue longer than extrafamilial abuse, Finkelhor reasoned that girl victims would be older than boy victims by the time the abuse came to light.

The size of the gap in ages between boy and girl victims in the American Humane Association data is most likely an artifact of the passage of time between onset and reporting of abuse, as Finkelhor surmised. It should be noted, however, that the AHA figure of 8.46 mean age for boy victims is consistent with the findings of the majority of these studies, and that Finkelhor's finding of a 11.2 mean age for boy victims stands out as the highest average in any of the major studies of male sexual abuse. The conclusion most consistent with the aggregate findings is that the AHA data were fairly accurate in terms of the age of boy victims but overestimated the age of girl victims because of the long period that elapsed between the onset of their victimization and its report or discovery. Concluding that boy victims are consistently younger than or older than girl victims would not appear to be well founded on the basis of extant research. All that can be concluded with certainty is that, like girls, boys of all ages are vulnerable to sexual abuse. Findings related to victims' age are displayed in Table 3.3.

TYPE AND SEVERITY OF ABUSE

A number of studies have examined the types of sexual maltreatment to which boys are subjected. These studies may be divided into two distinct categories—case-report and retrospective self-report studies—with quite different findings in terms of severity of abuse.

Case-Report Studies

The aggregate findings of studies of reported cases of sexual abuse, such as the hospital-based research of DeJong et al. (1982), Ellerstein and Canavan (1980), Farber, Showers, Johnson, Joseph, and Oshins (1984),

Table 3.3 Age of Male Victims

Study	Mean Age (in years)	Comments
AHA (in Finkelhor, 1984)	8.46 (boys) 12.4 (girls)	Child Protective Services cases
Condy et al. (1987)	12.53 12.63	College students Prisoners; both studies include female perpetrators only
DeJong et al. (1982)	8.7 (boys) 10.5 (girls)	Hospital-based study
Ellerstein & Canavan (1980)	9.7	Hospital-based study
Faller (1989)	6.3 (boys) 5.5 (girls)	Referrals for sexual abuse evaluation
Finkelhor (1979)	11.2	College students
Finkelhor et al. (1990)	9.9	National sample
Fromuth & Burkhart (1989)	50% ≤ 13	College students
Groth (1979b)	15% ≤ 6 68% ≤ 13	Adult male sex offenders
Kelly & Gonzalez (1990)	8.3	Out-patient therapy groups for male sexual abuse survivors
Pierce & Pierce (1985)	8.6 (boys) 10.6 (girls)	Calls to child abuse hot line
Ramsey-Klawsnik (1990b)	5.9	Child Protective Services; only cases involving victim ≤ 12
Reinhart (1987)	5.9	Referrals for sexual abuse evaluation
Risin & Koss (1987)	9.8	Higher education sample; only cases involving victim ≤ 14
Rogers & Terry (1984)	83% ≤ 12 26% ≤ 6	Hospital-based study
Spencer & Dunklee (1986)	7.2	Hospital-based study

Showers, Farber, Joseph, Oshins, and Johnson (1983), and Spencer and Dunklee (1986); the Child Protective Services research of Ramsey-Klawsnik (1990b); and Pierce and Pierce's (1985) examination of referrals from a child abuse hot line, suggest that boys are abused more severely than girls. The *Virginia Child Protection Newsletter's* review article on sexually abused boys (Grayson, 1989) concluded that the abuse of boys is more severe and more likely to include multiple forms of sexual maltreatment.

Pierce and Pierce (1985) found that boys were subjected to three or more types of sexual maltreatment in 92% of cases, versus 48% of the cases involving girls. Several studies have found that boys are more likely to experience physical as well as sexual abuse (DeJong et al., 1982; Dixon et al., 1978; Pierce & Pierce, 1985; Showers et al., 1983; Vander Mey, 1988). DeJong et al. (1982) state that 55.6% of male victims report violence compared to 31.7% of female victims. Evidence of physical trauma was also more commonly found in male victims (31.9% compared to 22.7%). Ramsey-Klawsnik's (1990b) sample of cases of male victims in the Massachusetts Protective Services system found extreme sexual victimization. Of these boys, 89% had experienced oral-genital contact; 22% had vaginal intercourse with an older female; 19% were subjected to anal intercourse; 25% had been anally raped with objects; 22% were forced to have sex with other children; and 17% had been ritually abused. Extreme abuse was also found in a study of men who had not been identified on the basis of their victimization. Petrovich and Templer (1984), who found a very high prevalence of female-perpetrated sexual abuse in the childhoods of convicted rapists, also indicated that the abuse was quite extreme. Sixty of the 73 cases of sexual abuse involved vaginal or anal intercourse, with 38 cases including fellatio and/or cunnilingus.

One conclusion that could be drawn from these studies is that boys are, in fact, subjected to more severe abuse than girls. I think it far more likely, however, that this finding reflects the fact that these studies are based solely on reported cases of sexual abuse. If boys are less likely to report abuse; if males are less likely to construe sexual interaction as abusive (especially "milder" sexual activity); and if parents and professionals are much slower to suspect sexual abuse or to respond to their suspicions, then abuse must be quite severe before it is recognized as such. As discussed above, Ramsey-Klawsnik (1990b) reached the same conclusion, arguing that abuse of boys must be more severe, obvious, and incontrovertible before it reaches protective services. She cited the higher confirmation rate of cases involving boys as further evidence for this hypothesis. Pierce and Pierce's (1985) finding that boys were removed from their homes following discovery of abuse much less frequently than girls, despite the much greater severity of their abuse, led them to a similar conclusion regarding professionals' lack of urgency and concern regarding boys' vulnerability to harm.

Self-Report Studies

If boys are not actually subjected to more extreme and severe sexual abuse, then self-report studies should reveal a different pattern than do those that rely on reported cases of abuse. We should expect that such studies would indicate a broader range of childhood sexual interaction, including noncontact as well as contact offenses; and touching, kissing, or fondling, as well as penetration. Large-scale retrospective studies, such as those of Risin and Koss (1987) with a higher education sample; Finkelhor (1979, 1981) with samples of college students and parents, respectively; Fromuth and Burkhart (1987, 1989) with two college samples; and Finkelhor et al. (1990) in a general population survey; and clinical studies such as Olson's (1990) and Krug's (1989), indicate that this is the case. Boys are exposed to a wide range of childhood sexual interaction, much of which they do not construe as negative, and extremely little of which was ever reported.

As discussed in the previous chapter, several researchers (Bolton et al., 1989; Fritz et al., 1981; Fromuth & Burkhart, 1987, 1989) have noted that age-discrepant sexual activity involving boys as opposed to girls is likely to be construed very differently by the victims themselves and by the society at large. Bolton et al. (1989) note that noncontact situations that are considered to be abusive to females are not viewed as offensive or disruptive to males. They cite exhibitionism as an offense that is only recognized within the framework of adult male perpetrator-girl victim (see also Schultz, 1979). Fromuth and Burkhart (1987) found that male college students' recall of childhood experiences included a much

> wider range of experiences involving more cross-gender experiences, many of which are perceived as non-abusive. Even when experiences are restricted to events occurring before age 13, the majority are not viewed negatively. Thus, whereas women report age-discrepant childhood sexual experiences as almost inevitably negative, men do not. (p. 252)

Therefore, based on their studies and reviews of self-recalled childhood sexual activity, these researchers concluded that males—less likely in general to report sexual abuse—are especially unlikely to report or have recognized their experiences of noncontact (and milder forms of contact) abuse. Such experiences, though virtually absent in the official data, are prevalent in retrospective studies.

Risin and Koss (1987), in their self-report study of higher education students, categorized the most serious abusive experience the men in their sample had undergone. Among sexually abused men, the most serious was exhibition in 34.7% of cases, fondling also in 34.7%, and penetration in 30.7%. Fromuth and Burkhart (1987) estimated the prevalence of sexual victimization on the bases of various abuse criteria. They did not provide a breakdown of abuse by specific acts. However, sexual interactions that are perceived negatively and that involve physical contact account for only 15% and 20% of all reports of sexual interaction in their two samples. The vast majority of sexual activity was not recalled negatively and much did not involve physical contact. Similarly, Fritz et al. (1981) found a great deal of recalled activity that was perceived as initiation rather than as abuse. Finkelhor et al. (1990) found that 9.5% of the male respondents had experienced sexual intercourse that they considered to be sexually abusive in childhood; an additional 4.5% had been touched, grabbed, or kissed in a way they construed as abuse; another 0.4% reported abusive acts of oral sex or sodomy; and an additional 2% reported such acts as exhibitionism, nude photos, or being forced or manipulated to perform sexual acts with other people. Finally, despite the fact that much of male sexual activity in childhood is recalled as benign or even positive, this attribution may be a sort of defensive patina upon disturbing and traumatizing events (Bolton et al., 1989; Fromuth & Burkhart, 1989; Risin & Koss, 1987; Sarrel & Masters, 1982). The impact of childhood sexual activity on males will be explored in Chapter 5. Findings related to type and severity of abuse are displayed in Table 3.4.

GENDER OF PERPETRATOR

As the discussion in the previous chapter on barriers to the recognition of female perpetration indicated, gender of perpetrator appears to be vastly underreported and underidentified. The barriers consist of societal attitudes regarding femininity that are incompatible with sexual abuse, and "male sexual socialization [that] encourages men to define sexual experiences as desirable as long as there is no homosexual involvement" (Fromuth & Burkhart, 1987, p. 252).

Case-Report Studies

Studies of sexual abuse of males that address the question of gender of perpetrator confirm the hypothesis that the true rate of female perpetra-

Table 3.4 Type and Severity of Abuse
(Where not specified, percentage is for boy victims)

Study	Findings			Comments
Condy et al. (1987)		*College*	*Prison*	Surveys of 359 male college students and 212 prisoners regarding childhood sexual activity; numbers refer to % of those reporting sexual interaction
	Intercourse	68%	82%	
	Oral Sex	53%	62%	
	Genital contact	84%	81%	
DeJong et al. (1982)	*Finding*	*Boys*	*Girls*	Hospital-based study
	Violence	56%	32%	
	Evidence of physical trauma	32%	23%	
Farber et al. (1984)	Boy victims experienced a greater frequency of oral-genital contact than girl victims			Hospital-based study
Finkelhor et al. (1990)	Sexual intercourse		9.5%	% of general population; miscellaneous includes exhibitionism, nude photographs, and forced sexual contact with others
	Touched, grabbed, or kissed		4.5%	
	Oral sex or sodomy		0.4%	
	Miscellaneous		2.0%	
Pierce & Pierce (1985)	*Finding*	*Boys*	*Girls*	Calls to a child abuse hot line
	Oral sex	52%	17%	
	Masturbation	40%	21%	
	Use of force	45%	30%	
	Use of threats	43%	35%	
	3 or more forms of abuse	92%	48%	
Ramsey-Klawsnik (1990b)	Oral-genital contact		89%	Child Protective Services cases
	Vaginal intercourse		22%	
	Anal intercourse		19%	
	Anal rape w/object		25%	
	Forced sex with other children		22%	
	Ritual abuse		17%	
Reinhart (1987)	Anal penetration		40%	Referrals for sexual abuse evaluation
	Oral-genital contact		35%	
Risin & Koss (1987)	*Most severe abuse experienced:*			Self-report higher education sample
	Exhibitionism		35%	
	Fondling		35%	
	Penetration		31%	
Rogers & Terry (1984)	Anal intercourse		56%	Hospital study
		Boys	*Girls*	
	Threats of physical harm	51%	31%	
Showers et al. (1983)	Anal penetration		47%	Hospital study
	Oral-genital contact		41%	

tion among male victims is severely underrepresented in reported cases of sexual abuse. As was the case with respect to type and severity of abuse, studies of male victims and survivors may be divided into two categories with distinct findings with respect to gender of perpetrator. Studies that are reliant upon reported cases or based upon investigation of sexual abuse evaluations indicate a preponderance of male perpetrators (De Francis, 1969; DeJong, 1982; Ellerstein & Canavan, 1980; Faller, 1987; Farber et al., 1984; Reinhart, 1987; Showers et al., 1983; Spencer & Dunklee, 1986).

In 1981 Finkelhor reviewed the literature on the topic and concluded that the aggregate findings of earlier studies indicated that approximately 16% of the perpetrators in cases involving male victims were female. Although several researchers had speculated that the incidence of reported female perpetration would increase along with greater candor about the subject (Groth, 1979a; Justice & Justice, 1979), Finkelhor noted that recent years had not witnessed an increase in reports and concluded that female perpetration was, in fact, quite rare. Finkelhor and Russell (1984) returned to an exploration of female perpetration a few years later. They astutely observed that official data of the American Humane Association indicating that 46% of abuse of boys was committed by women overstated the incidence of female perpetration by including cases in which a caretaker "permitted acts of sexual abuse to occur." Therefore, Finkelhor and Russell looked only at cases in which females were identified as the sole perpetrator. The adjusted data yielded a prevalence rate for female perpetration of 13%, which is consistent with most of the other studies reviewed by Finkelhor and Russell. They conclude that sexual abuse by women constitutes at most 20% of the cases involving boy victims.

Self-Report Studies

Self-report measures reveal a very different picture of the abuse of boys and the prevalence of female perpetration. Finkelhor and Russell's (1984) review of this topic cites six studies. Of these, half found prevalence rates greater than 25% for female offenders. Two of the studies that indicated lower rates of female perpetration were Finkelhor's surveys of college students (Finkelhor, 1979) and parents in Boston (Finkelhor, 1984), which found rates of 16% and 15%, respectively, for female perpetration.

The third sample that showed a relatively low rate of female perpetration was Bell et al.'s (1981a, 1981b) sample of sexually abused homosexual men among whom women had been the perpetrators in 14% of cases. In contrast, Bell et al.'s 1981 study of sexually abused heterosexual men found a prevalence rate of 27%. Gebhard, Gagnon, Pomeroy, and Christenson's (1965) survey of adult men found the same rate of female perpetration. Finally, Fritz et al. (1981), in a sample of college students, found the prevalence of female perpetration to be 60%. This result was so discrepant from all other studies on the topic that Finkelhor and Russell (1984) surmised that these "findings resulted from an unusual sample or an error in tabulation" (p. 176).[3]

With the benefit of the hindsight afforded by the passage of time since Finkelhor and Russell's review article, it now appears that Fritz et al.'s study differed from other studies largely in being ahead of its time. Though the methodology and abuse criteria used in recent self-report studies have been similar to those used in studies cited by Finkelhor and Russell, with one exception (Finkelhor et al., 1990) all such studies since Finkelhor and Russell's review have yielded much higher rates of female perpetration. Fromuth and Burkhart (1987, 1989) surveyed a total of 582 male college students at two different universities. The rates of female involvement among men reporting childhood sexual activity in the two samples were 78% and 72%. Seidner and Calhoun's survey of college men (1984) found that older females were involved in 82% of the childhood sexual activity. Olson (1990), in a clinical study of 44 sexually abused men, noted that 30 had been victims of incest. Of these, the mother was the perpetrator in 61.5% of cases, with the father perpetrating in 52%. Olson does not provide any further information regarding gender of perpetrator.

Groth's (1979b) study of convicted sex offenders contains an intriguing finding. Out of a total of 348 male sex offenders, 98 had been sexually abused in childhood. Of these 98, 47 had sexually assaulted adults ("rapists"), whereas 49 had sexually assaulted children ("child molesters"). Rapists were much more likely to have been victimized by females; 66% of the rapists reported female perpetrators. By way of contrast, only 33% of the 39 child molesters reported female perpetrators. One hundred seventy men in his original sample were convicted rapists. Of these, 31 or 18% had been sexually abused by females. Groth notes that the later sexual offenses often closely match the childhood victimization experience and speculates about causal links between the two. Similarly, Petrovich and Templer (1984) found that 59% of rapists in their study had been sexually abused by females in childhood. Briere and Smiljanich (1993) examined self-reported sexually aggressive behavior among men. They found that sexually abused men were significantly more likely than nonabused men to report having pressured women by way of continual argument into sexual intercourse. Strikingly, among the sexually abused men who reported sexual aggression against women, 80% had been sexually abused during childhood by a female perpetrator. In other words, sexual activity during childhood with an older female strongly predicted later sexual aggression against adult women. Data from these studies suggest that *childhood sexual victimization by females is a particular risk factor for later sexual assault directed at adult female victims.*

Condy et al. (1987) indicate that 16% of male college students and 46% of male prisoners (including 47% of those convicted for crimes other than sexual offenses) report sexual interaction with older females during childhood. Risin and Koss's (1987) study of 2,972 men in higher education found that 43% of those victimized were abused by a female alone, 56% by a male alone, and 4% by both. Finally, Ramsey-Klawsnik's (1990b) archival study of Child Protective Services cases in Massachusetts represents a departure from the general pattern of case-report studies yielding low estimates of the prevalence of female perpetration. Male victims were abused by females only in 34% of cases, by males only in 25% of cases, and by both in 41% of cases.

The one exception to the pattern of recent studies indicating higher rates of female perpetration than earlier studies is Finkelhor et al.'s (1990) *Los Angeles Times* national survey, which found that 83% of the offenders against boys were male. This result appears to be easily explicable, however. This survey, as noted above, asked only about sexual interactions that the respondent considered to have been abusive. Males are likely to see childhood sexual activity with older females as benign or even positive. Therefore, questions regarding sexual abuse rather than sexual activity inevitably underestimate the incidence of female perpetration (see also Fromuth & Burkhart, 1987). In fact, in his survey of attitudes regarding sexual abuse, Finkelhor (1984) himself found that "the relationships considered as the least abusive were those involving women as perpetrators" (p. 116). This finding makes it puzzling that Finkelhor would word his survey in this fashion.

It appears that studies of *sexual activity* in childhood and those specifically addressing *activities construed to be sexually abusive* constitute distinct databases. The former category, as exemplified by the studies of Fromuth and Burkhart (1987, 1989) and Risin and Koss (1987), consistently yields a broader range of sexual activity and a much higher rate of female perpetration. The latter category comprises predominantly male perpetration and more severe acts of abuse. In other words, the findings of studies investigating only those sexual acts construed as abusive are similar to studies based only on reported cases of childhood sexual abuse. The two phenomena that emerge when self-report as opposed to case-report data are examined—female perpetration and milder forms of abuse—seem to be connected. It appears that sexual activity between women and boys is generally less severe than that between men and boys (Fromuth & Burkhart, 1987; Mathews et al., 1990). Severe abuse between women and boys does occur more often than earlier writers suspected, however (Ramsey-Klawsnik, 1990a; Petrovich & Templer, 1984). Systematic studies are needed in order to assess variations in type of abuse by gender of perpetrator.

Risin and Koss (1987) were struck by the high proportion of female perpetrators in their sample, noting that this was the "one large distinction between the characteristics of the abusive incidents reported in the present study and those recorded by Finkelhor (1979)," despite the fact that almost identical criteria for abuse were used in the two studies (Risin & Koss, 1987, p. 320). They speculated that one source of this difference could be that "Finkelhor's data were collected before sexual abuse had received widespread attention in the media. Media coverage could influence the events recalled and give permission to discuss them" (p. 322). Although this may be overly optimistic, one could hope that Ramsey-Klawsnik's (1990a, 1990b) studies reflect a similar change in reported cases: That is, perhaps the increased attention to male sexual abuse in the past few years has begun to result in increased recognition of the full spectrum of this phenomenon, including abuse by females.

Although it is impossible to state with exactitude the true frequency of female victimization of boys, it is clear that earlier studies, particularly studies that relied upon reported cases of sexual abuse, significantly

Table 3.5 Gender of Perpetrator

Type of Study	Study	Percentage of Female Perpetrators	Comments
Case-Report Studies	American Humane Association, reported in Finkelhor (1984)	46%	Includes cases of female caretaker "permitting" acts to occur
	AHA, revised by Finkelhor (1984)	13%	Females as sole perpetrator
	De Francis (1969)	3%	Child Protective Services cases
	DeJong et al. (1982)	< 1% of all victims	Hospital study; no breakdown by gender of victim
	Ellerstein & Canavan (1980)	0	Hospital study
	Faller (1989)	8% female only 63% male only 29% both	Referrals for sexual abuse evaluation
	Farber et al. (1984)	2% female only 92% male only 6% both	Hospital study
	Ramsey-Klawsnik (1990b)	34% female only 25% male only 41% both male and female	Child Protective Services cases
	Reinhart (1987)	4%	Referrals for sexual abuse evaluation
	Showers et al. (1983)	11%	Hospital study
	Spencer & Dunklee (1986)	1.5%	Hospital study

underestimated the incidence of female perpetration. The previous section demonstrated, I hope, that the frequent finding that boys were abused more severely than girls is an artifact of the low rate of reporting and recognition of male victimization. Similarly, the almost universal finding that female perpetration is quite rare appears to reflect the fact that sexual interactions between women and boys are but rarely reported or recognized. The proportion of female offenders within samples of abused males has risen dramatically over the course of the 1980s and early 1990s. I would speculate that this is a result of increasing acknowledgment of the sexual victimization of males, in all its forms and variations. The findings of case-report studies and self-report studies with regard to gender of perpetrator are presented in Table 3.5.

Table 3.5 Continued

Type of Study	Study	Percentage of Female Perpetrators	Comments
Self-Report Studies	Bell et al. (1981a, 1981b)	14% 27%	Homosexual men Heterosexual men
	Finkelhor (1979)	16%	College students
	Finkelhor (1984)	15%	Fathers
	Finkelhor et al. (1990)	17%	General population sample
	Fritz et al. (1981)	60%	College students
	Fromuth & Burkhart (1987)	78%, 72%	Two college samples
	Gebhard et al. (1965)	27%	Kinsey studies; general population
	Groth (1979b)	66% 33%	Convicted rapists Convicted child molesters
	Kelly & Gonzalez (1990)	69% male only 5% female only 26% both male and female	Out-patient therapy groups for male survivors of child sexual abuse
	Olson (1990)	61.5% mothers	Out-patient clinical sample; does not provide data by gender of perpetrator
	Petrovich & Templer (1984)	59%	Convicted rapists (figure represents % of sample of rapists abused by females during childhood)
	Risin & Koss (1987)	43% female only 56% male only 4% both	Higher education sample
	Seidner & Calhoun (1984)	82%	College students

RELATIONSHIP BETWEEN
PERPETRATOR AND VICTIM

Studies that assess the relationship between perpetrator and victim have examined the following questions: How frequently are boys abused by strangers as opposed to someone they know? What proportion of the abuse of boys is intrafamilial and what proportion extrafamilial? What is the specific role relationship between perpetrator and victim?

Stranger Versus Acquaintance

One notion that appears to have been adequately dispelled by the research is that boys are predominately sexually assaulted by strangers. Though many studies indicate a high rate of extrafamilial abuse (e.g., Finkelhor, 1979; Finkelhor et al., 1990; Rogers & Terry, 1984), in the vast majority of cases the perpetrator is known to the victim prior to the onset of sexual activity (Faller, 1989; Farber et al., 1984; Finkelhor, 1979; Fromuth & Burkhart, 1987, 1989; Neilsen, 1983; Risin & Koss, 1987; Rogers & Terry, 1984; Showers et al.,1983; Spencer & Dunklee, 1986). In Fromuth and Burkhart's two college samples (1987, 1989), for example, strangers perpetrated the abuse in only 17% and 4%, respectively, of the cases.

The only exceptions to this pattern of findings appear to be Ellerstein and Canavan's (1980) and DeJong et al.'s (1982) hospital-based studies and Finkelhor et al.'s national survey (1990). Ellerstein and Canavan found strangers to constitute 44% of the perpetrators in cases involving boy victims. DeJong et al. do not provide data by gender of victim in terms of familiarity with the perpetrator. Sexual assault was perpetrated by strangers in 53.9% of the cases in their study, however, and they state that no significant gender differences were found for this variable, indicating that a high proportion of boys as well as girls were abused by strangers. Both of these studies were conducted with child victims who had arrived in hospital emergency rooms due to sexual assault. It is likely that the high rate of perpetration by strangers is due to this factor. Finkelhor et al. (1990) found that 40% of victimized boys versus 21% of girls had been abused by strangers. This study looked only at sexual activity considered by the respondent to be abusive, however, which is likely to inflate the relative frequency of reported sexual interactions with strangers. These findings are presented in Table 3.6.

Intra- Versus Extrafamilial

Like most aspects of the sexual abuse of boys, studies that assess the ratio of intrafamilial to extrafamilial abuse have produced a mixed bag of results. A number of studies have found that boys are more likely than girls to be abused by a nonfamily member (American Humane Association, cited in Finkelhor, 1984; DeJong, 1982; Farber et al., 1984; Faller,

Table 3.6 Proportion of Males Abused by Strangers

Study	Percentage of Strangers	Comments
DeJong et al. (1982)	54% of victims	Not separated by gender of victim
Ellerstein & Canavan (1980)	44%	Hospital emergency room
Farber et al. (1984)	20%	Hospital-based study
Finkelhor (1979)	25%	College students
Finkelhor et al. (1990)	40% 21% of girls	General population sample; only sexual activity considered abusive
Friedrich et al. (1988)	3%	Sexual assault center sample
Fromuth & Burkhart (1989)	17%, 4%	Two college samples
Reinhart (1987)	4%	Referrals for sexual abuse evaluation
Risin & Koss (1987)	15%	Higher education sample
Rogers & Terry (1984)	15%	Hospital-based study
Showers et al. (1983)	20%	Hospital-based study
Spencer & Dunklee (1986)	12%	Hospital-based study

1989; Finkelhor, 1979; Rogers & Terry, 1984). Several additional studies, although not comparing the rate with that for girl victims, found that extrafamilial abuse constituted the majority of sexual victimization experiences in samples of boy victims (Farber et al., 1984; Risin & Koss, 1987; Showers et al., 1983).

Several studies, however, indicate equivalent proportions of intra- and extrafamilial abuse or a preponderance of the former. The AHA data cited by Finkelhor (1984) indicate that 23% of sexually victimized boys are abused outside the home. Finkelhor argues that because these figures reflect only abuse by caretakers, they are likely to understate the prevalence of extrafamilial abuse considerably. Spencer and Dunklee (1986) found that 49% of abuse was perpetrated by a relative. Pierce and Pierce (1985) found that only 20% of perpetrators were nonfamily members. Faller (1989) found that 36.8% of perpetrators were nonfamily members. Olson's (1990) clinical study of 44 sexually abused men found that 30 had been abused by a family member and 31 by someone outside the family (most of the men in the study recorded abuse by more than one perpetrator).

Thus, there is a wide range of findings with respect to the relationship of perpetrator and victim. Estimates of the proportion of extrafamilial abuse of boys extend from 89% (Finkelhor et al., 1990) to 20% (Pierce

& Pierce, 1985). The studies that found the highest rates of intrafamilial abuse were conducted on samples from child protective services or other sources focused on in-home, or caretaker abuse. The AHA data (in Finkelhor, 1984) explicitly concern abuse related to a child's caretaker, whereas Pierce and Pierce's study (1985) was based on calls to a child abuse hot line. A large percentage (43.7%) of Faller's sample (1989) came from child protective services. The two remaining studies indicating high percentages of intrafamilial abuse (Olson, 1990; Spencer & Dunklee, 1986) each found approximately equal proportions of intra- and extra-familial victimization. It cannot be stated with certainty what the relative proportions of these two types of abuse are in the population of abused men. It appears, however, that boys who are abused are in fact more likely than girls to be victimized by a nonfamily member and that a high proportion of male sexual abuse is extrafamilial. It is significant that studies that relied on self-report rather than reported cases (Finkelhor, 1979; Risin & Koss, 1987) found higher proportions of extrafamilial abuse, 83% and 78% respectively. It is unfortunate that Fromuth and Burkhart's (1987, 1989) large self-report study of college men did not provide data on intra- versus extrafamilial victimization. Studies providing data regarding the proportions of intra- and extrafamilial perpetration are presented in Table 3.7.

*Specific Relationship Between
Perpetrator and Victim*

A number of studies have looked at more specific features of the relationship between perpetrator and victim. Ramsey-Klawsnik's (1990b) study indicated that 37% of the offenders of boy victims were adult females, 19% were adolescent females, 33% adult males, and 12% adolescent males. The most frequent perpetrators were biological mothers and fathers. The *Virginia Child Protection Newsletter* (Grayson, 1989) noted that a significant difference between boy and girl victims was the lower rate of perpetration by natural father. Ellerstein and Canavan (1980) found the natural father to be the perpetrator in 7% of cases; Spencer and Dunklee (1986) in 14%; and Pierce and Pierce (1985) in 20%. There have been several exceptions to this finding—including Friedrich, Beilke, and Urquiza (1988), who found father perpetrators to constitute 48% of offenders and Faller's (1989) study, in which natural fathers constituted 28.7% of the perpetrators. Olson's (1990) study of 44 men in out-patient

Table 3.7 Intra- Versus Extrafamilial Abuse

Study	Percentage Abused by Nonfamily Member	Comments
AHA (in Finkelhor, 1984)	23%	Reported cases
DeJong et al. (1982)	87.5% of boys 74.5% of girls	Hospital-based study
Faller (1989)	37%	Referrals for sexual abuse evaluation
Farber et al. (1984)	58%	Hospital-based study
Finkelhor (1979)	83% of boys 56% of girls	College students
Finkelhor et al. (1990)	89% of boys 71% of girls	General population sample
Kelly & Gonzalez (1990)	23%	Out-patient therapy groups for male survivors
Pierce & Pierce (1985)	20%	Child abuse hot line calls
Reinhart (1987)	38%	Referrals for sexual abuse evaluation
Risin & Koss (1987)	78%	Higher education sample
Rogers & Terry (1984)	78% of boys 48% of girls	Hospital-based study
Showers et al. (1983)	63%	Hospital-based study
Spencer & Dunklee (1986)	48%	Hospital-based study

therapy found that 61.5% had been victimized by their mothers and 52% by their fathers. The most frequent nonfamily perpetrators were neighbors (gender not specified), who offended in 23.8% of cases.

Several researchers have found a high percentage of adolescent perpetration among male victims (Ellerstein & Canavan, 1980; Ramsey-Klawsnik, 1990b; Reinhart, 1987; Rogers & Terry, 1984; Showers et al., 1983; Simari & Baskin, 1982; Spencer & Dunklee, 1986). Rogers and Terry (1984) found that 56% of boy victims were abused by juveniles compared to 28% of girls. Simari and Baskin's (1982) study of the incest histories of homosexuals found that 46% of male homosexuals reported incestuous experience. Thirty-six percent of these experiences were within the nuclear family, with 64% occurring with extended family members. The vast majority of sexual interaction occurred with brothers (32% of the incestuous experiences) and male cousins (60% of the incestuous experiences). Simari and Baskin's (1982) study is different than most of those cited here in explicitly examining incest rather than sexual abuse. For the most part, the childhood or adolescent sexual experiences described by respondents were perceived as mutually consensual activities between similar age relatives, without coercion or power differentials. Thus, by most definitions they could not be construed as abusive. This study is relevant primarily in documenting the common occurrence of intrafamilial homosexual activity reported retrospectively by adult homosexuals.

Pierce and Pierce (1985), Risin and Koss (1987), and Faller (1989) provide more detailed data on the role relationship of the perpetrator. The most frequent abuser in Pierce and Pierce's study was the stepfather, who perpetrated in 28% of cases, with the natural father and "someone outside the family" each constituting 20% of the offenders. Sibling perpetrators comprised 8% of the total, with the mother abusing in 4% of cases. Risin and Koss (1987) divided the perpetrators into six categories. Strangers abused in 15.3% of cases; neighbors, teachers, or friends of the parent in 25%; family members in 22.2%; baby-sitters in 23.1%; friends of siblings in 8.8%; and peers in 5.6%. Intrafamilial abuse is further broken down as follows: 7.4% of the total perpetrators were parents (relative frequencies for mother and father not given); 6.9% were aunts, uncles, or grandparents of the victim; 6.0% of perpetrators were siblings; and 1.9% were stepparents. In Faller's study (1989), natural fathers perpetrated in 28.7% of male abuse cases; stepfathers in 7.2%; mothers in 5%; mothers and fathers jointly in 9.2%; other relatives in 3.4%; friends or acquaintances of the family in 11.5%; and professionals (including teachers, day-care providers, camp counselors, and scout leaders) in 24.1%. These findings are presented in Table 3.8.

Several researchers have noted that an abused boy is frequently one of several victims of a perpetrator (Dixon et al., 1978; Faller, 1989; Farber et al., 1984; Finkelhor, 1984; Neilsen, 1983; Pierce & Pierce, 1985; Spencer & Dunklee, 1986). Estimates of the frequency with which boys are one of multiple victims rather than solo victims range as high as 60% (Neilsen, 1983) and 84% (Dixon et al., 1978). It is possible, however, that although boys are often victimized along with others, this finding is overstated because of the tendency not to report or recognize male victimization. Several researchers have noted that one of the most frequent ways in which abuse of boys comes to light is consequent to an investigation of their sisters' victimization (Finkelhor, 1984; Grayson, 1989; Pierce & Pierce, 1985; Sepler, 1990; Vander Mey, 1988). In other words, a male solo victim may be less likely to be identified, thus artificially inflating the rates of multiple victimization among males.

Table 3.8 Relationship Between Perpetrator and Victim

Study	Relationship		Source
Ellerstein & Canavan (1980)	Natural father	7.0%	Hospital-based study
Faller (1989)	Natural father	28.7%	Referral for sexual abuse
	Stepfather	7.2%	evaluations
	Mothers	5.0%	
	Both parents	9.2%	
	Other relatives	3.4%	
	Friends of family	11.5%	
	Professionals	24.1%	
Friedrich et al. (1988)	Natural father	48.0%	
Pierce & Pierce (1985)	Stepfather	28.0%	Calls to a child abuse hot
	Natural father	20.0%	line
	Nonrelative	20.0%	
	Sibling	8.0%	
	Mother	4.0%	
Ramsey-Klawsnik (1990b)	Adult females	37.0%	Massachusetts Child
	Adult males	33.0%	Protective Services
	Adolescent females	19%	cases: 1984-1989
	Adolescent males	12.0%	
Risin & Koss (1987)	Strangers	15.3%	Self-report higher
	Neighbor/teacher/		education sample
	friend of parents	25.0%	
	Baby-sitters	23.1%	
	Friends of siblings	8.8%	
	Peers	5.6%	
	Family members	22.0%	
	Parents	7.4%	
	Aunts/uncles/		
	grandparents	6.9%	
	Siblings	6.0%	
	Stepparents	1.9%	
Rogers & Terry (1984)	*Juvenile perpetrator*		Hospital-based study
	Male victim	56.0%	
	Female victim	28.0%	
Spencer & Dunklee (1986)	Natural father	14.0%	Hospital-based study

NUMBER OF PERPETRATORS

Researchers have also found that boys may be more likely to be victimized by several perpetrators (Burgess, 1984; Faller, 1989; Finkelhor, 1984; Rogers & Terry, 1984). Rogers and Terry found that 20% of their sample of boy victims had multiple abusers compared to 13% of their female sample. Faller found multiple perpetration in 33% and 26% of her male and female samples, respectively. Burgess and her colleagues have discussed the existence of "sex-rings" in which large amounts of victimization by multiple abusers occurs. It appears from their studies that boys are more vulnerable to this form of abuse. Olson (1990) did not provide data on numbers of abusers, but indicated that 30 of his sample of 44 sexually abused men had experienced incest, along with 31 who had been victimized outside of the family, clearly indicating a high prevalence of multiple perpetration. Some studies, however, have found moderate to low percentages of multiple perpetrators in samples of boy victims. Ramsey-Klawsnik (1990b) found that 6 out of 43 (or 14%) abused boys had more than one perpetrator. Risin and Koss (1987) report that 17.6% of their sample of sexually abused male students in higher education had multiple perpetrators. Of the 140 boys in Spencer and Dunklee's (1986) study, only one reported abuse by more than one perpetrator.

It is unclear what accounts for the discrepancies across studies of reported number of perpetrators. There may be a bimodal distribution of boy victims, including one category of boys who experience abuse at the hands of one, or perhaps two perpetrators. The second category would comprise those who are inducted into sex-rings such as those studied by Burgess (1984) and her colleagues. Another possibility is that raised by Ramsey-Klawsnik (1990b). Based on her experience investigating sexual abuse allegations, she argues that the incidence of both multiple victimization and multiple perpetration are severely underestimated. She advocates inquiring directly within any sexual abuse evaluation whether the child has any knowledge of other perpetrators or other victims.

In concluding this review of the literature on child sexual abuse, it is worth emphasizing once again the chasm between official data from reported cases of sexual abuse and data garnered from self-reports of sexual activity. It appears that the two sources yield distinct databases. First, although by either measure a higher percentage of girls is sexually abused, this difference is less pronounced in self-report studies. That is, a higher percentage of male victimization goes unreported and/or unrecognized. Second, there are significant differences between the two sources of information in terms of the specifics of the sexual abuse of boys. The vast majority of reported cases are male-perpetrated and the abuse is generally quite severe. Self-report studies, in contrast, indicate a much broader range of sexual activity, mild as well as brutal. The perpetrators in self-report studies are much more likely to be female than in case-report studies. Women represent as much as one half (Risin & Koss, 1987) or even three quarters (Fromuth & Burkhart, 1989) of all perpetrators in self-report studies. Finally, men who identify sexual activity in their childhood on self-report questionnaires are likely to construe these activities as neutral or positive rather than abusive, though it should be borne in mind that this benign attribution does not preclude negative sequelae of the childhood sexual interactions (Fromuth & Burkhart, 1989).

Notes

1. Eight of the 106 cases involved physiological injury or sexual handicap (such as endocrine imbalance resulting in development of breasts, or penile prosthesis due to vehicular accident). In these cases, there was no sexual abuse per se. Eliminating these 8 cases leaves 98 cases of perpetrated sexual abuse, or 28% of the total population under investigation.

2. *Sexual abuse* was defined in this study as "the exposure of a child to sexual stimulation inappropriate for the child's age, level of psychosocial development, and role in the family" (p. 255). Unlike any other study to my knowledge, Ellerstein and Canavan used an age limit of 21 years for their research.

3. Finkelhor and Russell (1984, p. 176) cite two other studies—Groth's study of sex offenders and MacFarlane's sample of Parents United, an organization for incest offenders and their families—that find high incidence rates of female perpetration among abuse survivors (25% and 33%, respectively). They argued that these studies were unique and unrepresentative due to the nature of their samples.

Ned's Story

Ned completed a questionnaire but was not interviewed. He indicated that he is a survivor of ritual abuse and included the following passage to describe his childhood experiences.

It started when the man was a child. A very young child. He couldn't verbalize what he saw. Too young to be able to draw any coherent picture. The images too vivid to leave. Although the rest of the class would be considering the lessons of the day his mind would be occupied by twisted scenes and gore.

On All Saints' Day you need a newborn animal, preferably a lamb, and a newborn baby girl. These were essential for the rites to have the necessary potency. The usual procedure is to have initiation rites, then have the people take of the newborns. First the lamb is killed, after defiling it. The blood is mixed with urine and feces, then smeared on the human baby. The youngest initiate is required to carry the baby around for all the elders to kiss and fondle and if desired they may also defile the baby. After the High Priest has had his way with the child and the baby, the baby is then thrown into the fire. It is only when the baby has stopped crying the orgy may begin.

4 Explanatory Models of the Impact of Child Sexual Abuse

This chapter and the next address the impact of child sexual abuse upon males. Chapter 4 reviews models and conceptual frameworks that have been developed in order to further the understanding of the effects of sexual abuse upon its victims. For the most part, these have been formulated with respect to female victims and survivors. Chapter 5 reviews the literature on the initial and long-term consequences of sexual abuse of boys.

No clear line exists between conceptual models of the impact of sexual abuse and less ambitious descriptions of the various consequences of such abuse. Most studies that assess the effects of childhood sexual victimization group these sequelae into patterns, syndromes, or constellations; only a small percentage of studies proclaim themselves explanatory models. Therefore, the decision of what to include in this discussion and what to defer to the following chapter is somewhat arbitrary. The theoretical models reviewed here are a combination of those that are most comprehensive in their coverage of the aftereffects of sexual abuse, those that have been most influential in the understanding of sexual abuse, and those that appear to be most relevant in updating the state of the field to incorporate the experience of male victims.

If there is such a fine line between explanatory models and studies that assess and describe consequences of abuse, one question that might be posed is why such models are needed. Why not simply cite the accumulated data on short- and long-term consequences of sexual abuse and leave it at that? What is gained through the development of theoretical frameworks for understanding sexual abuse? In short, do we need such models at all?

I believe that theoretical models such as those outlined in this chapter are of critical importance, both to the furtherance of the study of sexual abuse and to more effective intervention with its victims and survivors. I believe that such models must be returned to, reviewed, revised and, if necessary, replaced. Conceptual frameworks provide a lens through which to view the disparate phenomena that comprise child sexual abuse. It is only through creating such a lens—and then continually honing and polishing it—that our understanding of child sexual abuse is advanced. There is, or must be, a recursive mutual feedback loop between data collection and analysis on the one hand and theory formation on the other. Optimally, the model or framework should guide us in our choices of questions and research strategies; the resultant data should then be fed back into the loop and our theories revised accordingly. Out of the meld of theory and research arises increased knowledge of child sexual abuse and, thus, more effective avenues for intervention.

In the context of the present work this recursive loop works as follows: The models described below provided something of a foundation or starting point for the study described in the second portion of this book. One of my central points of criticism of research on sexual abuse is that it has inadequately incorporated the experiences of male victims and survivors. It is my hope, therefore, that the findings of this study can provide a feedback function and lead to an expansion of such models to include sexually abused males. Better, more timely, intervention with males could then ensue.

The Four Traumagenic Dynamics

Finkelhor and Browne's model (1985; Finkelhor, 1986, 1988), in which the various effects of sexual abuse are divided into four traumagenic (trauma-causing) dynamics, is perhaps the most influential and comprehensive framework for understanding the impact of such abuse.

The authors present these dynamics as "clusterings of injurious influences with a common theme" (1985, p. 33) and describe the psychological impact and the behavioral manifestations associated with each of these "clusterings." The four dynamics are traumatic sexualization, betrayal, powerlessness, and stigmatization. Let us allow Finkelhor and Browne (1985) to describe each:

> Traumatic sexualization refers to a process in which a child's sexuality (including both sexual feelings and sexual attitudes) is shaped in a developmentally inappropriate and interpersonally dysfunctional fashion as a result of sexual abuse. . . . Children who have been traumatically sexualized emerge from their experiences with inappropriate repertoires of sexual behavior, with confusions and misconceptions about their sexual self-concepts, and with unusual emotional associations to sexual activities. (p. 531)

Traumatic sexualization may result in an increased salience of sexual issues, and confusion about sexual identity, sexual norms, and the differences between sex and affection. This may be expressed via sexual preoccupations and compulsions, precocious or aggressive sexual behavior, promiscuity, prostitution, fear of sexual interaction, and sexual dysfunctions.

> Betrayal refers to the dynamic by which children discover that someone on whom they were vitally dependent has caused them harm. . . . Sexual abuse experiences that are perpetrated by family members or other trusted persons obviously involve more potential for betrayal than those involving strangers. . . . Children who are disbelieved, blamed, or ostracized undoubtedly experience a greater sense of betrayal than those who are supported. (pp. 531-532)

The sequelae of betrayal may include extreme dependency or impaired ability to trust others, difficulty judging the trustworthiness of others, anger, hostility, grief, and depression. These psychological states may be expressed via clinging behavior, vulnerability to subsequent abuse and exploitation, isolation, discomfort with intimate relationships, marital problems, delinquency, aggressive behaviors, and exposing one's children to victimization.

> Powerlessness . . . refers to the process in which the child's will, desires, and sense of efficacy are continually contravened. . . . [A] basic kind of powerlessness occurs in sexual abuse when a child's territory and body

space are repeatedly invaded against the child's will. This is exacerbated by whatever coercion and manipulation the offender may impose as part of the abuse process. Powerlessness is then reinforced when children see their attempt to halt the abuse frustrated. (p. 532)

Powerlessness may lead to anxiety, fear, a lowered sense of efficacy, a perception of oneself as a victim, a need to control, and identification with the aggressor. Behavioral manifestations of powerlessness may include nightmares, phobias, somatic complaints, eating and/or sleep disorders, depression, dissociation, running away, school problems, employment problems, vulnerability to subsequent victimization, aggressive behavior, delinquency, and becoming an abuser.

> Stigmatization . . . refers to the negative connotations—e.g., badness, shame, and guilt—that are communicated to the child around the experiences and that then become incorporated into the child's self-image. These negative meanings . . . can come directly from the abuser, who may blame the victim for the activity, demean the victim, or furtively convey a sense of shame about the behavior. . . . But stigmatization is also reinforced by attitudes that the victim infers or hears from other persons in the family or community. . . . Keeping the secret of having been a victim of sexual abuse may increase the sense of stigma, since it reinforces the sense of being different. (pp. 532-533)

Stigmatization may lead to feelings of guilt and shame, poor self-esteem, and a sense of being different than others. Behavioral manifestations of stigmatization may include withdrawal and isolation, substance abuse, criminal involvement, self-mutilation, and suicide.

Finkelhor and Browne's model is not presented as gender specific. That is, the four traumagenic dynamics are considered to be applicable to both male and female victims and no discussion is provided of differential impact upon males and females. The same authors acknowledge elsewhere, however, that the literature on impact of child sexual abuse is based almost entirely on female victims. Therefore, they "decided to limit [their] review to female victims. Few clinical, and even fewer empirical, studies have been done on male victims . . . and it seems premature to draw conclusions at this point [regarding male victims]" (Browne & Finkelhor, 1986, p. 66). Although it seems reasonable to hypothesize that the four traumagenic dynamics are present in male victims, it is likely that several differences exist between males and females in terms of the relative salience or potency of the four. First, it would appear that the degree of stigmatization surrounding male sexual victimization is far greater than that experienced by females. If keeping one's sexual abuse a secret increases the sense of stigma, as Browne and Finkelhor assert, then the tendency noted by many researchers of males not to report or disclose their abuse (e.g., Finkelhor, 1979; Nasjleti, 1980; Swift, 1979) would augment their stigmatization. The denial or minimization within society of male victimization is likely to make abused males feel much more isolated, unusual, and deviant. Moreover, Finkelhor and Browne state that stigmatization is reinforced by attitudes of the community: The boy victim is thus likely to be additionally stigmatized by being held accountable for the sexual interactions (Finkelhor, 1984; Nasjleti, 1980). Second, although one cannot state whether the dynamic of powerlessness is a more critical dynamic for males than females, this dynamic certainly has different meanings for each. For males, the experience of powerlessness is likely to be enormously dissonant, standing as it does at odds with the male role expectation of powerful competence and self-reliance. This issue will be discussed in depth in Chapter 9.

Post-Traumatic Stress Disorder and Sexual Abuse Symptomatology

POST-TRAUMATIC STRESS DISORDER

A second model that has been utilized to characterize the effects of child sexual abuse is borrowed from the psychiatric literature. Post-traumatic stress disorder, or PTSD, was first proposed as a syndrome commonly affecting veterans of wars. Veterans displayed characteristic symptoms months, years, even decades after their stint on the battlefield had ended. Gradually, psychiatrists and others in the helping professions recognized that the concept of PTSD has descriptive and heuristic value extending beyond military veterans. PTSD is currently defined as

> the development of characteristic symptoms following a psychologically distressing event that is outside the range of usual human experience. . . . The stressor producing this syndrome would be markedly distressing to almost anyone, and is usually experienced with intense fear, terror, and helplessness. The characteristic symptoms involve re-experiencing the trau-

matic event, avoidance of stimuli associated with the event or numbing of general responsiveness, and increased arousal. (American Psychiatric Association, 1987)

Researchers and clinicians working with survivors of natural disasters, accidents, and the Holocaust, and with victims of rape and other forms of assault, observed similar symptom patterns, leading to an extension of the concept to many different experiences beyond its original application to battle. Eventually, writers such as Lindberg and Distad (1985), Donaldson and Gardner (1985), and Eth and Pynoos (1985) came to apply the concept of PTSD to childhood abuse experiences including sexual abuse.

These writers noted considerable similarity between the presentation of adult survivors of sexual abuse and that of battle veterans. Symptoms such as intrusive memories of the trauma, flashbacks to the traumatic events, and dissociative states are common to both groups. Survivors of childhood abuse, like veterans, may avoid stimuli that trigger memories of the earlier trauma, and both may experience a psychological numbing and decreased emotional responsiveness. Both groups may experience startle responses, difficulty with sleep, and other indications of increased arousal. Survivors of childhood sexual abuse often appear to meet criteria for PTSD. They have clearly undergone a traumatic event outside the range of usual human experiences; the impact of this trauma elicits a constellation of symptoms similar to those reported in large numbers of battle veterans and survivors of disasters.

PTSD appears to have limited utility in explaining the *particular* characteristics of childhood sexual abuse, however. The fact that the traumatic experiences of abuse survivors occur during childhood, the sexual nature of the trauma, the tendency of sexual abuse to comprise an ongoing relationship rather than a single event, and the involvement of trusted caregivers and family members in most instances of the trauma make childhood sexual abuse quite distinct from military battles and natural disasters. The concept of PTSD elucidates some characteristic responses to uncontrollable trauma but does not have a great deal to say about the unique nature of sexual abuse.

Drawing upon the work of Alexander (1992), Urquiza (1993) divides the impact of childhood sexual abuse into two categories: PTSD symptoms in response to the experience of violence and coercion, and interpersonal sequelae stemming from the relationship between perpetrator and victim. Examples of the second type of impact include distrust, revictimization experiences, promiscuity, and a distorted view of the motivations and behaviors of others. Finkelhor (1988) provides a detailed critique of the application of PTSD to child sexual abuse.

SEXUAL ABUSE SYMPTOMATOLOGY

Briere and Runtz (1989; Briere, 1989), also working within the framework of psychiatric diagnosis and nosology, have attempted to identify the symptoms characteristic of survivors of childhood sexual abuse. They created a 33-item self-report symptom checklist the Trauma Symptom Checklist-33 (TSC). (Briere [1989] has added seven experimental items. The resultant experimental scale is the TSC-40.) Four constellations of symptoms were found to occur with frequency in this population: *dissociation, anxiety, depression,* and *sleep disturbance.* Briere and Runtz (1989) proposed an additional subscale consisting only of those items most highly characteristic of survivors of childhood sexual abuse, which they called *post-sexual abuse trauma-hypothesized* (PSAT-h). The symptoms most frequently reported by this population were: nightmares, flashbacks (sudden, vivid, distracting memories), sexual problems, fear of men, feelings that things are "unreal," and memory problems.

Assumptive Worlds

Janoff-Bulman (1985, 1989) focused on the cognitive aspect of the impact of various forms of trauma, including sexual abuse. All individuals carry within them certain assumptions or schemas about the world. Ordinarily, these "assumptive worlds," as she calls them, are unchallenged and unquestioned. Trauma forces its victims to reappraise their view of the world. They must either assimilate the trauma into their existing schemas or revise the schemas so as to accommodate the trauma. Janoff-Bulman focused upon three categories of assumptions, each of which are fundamentally challenged by experiences of victimization, including child sexual abuse: (1) *perceived benevolence of the world;* (2) *meaningfulness of the world;* and (3) *worthiness of the self.* Each of these are further divided into particular assumptions. The benevolence of the world comprises the perceived *benevolence of the impersonal world* and the *benevolence of people*. The meaningfulness of the world includes conceptions of *justice*—whether outcomes are distributed according to principles of justice and deservingness; *controllability*—whether outcomes correspond to a person's behavior rather than his or her character; and randomness or *chance*—whether it is possible to make sense of why particular events happen to particular people. Finally, the component parts of the "worthiness of the self" category are *self-worth; self-controllability*—the extent to which the individual sees him- or herself as exercising appropriate precautions to leave him or her minimally vulnerable in a controllable world; and *luck*—whether the individual perceives him- or herself to be lucky or unlucky.

Janoff-Bulman hypothesized that each of these would be likely to be affected by sexual abuse. She developed a self-report measure, the World Assumptions Scale, for use in assessing individuals' assumptions about the world. In her 1989 study she found that three of the eight constructs reliably distinguished victims and nonvictims. The most robust predictor was self-worth, with victims seeing themselves less positively than nonvictims. Second, victims saw the impersonal world as a significantly less benevolent place than did nonvictims. Third, victims and nonvictims differed in terms of the extent to which they perceived events as occurring by chance. Here, however, the direction of the effect depended on the gender of the respondent: Male victims, compared to male nonvictims, saw outcomes as due primarily to chance, believing that there was no way to make sense of why a given event happens to a particular person. Female victims, conversely, were less likely to perceive outcomes as randomly determined than were female nonvictims.

The notion of assumptive worlds has strengths and weaknesses similar to those of the PTSD model. It highlights an important dimension of the impact of sexual abuse. Child abuse in general, including child sexual abuse, is certainly likely to cause an individual to question and, possibly, to revise his or her perspectives on the world and on him- or herself. Moreover, this model explicitly recognizes the impact of trauma years after its occurrence, which is consistent with the findings regarding long-term sequelae of child sexual abuse. It does not incorporate the full range of effects of sexual victimization in childhood, however; it is really a model of the cognitive impact of victimization. Second, it is a conceptualization of trauma and victimization in general and therefore does not capture or convey the particular impact of child sexual abuse, including such commonly noted sequelae as fear, depression, self-blame, sexual problems, guilt, and suicidality.

Feminism

One of the most influential frameworks for understanding incest is the feminist perspective of Judith Herman (1981). Herman argues that incest stems from power imbalances between parents and children and between males and females. Because parents inevitably have more power than their children, they are prone to abuse them. However, male supremacy within society and a sexual division of labor in which women have primary responsibility for raising children result "in the asymmetrical application of the [incest] taboo to men and women" (p. 62). Thus, the paradigmatic incest situation is that between father and daughter, in which the power imbalance is greatest. Herman writes that "a frankly feminist perspective offers the best explanation of the existing data. Without an understanding of male supremacy and female oppression it is impossible to explain why the vast majority of incest perpetrators . . . are male, and why the majority of victims . . . are female" (p. 3). In her 1981 book, Herman presented the results of a study she and Hirshman conducted. They compared families in which father-daughter incest occurred and those in which the father behaved seductively or in a "covertly incestuous" manner toward his daughter but did not perpetrate overt incest.[1] They found the distinguishing feature between the two groups to be the degree of power held by the mother.

> The families in which mothers were rendered unusually powerless, whether through battering, physical disability, mental illness, or the burden of repeated childbearing, appeared to be particularly at risk for the development of overt incest. In families where a more nearly equal balance of parental power was preserved, overt incest did not develop, even though the fathers' sexual interest in their daughters was quite apparent. (p. 124)

I concur with the essence of Herman's perspective, that sexual abuse should be considered an abuse of power. As she states, "it is regarded as axiomatic that parents have more power than children" (p. 3). I also agree that the sexual division of labor and the superior position held by men contributes to the higher rate of male perpetration. In terms of understanding the impact of abuse, however, a feminist perspective appears to work best with respect to father-daughter incest and to have decreased applicability to other forms of sexual abuse. In the years since Herman's landmark work there has been increasing recognition of male victimization and female perpetration. Thus, her observations that "boys are rarely molested by their parents" (p. 10) and that she was able to find only 22 documented cases of mother-son incest in the literature appear dated. The feminist perspective retains heuristic value with respect to fathers abusing their sons, which can be seen as fathers exercising their patriarchal rights over their property. This perspective has less explanatory power when it comes to female perpetration and extrafamilial abuse, both of which appear to occur at higher rates to male victims.

The "Persisting Negative Effects" of Incest

Gelinas (1983) proposed what she hoped would provide a "coherent, explanatory and heuristic framework to identify and explain the negative effects of incest on the victim" (p. 312). In this model, the various expressions of distress commonly found among incest survivors arise out of three underlying, persisting negative effects: chronic traumatic neurosis (with secondary elaborations arising from lack of treatment), continuing relational imbalances (with secondary elaborations arising from lack of treatment), and increased intergenerational risk of incest.

Traumatic neurosis is a concept borrowed from psychoanalytic writings, including those of Ferenczi (1949) who discussed the feelings of helplessness within incestuously abused children as a result of the "overpowering force and authority of the adult [which] makes them dumb and can rob them of their senses" (p. 221; cited in Gelinas, 1983, p. 315). The traumatic neurosis, within this view, is a response to the emergence of previously repressed memories, typically within therapy. The recovery of the memories and the intense effect accompanying them are seen as the "potentially curative, cathartic emergence of a long-buried traumatic neurosis" (Gelinas, 1983, p. 315). In the absence of disclosure and effective treatment, numerous symptoms may be manifested. It is these symptoms that typically lead the survivor to seek treatment, rather than the recovery of memories and associated affect. Gelinas lists a broad range of symptoms that are manifested by incest survivors. These symptoms include depression, dissociative episodes, emotional numbing, sexual dysfunction, intense guilt, low self-esteem, substance abuse, anxiety, somatic complaints, learning disabilities, and marital difficulties. In addition, aspects of the traumatic experience may be reenacted in various ways, such as through nightmares, hallucinations, recurrent unbidden images and obsessive ideas, panic attacks, weeping episodes, and compulsive verbalizations regarding the abuse. Gelinas argues that these symptoms represent a "disguised presentation" and tend to dissipate when the survivor discloses and begins to work through the traumatic experience. These symptoms are then replaced by painful, frightening affect associated with the memories of the abuse. Working through of these feelings leads to recovery.

Gelinas discusses only female survivors. If it is true that men who were abused disclose (or discover) their childhood sexual victimization less frequently than do their female counterparts, than "disguised presentations" may be even more characteristic of male victims. The particular "masks" worn by male survivors are also likely to differ, with men tending toward aggressive and "acting-out" behaviors.

The second characteristic response pattern consists of "relational imbalances." These stem from the fact that incest is relationally based and "the traumatic events occur within the family and by a parent's agency—with all this implies about betrayal of trust, exploitation and skewed family relationships" (p. 319). Similarly, Herman (1981) states that "the horror of incest is not in the sexual act, but in the exploitation of children and the corruption of parental love" (p. 4). In Gelinas's view, incest arises out of a mixture of individual and family processes, and one must understand the complex dynamics within incestuous families in order to understand the incest and its impact. The typical family process within an incestuous family is as follows: Mothers in such families have inadequate emotional and energy resources to provide for the needs of their husbands and children. Fathers feel abandoned as a result of this loss of a maternal caretaker and respond with increasing demands for attention, affection, and nurturance. Marital estrangement ensues and escalates, and a child, typically a daughter, is parentified, or selected to take over some parental responsibilities. "The inception of incest occurs gradually and usually in the context of father's emotional needs, mother's depletion and daughter's parentification" (p. 321). The preconditions for incest to occur within Gelinas's model are as follows: serious marital estrangement; parentification of a daughter; and a father who is "needy and shows poor judgment, impulsivity or a heightened sense of entitlement" (p. 321).

Growing up within such an environment has profound effects upon incest survivors. They are likely to have a hyperdeveloped caretaking capacity and sense of responsibility, but to have very low self-esteem. They are often very passive and unassertive. Gelinas asserts that they are almost universally extremely guilty. They tend to enter into relationships in which they are exploited, often in ways similar to their childhood experiences. They generally have few friends and difficulty with marriages and parenting. Finally, they often "repeat their mothers' pattern—to marry and meekly submit to men who are immature, needy and demanding" (p. 323).

THE INTERGENERATIONAL
TRANSMISSION OF INCEST

The repetition of this pattern, and the consequent recurrence of incest in the next generation, constitutes the third underlying negative effect of incest in Gelinas's model. "When the relational imbalances of her family of origin remain unfaced and untreated she is at risk for contributing to a family structure which will repeat the incestuous family constellation and in which her husband will sexually abuse one or more of their daughters" (p. 325). Because of her own experience of parentification and focus on caretaking, she tends to select an emotionally needy man as a spouse. With the birth of children, she has inadequate energy and time to meet his needs, marital estrangement ensues, a daughter is parentified, and the process begins anew.

The recurrence of abuse across generations has received considerable attention, with respect to physical abuse (Kempe & Kempe, 1978) as well as incest. Although for obvious ethical reasons one may not conduct a prospective study of untreated incest victims to determine what percentage of them will eventually be parents within incestuous families, retrospective studies have consistently shown high incidence rates of sexual abuse in the previous generation of incestuous families (Ballard et al., 1990; Gelinas, 1983; Gerber, 1990; Groth, Hobson, & Gary, 1982). As Ballard et al. (1990) state, stories of childhood sexual victimization within perpetrator populations "could be told and retold by almost any clinical therapist involved in treating incest perpetrators and victims" (p. 52).

The perpetuation of incest across generations may be understood from within several perspectives. The psychoanalytic notion of identification with the aggressor refers to a process in which a child allies himself with the aggressive, victimizing role in order to escape painful feelings of powerlessness, shame, humiliation, and passivity. A victim of sexual abuse may perpetrate sexual abuse in order to master unresolved psychological trauma (Ballard et al., 1990; Finkelhor, 1984; Groth et al., 1982; Howells, 1981). Although both boys and girls presumably need to master incidents of traumatic sexual victimization, male socialization is likely to make the experience of powerlessness and passivity particularly intolerable to boys (Bolton et al., 1989; Finkelhor, 1984; Lew, 1990b; Sepler, 1990). Therefore, males' attempts at mastery may be more likely to be in the direction of identification with the aggressor and reversal of roles than are females'. From an early age, boys learn to see themselves as they are seen by those around them: as powerful, active, and aggressive; they may move toward that pole both in order to master their traumatic experiences and to restore a sense of congruence to their self-image.

Second, the perpetuation of abuse across generations may be understood within the framework of cognitive schemata. Children who grow up in abusive households may have a dichotomous view of interpersonal relationships. People are either perpetrators or victims; there is no template or schema for relationships based on mutuality, respect, or love. If one views relationships in such terms, the choices for future relationships are stark: abuse or be abused. For the reasons discussed above, boys may be particularly likely to gravitate toward the role of perpetrator. If a child is abused but has alternate models of relatedness, he or she is less likely to develop such a black-and-white view of the world. If there are people in the child's life who provide warmth, security, and affection, without contaminating them via molestation, the child is freed to conceive of such relationships existing (see Egeland, Jacobvitz, & Sroufe [1988] for a discussion of relationship variables in the cycle of abuse). Within this framework, it is easy to see why studies on the impact of sexual abuse (which will be discussed in depth in Chapter 5) consistently find that abuse by a parent is the most damaging form of maltreatment. In such families, it is the primary figures in the child's life who create in him or her this dichotomous worldview. This is also one way of understanding the role of therapy in such individuals' lives. The beneficent and supportive therapist offers the survivor the model and the hope for relationships based on respect and trust.

Third, sexually abusive behaviors may be learned in a straightforward fashion through the processes of modeling and social learning (Bandura, 1977). Within this view, children are not only being abused but also trained in the practice of abuse (Ballard et al., 1990; Holmes, 1983; Ramsey-Klawsnik, 1990b). Ramsey-Klawsnik's study found a high incidence of children being forced to engage in sexual activities with other children. She believes this to be an extremely underidentified phenomenon and advocates inquiring into it in any sexual abuse evaluation. She views these events as "training" in abuse and speculates that fancy theories may be unnecessary for explaining the recurrence of abuse across generations when abused children are simply taught to perpetrate.

The concepts of modeling and identification with the aggressor are both "direct" theories of the intergenerational transmission of abuse: that is, they attempt to explain how an abused child goes on to perpetrate abuse in his adult life. The family system theory of the continuity of abuse across generations, as described by Gelinas (1983) and outlined above, is far more circuitous. To review, a girl is parentified and incestuously abused by her father. The process of parentification both contributes to the incest and is fostered by the incest. As a result of her parentification, she marries a dependent man. With the birth of children, her internal resources are inadequate to meet the needs of both her husband and the children. Marital estrangement escalates and a daughter becomes parentified to help meet the parental and largely maternal tasks of the household. Eventually, these responsibilities come to include a spouse-like relationship with the father, which progresses to the point of overt incest, and the cycle continues.

This view has been criticized by feminist writers in this area (e.g., Herman, 1981; Jacobs, 1990; Russell, 1984) because it diffuses responsibility for the incest among various family members rather than placing it squarely upon the shoulders of the actual perpetrator. Therefore, feminist critics argue that the family systems framework constitutes mother-blaming.[2]

Ironically, the opposite criticism can be directed at the family systems perspective: that it excuses mothers. This perspective applies only to the paradigmatic male perpetrator-female victim domain of sexual abuse. Gelinas's model, like Herman's, is explicitly an analysis of the incestuous abuse of girls by adult men. As Finkelhor (1984) notes, "the family-systems theory, which is entirely about father-daughter incest, is virtually useless in trying to account for the sexual abuse of boys in their own family" (p. 62). Along with its limited applicability with respect to male victimization, the family-systems model as outlined by Gelinas has nothing to say about female perpetration. As a result, the family-systems theory is inevitably circuitous: It posits female victims as conduits for the recurrence of male perpetration. The progression from parentification to incest to poor object choice to parentification and incest in the next generation may well apply to a large segment of incestuous families. Recent evidence of much higher rates of male victimization and female perpetration than had previously been suspected, however, leads to the conclusion that more direct means of transmission of abuse should also be examined. In other words, male perpetrators often have a history of sexual victimization; female victims may be likely to perpetrate sexual abuse in their adult lives rather than, or in addition to, marrying abusive men. The latter speculation clearly needs a great deal of further investigation.

Abuse Characteristics and Long-Term Impact

Herman, Russell, and Trocki (1986) explored various factors in terms of which severity of abuse could be assessed and degree of long-term negative impact predicted. The factors they analyzed included age at onset of abuse, duration and frequency of abuse, age difference between victim and perpetrator, degree of force or violence involved, degree of bodily penetration involved, and the familial relationship between victim and perpetrator. They analyzed previously conducted interviews of 152 women who had identified themselves as incest survivors in a community survey (Russell, 1984) and the cases of 53 women who had participated in out-patient short-term therapy groups for incest victims (Herman & Shatzow, 1987). They found the following factors to be correlated significantly with perceived negative effects of the incest in the community sample: father or stepfather as perpetrator; severe bodily violation (vaginal, anal, or oral intercourse); forceful or violent abuse; duration of incest greater than 2 years; and an age difference of more than 10 years between perpetrator and victim. In addition, a statistically nonsignificant trend was found between early onset of abuse and estimate of negative impact.

A comparison of the community and out-patient samples echoes the findings regarding risk factors. Those in treatment reported much higher rates of the various risk factors than did the women in the community sample. For example, 75% of the women in treatment reported incest by father or stepfather, compared to 28% of the community sample; 21% reported violent abuse versus 3% of the community sample; and abuse of long duration was reported by 51% of the patient sample versus 19% of the community sample.

Herman et al.'s (1986) findings suggest that incest perpetrated by a girl's father or stepfather, beginning at an early age, occurring frequently over a long period of time, and characterized by penetration and force and/or violence presents the worst prognosis for long-term adjustment. Conversely, one-time or infrequent incidents, those occurring at a later age at the hands of a more distant relative (or brother), those in which the abuse is limited to milder forms of sexual activity, and those that include less physical violence are likely to lead to less severe negative sequelae. Herman et al.'s study (1986) provides an excellent starting point for considerations of factors associated with negative repercussions in adult life. It appears likely that several of these factors would be indicators of poor prognosis for male victims as well. However, the results of this study may not be applied whole-cloth to the experience of males. First, these surveys were conducted solely on female survivors. Second, only intrafamilial sexual abuse was explored. Third, only male perpetrators were identified within the survey. It is thus unclear to what extent the experience of male survivors in general and particularly those abused by females or by nonfamily members is addressed by these studies. There has been only one study to date (Kelly & Gonzalez, 1990) to address risk factors for male victims of child sexual abuse. The current study, contained in the second portion of this book, examines factors associated with negative sequelae for males.

Other researchers have also proposed risk factors, sometimes contradictory, for later trauma. Factors associated with the abuse that have been found to correlate with later disturbance include abuse that continues for a long period of time; abuse by a closely related person; penetration; abuse that is accompanied by force or violence; participation of the child in the abuse; unsupportive parental reaction to disclosure of the abuse; older age of victim making him or her cognizant of the violation of cultural taboos; younger age of victim; more frequent abuse; and abuse by males (Browne & Finkelhor, 1986; Finkelhor, 1979; Friedrich, Urquiza, & Beilke, 1986; MacFarlane, 1978; Russell & Finkelhor, 1984; Seidner & Calhoun, 1984; Tsai, Feldman-Summers, & Edgar, 1979). Conte and Schuerman (1987) examined other factors in the lives of children who had experienced sexual abuse and found the following factors to be most highly correlated with negative outcome: number of stressful life events the victim has faced; number of problems in the victim's family; pressure on the victim to recant the story of the abuse; and the victim perceiving him- or herself as responsible for the abuse. Most of these studies focused primarily or exclusively on female victims.

The models reviewed thus far are based primarily and in some cases solely upon the experiences of female victims/survivors of sexual abuse. Gelinas (1983) and Herman et al. (1986) considered female incest survivors exclusively, whereas Finkelhor and Browne (1985; Browne & Finkelhor, 1986) acknowledged that little was known about male victimization. Post-traumatic stress disorder was originally formulated with respect to war veterans, who were primarily male. Applications of this schema to sexual abuse survivors (Donaldson & Gardner, 1985; Lindberg & Distad, 1985), however, largely concern females. One exception is a study conducted by Williams (1991), which assessed 61 male survivors of childhood sexual abuse and found that the majority met DSM-III-R criteria for PTSD. Kelly and Gonzalez (1990) have also considered male survivors within the perspective of PTSD. The Trauma Symptom Checklist (Briere & Runtz, 1989), though first administered to female incest survivors, is readily applicable to males.

Janoff-Bulman's (1989) Assumptive Worlds Model is also equally applicable to males and females, though it does not appear to constitute a comprehensive framework for understanding the impact of child sexual abuse. As noted above, virtually nothing is known—with respect to male survivors—about the differential impact of childhood sexual abuse depending upon variations in abuse characteristics. In recent years, along with the increased examination of male victimization, a few frameworks for explaining its impact have emerged. Two of these, Bolton et al.'s (1989) abuse of sexuality model and Sepler's revision and application of a victim advocacy perspective to male victims (1990), are reviewed here.

Abuse of Sexuality

Bolton et al. (1989) proposed a framework they call the abuse of sexuality model. The need for a new model, in the view of these authors, stems from the fact that male victims view their childhood sexual interactions differently and respond to them differently than do female victims. In addition, legal and mental health professionals also have a double standard with respect to male and female victimization. Bolton et al. call for clinicians to focus more attention on environments that are detrimental to an individual's developing sexuality without escalating to overt sexual activities. They see the need for increased attunement to such backgrounds as particularly pressing for males. Bolton et al. assert that looking only at sexual interaction that is considered by the victim or survivor to be abusive inevitably underserves males, who are less likely to view such interactions as abuse. In the absence of such overt abuse, clinicians may overlook subtly sexually victimizing experiences that occur in the lives of their clients.

The abuse of sexuality model includes direct sexual contact as one end of "a continuum of environments that range from the promotion of normalized sexual development in males and females to those which eliminate the possibility of normal development" (pp. 18-19). The authors offer three assumptions upon which their model rests: that sexuality is a constant developmental element from infancy forward, that developing sexuality may be either nurtured or hindered in multiple ways, and that the hindrances to normal sexual development may reach abusive proportions at any time prior to adulthood (p. 18). Bolton et al. describe eight different environments in terms of their impact upon developing sexuality. The first two, the ideal environment and the predominantly nurturing environment, are considered to be nonabusive. Environments 3 through 7 constitute the abuse of sexuality. These environments include the evasive environment, the environmental vacuum, the permissive environment, the negative environment, and the seductive environment. The eighth category, the overtly sexual environment, constitutes clear sexual victimization. Treatment and legal involvement with abuse victims have thus far concentrated almost exclusively on this last group; these authors suggest that clinical work will be facilitated by earlier consideration of the less obviously inhibiting environments.

The ideal and the predominantly nurturing environments provide the child, at least for the most part, with "the opportunity to learn about and experience his or her developing sexuality within a supportive, nurturing, understanding, and informative environment" (p. 19). The evasive environment provides sparse information about sexual matters and may misinform purposefully or accidentally. "Models for appropriate expression of behavior and feelings are virtually absent" in the environmental vacuum (p. 22). The permissive environment can overwhelm the child by providing "too much information too soon, overstimulating the child, and failing to model appropriate boundaries for sexual activities" (p. 23). The negative environment inculcates pejorative attitudes about sexuality. Within such families, children are taught that sex is bad and they may be punished for exploring their bodies. This atmosphere causes sexual feelings to become associated with guilt, shame, and aversive consequences. The seductive environment gives a child the message that an adult is interested in him or her in sexual ways, without this interest escalating to overt sexual activity. Finally, the overtly sexual environment includes clearly sexual interactions between adults and children.

Victim Advocacy and Male Sexual Victimization

In a compelling work, Sepler (1990) reviews the evolution in treatment of sexual abuse victims from its source in victim advocacy for female rape victims. She argues that principles appropriate to female victimization are inappropriately transferred to work with males where they may do more harm than good. Victim advocacy, according to Sepler, emerged from the feminist movement and the civil rights movement. Its base in the feminist movement was the "recognition that women who had been raped were not only victims of a physical violation but also were suffering the impact of concentrically delineated imbalances of power and equity" (p. 73). Gradually, the same understanding was applied to victims of incest and other forms of sexual abuse. As long as reported cases remained overwhelmingly of the adult male perpetrator-girl victim paradigm, the view of sexual crimes as sexual violence perpetrated by males against females could continue to serve as the prevailing frame of reference for intervention. . . . As a matter of either evolution or philosophical dogmatism, victimization, and the symptoms and responses to victimization, have been largely defined from the perspective of the adult female rape victim. (p. 75)

Sepler terms this phenomenon *the feminization of victimization* (p. 74). She writes that, "as rape was a feminist issue, violence, the central ideological core of rape crisis thinking about rape, came to be viewed as an exclusive province of male culture" (pp. 74-75). In other words, the corollary to the feminization of victimization could be called the "masculinization of oppression."

Over time, increasing numbers of male victims came to the attention of the mental health and criminal justice systems. Because of the feminization of victimization (and the masculinization of oppression), however, only a small percentage of male victims are recognized as such. Sepler points out that juvenile males tend to be recognized by each of these systems only as sexual aggressors, and their experiences of "victimization discounted or minimized in lieu of an immediate focus on the current aggressive acts" (p. 76).

In Sepler's view, the basic model for defining victimization, understanding its impact, and offering treatment—a model developed for use with female victims of rape and other forms of sexual assault—breaks down when confronted with male victims. She argues that male socialization leads males to experience their victimization "from an entirely different self-view and worldview than do female victims" (p. 76). Intervention efforts, however, equate "victim" with "female" and therefore misapply treatment strategies founded on female experience to males. Sepler characterizes work with female victims as focusing upon

crisis intervention, physical safety, gaining or regaining a sense of control, and dealing with the issues of shame, guilt, powerlessness, and anger. . . . Victims have been urged to reframe their experience and to think of themselves as survivors of an ordeal. . . . The unequivocal reinforcement of the blamelessness of the victim is accompanied by practical assistance and expression of appropriate anger. (p. 75)

To males in general and the male victim in particular, however, the notion of being powerless or helpless, a victim or survivor, is anathema, according to Sepler. There is nothing he fears more than being unable to do anything about the situation in which he finds himself. Interveners who work within the female model of victimization may be "assuring" men of just what they fear. Similarly, working with a survivor of childhood sexual abuse to encourage access to anger and rage, an effective strategy with females, is superfluous with male victims who often have access only to anger, though they do not consciously connect this affect with their abuse experience. "The general framework for victimization, laden with painful affect, powerlessness, shame, and self-blame, reflects a societal bias toward the female experience of victimization and casts doubt and skepticism on the manifestations of victimization that are natural for male victims" (p. 78).

Male socialization emphasizes mastery and control. Therefore, males are unlikely to acknowledge or accede to their powerlessness or recognize themselves as victims. Instead, males tend to view themselves as consensual partners and even initiators in the sexual activity. They then act in such a way so as to reinforce this notion, including reenacting their own victimization against a vulnerable person. In other words, Sepler views much of male perpetration as a response to the intolerability of victimization for males. She argues that in order for male victims to be served effectively, the understanding of victimization and its presentation must be radically expanded. "The male victim . . . looks nothing like the sympathetic, traumatized, and vulnerable victim that the public recognizes but may instead appear aggressive, violent, masterful, commanding, and threatening" (p. 79). In order to attain an inclusive concept of victimization, professionals must learn to empathize with the diversity of gender responses to abuse and exploitation:

> It is, unfortunately, more comfortable to deal with an aggressive affect in terms of a female victim-male offender paradigm, in which the aggressive male victimizes the vulnerable female, than to recognize that aggression and antisocial conduct are viable and predictable male responses to victimization and that the disruption and damage is comparable to that suffered by a female victim. (p. 78)

Finally, Sepler directs her attention to the sexism in society that results in the denial and invalidation of male victimization and argues that this phenomenon has profound and far-reaching effects. In her view, the same forces that create a gender-specific model of victimization (victims are female; oppressors male) contributes to males responding to victimization with aggression and victimization of others. In other words, the societal denial of male victimization is itself a part of rape culture; the invalidation of the experience of the male victim contributes to sexual aggression by males.

Sepler's concept of the feminization of victimization provides a corrective for the overextension of feminist perspectives (and, perhaps ironically, those of the societal mainstream) on sexual abuse. In my opinion, where these models err is in equating victims with females. I believe that the feminist perspective is accurate in focusing upon power relationships and the differentials in power that make some people and some groups more prone to abuse and others more prone to be abused. In our society, women have less power than men and are, therefore, more vulnerable to abuse; men have more power and are thus more likely to abuse this power, including by way of sexual abuse. The fundamental underlying factor, however, is not gender but power. It is not that women are women, per se, that makes them more vulnerable to victimization, but that they are at a power disadvantage vis-à-vis another group—men. There is a very fine line, difficult to disentangle, between these two schemas. The distinction is critical, however, with respect to children. Anyone who has less power than those around him or her is vulnerable to victimization. Children are children before they are boys and girls. Children, as children, have less power than their parents, than other adults, and than older children. They are, therefore, susceptible to abuse, regardless of their gender.

Notes

1. It should be noted that a number of the behaviors described by Herman would meet the criteria of overt sexual abuse used by many researchers. Such behaviors include exhibitionism, voyeurism, and exposure to pornography.

2. Gelinas (1983) appears to have anticipated and attempted to parry this charge:

the adult who has the actual sexual contact has the primary responsibility, and blaming the adult (former victim) mother for her husband's actions constitutes scapegoating. Though mother and father share responsibility for the family constellation that often leads to incest, it is the offender who is responsible for the actual sexual contact. (p. 326)

Pete's Story

Pete is a 43-year-old homosexual cardiologist. He is the oldest of three brothers. He was sexually abused by his mother from around age two to age five. The abuse comprised being taken into bed by his mother, and fondled and masturbated. There was also a single occurrence of sexual fondling by his maternal uncle at around age four. He indicated that his mother had been continually raped as a child by her alcoholic father. In addition to the sexual abuse, Pete reported extreme physical and emotional abuse by both parents. This included severe beatings by both and a period of several years during which he was locked in his room each day from his return home from school until it was time to leave the following day. He said that both of his parents were rigid disciplinarians and that his father had an area of about 3 feet surrounding his chair with an imaginary boundary around it, the violation of which resulted in severe beatings. He stated that both of his brothers were also physically abused and that his mother beat his father, but that he was unaware of any other sexual abuse in his family. He appears to have been a parentified child, indicating that he was largely responsible for the care of his brothers and for much of the housework from the age of seven or eight.

Pete has participated in extensive therapy. He believes traditional psychological and psychiatric models to be inappropriate for work with abuse survivors and feels that self-help and process facilitation of the sort often conducted with people with addictions is a more productive format in which to work with these populations. In fact, he considers psychological and psychiatric systems of mental health as themselves representing outgrowths of addictions, and perceives himself as a recovering therapy addict. He continues to participate in 12-step groups and sees the proper role of the therapist or facilitator as the creation of a safe space in which the individual can do his or her own recovery work.

Unlike most of those in the self-help and 12-step movements, Pete has never had a difficulty with drugs or alcohol. Instead, he is a "process addict," which denotes a tendency to be addicted to certain mental or interpersonal processes, such as codependency (Bradshaw, 1988). Pete stated that his central problem is "romance addiction," which refers to a pervasive pretense that things are other than what they are. He feels that he has spent much of his life imagining that his father was really loving, that his mother was not so invasive, and that he was somewhere or someone else. This is the core legacy of his childhood abuse and the focus of much of his recovery work. Pete did not wish to respond to questions in the interview regarding how his life might be different had the sexual or the physical abuse not occurred, because engaging in such an endeavor would constitute, in his view, a return to the romance addiction that has characterized so much of his life.

About 5 years ago, while working with a process facilitator about feelings associated with his childhood abuse, Pete recognized that he had multiple personality disorder. He used a different name, Paul, to refer to himself and gradually discovered that he had two separate post office boxes, one in each name, several different wardrobes, and even a second set of eyeglasses with a different prescription. About 1½ years later, he became aware of a second alternate personality, Mike. One year after that, he became aware of a third personality, named Gildor, whom he described as primitive and "archaic." Pete indicated that throughout most of his life, it was as if no "Pete" existed. Instead, he lived from one personality to another, with no sense of a central, organizing self. As he said, "I did not recognize my self." He stated that as a child, he had so wished to be someone else that he had, in effect, become someone else and lost himself. Thus, Pete views multiple personality disorder as a severe outgrowth of romance addiction: The core fantasy of the romance addict—"I need to be someone or somewhere else"—when taken to an extreme, becomes multiple personality disorder.

Pete described Paul as extremely arrogant, full of hostility and anger. Mike, in contrast, is likable, seductive, flirtatious, gregarious, and loquacious. Over the course of his recovery work, he came to believe that Paul was the abuser and Mike the victim, and that he was acting out the abuse dynamics internally through taking on these personalities. Gildor is a very primitive personality. He is pious and asexual. Pete is least familiar with Gildor and feels that he should do more work to get to know him. He has some memories of the emergence of this personality in his early childhood (at the time of the abuse) but described Gildor as currently inactive. Presently, Pete describes himself as having a strong sense of self as a result of the enormous amount of recovery work he has done. Pete, rather than one of the other personalities, is present at all times. He can access Paul or Mike if he wishes, but does not feel the need to do so. He is able to recognize in advance when one threatens to emerge and can prevent this from occurring.

In addition to the profound impact of the abuse in terms of romance addiction and multiple personality disorder, Pete described numerous other sequelae of his disturbing upbringing. Until his recovery work, he reported that he was terrified of other people. He married a woman whom he described as dogmatic and dominating and felt unable to stand up to her or express his opinions or needs. His marriage lasted 7 years and he has two children. He thinks that without his therapeutic work he would have been abusive and said that he was initially quite rigid and authoritarian. His children live with him on weekends and during the summer and he attempts to give them clear boundaries, to teach them about "appropriate touch," and to encourage them to maintain access to their feelings and be able to express them.

He feels that his sexual abuse and the consequent confusion regarding sex and sexuality obscured his true sexual orientation. He did not realize that he was gay until he was 32. He felt that he was so focused upon the abuse and his victimization that he was unable to recognize his inner feelings. He began to recognize that he felt more similar to and comfortable or "simpatico" with gay men. He feels that his underlying sexual orientation is probably bisexual but that his preference is for men. He reports that he has been in a good and satisfying relationship for the past

4 years. Pete reported that, unlike his marriage, this relationship does not revolve around codependency. Neither he nor his partner are focused on taking care of each other or rescuing the relationship, but instead meet their own needs within the context of the relationship. He stated that his sex life, however, has been quite hindered. He reported not feeling very sexual and said that other needs—holding and affection, for example—take precedence for him over sex.

Pete's feelings about both men and women have been strongly affected by his childhood experiences. He indicated that until his recovery work he had envied men for their power and prestige and felt that he inevitably came up short compared to the men around him. Now he views this as an illusionary outgrowth of the white male patriarchal system. He said that "men are OK," and feels that he is now able to relate very well to some men—those who have broken out of their stereotypical roles. He seeks friendships with both men and women who have worked on their own recovery, and who are centered, able to speak from their hearts, and in touch with their feelings. Although he indicated that his feelings about women have also changed since he began his recovery, he appears to have much more hostility toward women. He stated that "most are bitches," and said that he feels no sense of boundaries with women. With some apparent anger, he stated that "women objectified me." He said that he now has more respect for women, at least healthy ones, than before, and that he has come to believe that they have a different reality than men's. They see life as a series of processes rather than events, and emphasize feelings over logic, in Pete's view.

Pete also sees a major impact of his abuse experiences upon his education and career. As he put it, he is "degreed to death." In addition to his M.D., Pete has received a Ph.D. and a D.D.S. He stated that he felt that he had to produce and to excel in order to be recognized and to have any sort of positive self-regard. With the increased insight that has come with therapeutic work, he recognizes that he has pursued his education and career for all of the wrong reasons. He hates being a cardiologist and indicated that he will soon leave his job to become a process facilitator.

5 The Impact of Sexual Abuse on Males

A Review of the Literature

In 1986, Angela Browne and David Finkelhor undertook a review of the literature on the effects of child sexual abuse that remains the most comprehensive and thorough coverage of this topic. As noted in Chapter 4, however, their review was limited to female victims. In the years since, a number of clinical and empirical studies have been conducted with boy victims and adult male survivors of child sexual abuse, reflecting the increased recognition of the phenomenon over this time period.

Recently, two teams of researchers have published reviews of the literature on the impact of sexual abuse on males (Bolton et al., 1989; Urquiza & Capra, 1990). Urquiza and Capra's review is presented explicitly as an extension of or companion piece to Browne and Finkelhor's (1986) article and is organized in similar clusters of effects. Initial effects are categorized in terms of behavioral disturbances and aggression, emotional reactions and self-perceptions, physical consequences and somatic complaints, and effects on sexuality. Long-term effects are grouped under depression and somatic disturbances, effects on self-esteem and self-concept, impact on interpersonal relationships, effects on sexuality, and addictive behaviors. Bolton et al. (1989) utilize the following categories of effects: emotional distress, behavior problems, sexual problems, cyclical victimization, and sexual orientation conflicts. It appears that Bolton et al.'s examination is more attuned to the unique reactions of abused males than is Urquiza and Capra's.

The current review follows the lead of Browne and Finkelhor (1986) and considers initial and long-term effects separately. The first section focuses upon initial reactions of boy victims, and the second looks at the long-term sequelae in adult male survivors of child sexual abuse. Responses are grouped according to the categories most often described with respect to male survivors. Initial effects are divided into emotional and psychological distress, and sexual problems. Long-term effects are organized in terms of emotional and psychological distress, problems and concerns related to sexuality and sexual orientation, addictive behaviors, and cyclical victimization (recapitulation of the victimization experience). To a degree, these categories are artificial and blend imperceptibly one into another. Behavior problems, for example, presumably indicate inner distress. Nonetheless, organizing the results of studies in this way provides some order with which to view the findings. This review is not intended as a general summary of research findings with respect to the impact of child sexual abuse, but as a consideration of the particular responses of abused males to their victimization. For an examination of this topic with primary reference to female victims, readers are referred to Browne and Finkelhor (1986).

A number of researchers who have studied sexual activity in childhood have asserted that sexual abuse is minimally harmful (Constantine, 1981; Henderson, 1983; Ramey, 1979) or even beneficial (Rascovsky & Rascovsky, 1950). Rush (1980) argued that sexual activity in childhood has profound negative consequences upon females but is experienced by males as inconsequential or positive. She opines that male children can dismiss incidents of sexual activity with adults as due to "childish helplessness" and reflect on the incident with "amused indifference" (p. 176). The opposite end of this spectrum is expressed by Kempe and Kempe (1984) who state that

> boys do worse than girls as victims of sexual abuse. . . . Incest leaves a boy with such severe emotional insult that emotional growth is often blocked. Some of the boys tend to be severely restricted and may be unable to handle

stress without becoming psychotic, while others may have symptoms but never be recognized as incest victims. (p. 190)

It appears to be an exercise in futility to attempt to determine whether males or females are affected more adversely by sexual abuse. As most researchers conclude, however, and as the studies reviewed here indicate, child sexual abuse has pronounced deleterious effects on its victims, regardless of their gender.

Initial Effects

EMOTIONAL AND PSYCHOLOGICAL DISTRESS

In a review of the literature on boy victims, Neilsen (1983) concluded that two thirds experience some form of emotional disturbance consequent to their victimization. The most common emotional reactions were guilt, depression, low self-esteem, sleep disturbances, and withdrawal. Conte and Schuerman's (1987) study of 85 male victims indicated that most children were affected negatively by their experience, with aggressiveness, withdrawal, poor self-esteem, and anxious efforts to please those around them the most frequent difficulties.

Most of these types of emotional and psychological distress have been found in multiple studies of boy victims, both clinical and empirical in nature. Frequent findings include problems with self-concept and self-esteem (e.g., Rogers & Terry, 1984; Sebold, 1987); guilt and shame (Froning & Mayman, 1990; Rogers & Terry, 1984; Sebold, 1987; Vander Mey, 1988); and marked anxiety (Burgess, Groth, & McCausland, 1981; Dixon et al., 1978; Froning & Mayman, 1990; Rogers & Terry, 1984). Several studies, including those of Froning and Mayman (1990), Ramsey-Klawsnik (1990b), Sebold (1987), Woods and Dean (1984), and Zaphiris (1986), found intense fear reactions in male victims. Depression was found in significant proportions of victimized boys by Adams-Tucker (1981), Rogers and Terry (1984), and Froning and Mayman (1990). Withdrawal and isolation were found by Friedrich et al. (1986), Froning and Mayman (1990), Rogers and Terry (1984), and Zaphiris (1986). A number of studies have found significant manifestations of anger and aggressiveness (Ramsey-Klawsnik, 1990b; Sebold, 1987; Summit, 1983).

Symptoms of emotional and psychological distress in boy victims are summarized in Table 5.1.

Burgess et al. (1981) conducted a study of children in sex rings and identified four patterns of impact: (1) integration of the trauma, so that it no longer caused problems; (2) avoidance, in which the victims are able to function adequately until confronted with trauma, at which time they become anxious or fearful; (3) recurrent symptoms, indicating a continuation of the trauma; (4) identification with the exploiter, which often leads to exploitation of others.

Boy victims of sexual abuse display a wide range of indications of emotional and psychological distress. For the most part, these do not appear to be distinctly different from those reported with respect to female victims (Browne & Finkelhor, 1986). Exceptions include an apparently greater incidence of issues related to homophobia and concerns about sexual orientation in males and, perhaps, more prevalent and powerful feelings of guilt. The latter pattern may be due to societal preconceptions that males are willing partners or initiators in sexual activity, which is internalized by the boy victim as self-blame for its occurrence. The following sections, on behavioral and sexual problems consequent to sexual abuse, provide evidence for a more characteristically male response pattern.

BEHAVIOR PROBLEMS

A characteristic finding regarding male victims is that they report their abuse less frequently than do females, and that their abuse is identified less readily than that of females. One result of this gender difference is that boy victims are more likely to come to the attention of helping professionals via behavioral indicators rather than through disclosure of the abuse (Ramsey-Klawsnik, 1990b; Vander Mey, 1988). Unfortunately, it may be even more likely that boys slip through the cracks of the mental health system altogether so that the first system they encounter is the criminal justice system.

Evidence of various behavioral problems has emerged in studies of boy victims. Sebold (1987) interviewed 22 therapists who had worked extensively with male sexual abuse victims, in order to assess indicators of child sexual abuse in males: The following indicators were seen as the most frequent responses to this form of victimization.

Table 5.1 Initial Effects: Emotional and Psychological Distress

Symptom	*Study*
Fear	Froning & Mayman (1990); Langsley et al. (1968); Ramsey-Klawsnik (1990b); Sebold (1987); Zaphiris (1986)
Self-concept/self-esteem problems	Bender & Grugett (1952); Burgess et al. (1981); Conte & Schuerman (1987); De Francis (1969); Rogers & Terry (1984); Sebold (1987); Symonds et al. (1980)
Guilt & shame	Bender & Grugett (1952); De Francis (1969); Froning & Mayman (1990); Rogers & Terry (1984); Sebold (1987); Vander Mey (1988)
Anxiety	Adams-Tucker (1982); Burgess et al. (1981); Conte & Schuerman (1987); Dixon et al. (1978); Froning & Mayman (1990); Rogers & Terry (1984)
Depression	Adams-Tucker (1982); Friedrich et al. (1986); Froning & Mayman (1990); Rogers & Terry (1984); Zaphiris (1986)
Sleep disturbance	Adams-Tucker (1982); Burgess et al. (1981); Dixon et al. (1978); Friedrich et al. (1986); Friedrich et al. (1987, 1988); Zaphiris (1986)
Suicidality	Adams-Tucker (1982); Dixon et al. (1978); Froning & Mayman (1990); Spencer & Dunklee (1986)
Withdrawal & isolation	Adams-Tucker (1982); Conte & Schuerman (1987); Friedrich et al. (1986); Froning & Mayman (1990); Rogers & Terry (1984); Zaphiris (1986)
Anger	Conte & Schuerman (1987); Ramsey-Klawsnik (1990b); Rogers & Terry (1984); Sebold (1987); Summit (1983); Zaphiris (1986)
Dependency	Conte & Schuerman (1987); Rogers & Terry (1984); Zaphiris (1986)

1. Homophobic Concerns. Homophobic concerns were considered the most dramatic indicator. Therapists describe a boy's anxious attempts to convince others that he is not gay, his lack of toleration for effeminate behaviors in others, and his insults and attacks directed at those he perceives as gay. Boy victims may also act in a stereotypically "macho" fashion or display (hetero)sexual braggadocio in an attempt to quell concerns regarding homosexuality.

2. Aggressive and Controlling Behavior. Abused boys often perceive themselves as small, helpless, and vulnerable to attack. They seek to gain control and to reassure themselves that they are not, in fact, as they feel themselves to be. Therefore, these boys often intimidate or overpower others, which gives them a temporary sense of power and control, but which also naturally leads to further isolation and an inability to gain more lasting reinforcement of their sense of self-worth. Sebold (1987) refers to this as the "cycle of aggression," an addiction-like pattern in which a temporary "shot" of power and control leads to further depression and a need "for a more powerful 'dose' of aggression in order to feel capable and in control" (p. 77).

3. Infantile Behavior. Sexually abused boys often display infantile speech and play patterns, and prefer relationships with younger children.

4. Paranoid/Phobic Behavior. Victimized males tend to be hypersensitive to environmental cues. They may adopt a counterphobic stance to deal with their underlying fearfulness, which may also be evidenced in frequent comments along the lines of "you can't make me." These boys may be terrified of getting caught for minor misdeeds and fear extreme punishment. This appears to be connected both with the severity of abuse and punishment many have received and with internalized feelings of guilt. Specific fears may be connected to homosexual concerns or related to the abuse being discovered or reoccurring. Fears may also arise around some environmental cue connected to the abuse.

5. Sexual Language and Behaviors. Boy victims of sexual abuse are often preoccupied by sexual thoughts, language, and behaviors. They may masturbate in public or to excess. Difficulties with concentration, increasing anxiety, and sleeping problems may also stem from these preoccupations.

6. Dreams. Several therapists reported that the dreams of abused boys often include themes of being chased, punished, or isolated.

7. Body Image Concerns. Body image concerns were commonly reported. Boys may be either compulsively neat or display little or no concern about their appearance. They may use sloppy appearance to decrease their appeal to possible molesters.

Table 5.2 Behavioral Problems Characteristic of Boy Victims (from Sebold, 1987)

- Homophobic concerns
- Aggressive and controlling behavior
- Infantile behavior
- Paranoid/phobic behavior
- Sexual language and behaviors
- Dreams of being chased, punished, or isolated
- Body image concerns

---

8. Other Indicators. Clinicians reported other possible indicators such as setting fires—a symptom that they see very rarely in female victims—running away, prostitution, enuresis and encopresis, and failure to develop trust and intimacy. These characteristics are presented in Table 5.2.

The issues raised by Sebold (1987) have been echoed by several researchers. Bolton et al. (1989) state that a central difference between male and female responses to sexual victimization is the tendency of the former to respond with aggressive, antisocial, and undercontrolled externalizing behaviors. It should be kept in mind that this tendency is not specific to sexually abused populations: In general, males are thought to display more of these type of "acting-out" behaviors, whereas females are more likely to internalize distress, with greater incidences of depression and somatic problems (Achenbach & Edelbrock, 1983).

Several studies have found severe behavioral problems in abused boys. Common problems include fighting and other displays of aggression (Friedrich et al., 1987, 1988; Friedrich et al., 1986; Kohan et al., 1987); suicide attempts or ideation (Adams-Tucker, 1981; Spencer & Dunklee, 1986); sleep disturbance and nightmares (Dixon et al., 1978; Friedrich et al., 1987, 1988; Friedrich et al., 1986; Zaphiris, 1986); hyperactivity (Friedrich et al., 1987, 1988; Friedrich et al., 1986; Ramsey-Klawsnik, 1990b); and regressive behaviors such as thumb-sucking, enuresis, or encopresis (Rogers & Terry, 1984; Ramsey-Klawsnik, 1990b; Spencer & Dunklee, 1986). Other reported behavior problems include declining school performance and school avoidance (Rogers & Terry, 1984); homicidal ideation (Dixon et al., 1978); running away from home

Table 5.3 Initial Effects: Behavioral Problems

Symptom	Study
Fighting/aggression	Friedrich et al. (1986); Friedrich et al. (1987, 1988); Froning & Mayman (1990); Kohan et al. (1987); Ramsey-Klawsnik (1990b); Rogers & Terry (1984); Zaphiris (1986)
Hyperactivity	Friedrich et al. (1986) Friedrich et al. (1987, 1988); Ramsey-Klawsnik (1990b)
Infantile behavior	Dixon et al. (1978); Friedrich et al. (1986); Friedrich et al. (1987, 1988); Geiser & Norberta (1976); Ramsey-Klawsnik (1990b); Rogers & Terry (1984); Spencer & Dunklee (1986)
Drug/alcohol abuse	Rogers & Terry (1984); Zaphiris (1986)
Delinquency	Bender & Blau (1937); Geiser & Norberta (1976); Rogers & Terry (1984); Zaphiris (1986)

(Rogers & Terry, 1984; Zaphiris, 1986); drug and alcohol use (Rogers & Terry, 1984; Zaphiris, 1986); and delinquency (Geiser & Norberta, 1976; Zaphiris, 1986). Findings with respect to behavior problems in sexually abused boys are displayed in Table 5.3.

One problem posed by these findings is that it is difficult to determine to what extent the various indications of disturbance stem from sexual abuse. Large percentages of victimized children come from families with multiple problems, including drug and alcohol abuse, poverty, enmeshment, and physical abuse, to name just a few (Bolton et al., 1989). Moreover, each of the behavioral problems noted here are also displayed by boys who have not been sexually abused. Sebold's (1987) interviews of clinicians experienced in work with victimized boys was an attempt to elucidate the behavioral indicators that distinguish sexually abused boys. In a series of studies, Friedrich et al. (1987, 1988; Friedrich et al., 1986) also compared sexually abused boys with a clinical sample of nonabused boys (identified as conduct-disordered) and with nonclinical control groups. They found the abused boys to be equivalent to the nonabused clinical sample in terms of depression and anxiety; to display less hyperactivity and aggression; and to be more sexualized. Abused boys displayed more externalized behavior problems and were more sexualized than the nonclinical control sample.

Summit (1983) views aggression and antisocial behavior as the modal response of male victims. Any victim must "accommodate" his or her sexually abusive experience. Dealing with the sense of helplessness is a pivotal part of the accommodation process. This process is more difficult for the male because of his tendency to blame himself for his inability to self-protect. The sudden loss of power and control are devastating for the boy victim because of the prominence of these elements in male socialization. The resultant clinical presentation tends to be one of rage and guilt. Acting-out behaviors often ensue because of the intolerability of the victim state for males (see also the review of Sepler [1990] in Chapter 4 for a discussion of this pattern in males).

SEXUAL PROBLEMS AND CONCERNS

This category comprises both sexualized behaviors such as increased masturbation and sexual aggression consequent to sexual abuse, and internal concerns including sexual preoccupations and confusion about sexual identity and sexual orientation. Rogers and Terry (1984) identified three reactions characteristic of boy victims:

1. *Confusion/Anxiety Over Sexual Identity.* In their study, Rogers and Terry (1984) found that male victims frequently seek explanations of why they were selected for abuse. They often blame themselves and believe the abuse was due to some indication of femininity or homosexuality on their part. This concern is reinforced by the absence of physical resistance and the inability to protect oneself, which in our culture are equated with failures in masculinity. Boy victims also express anxiety over sexual identity as a result of finding their experiences pleasurable.

2. *Inappropriate Attempts to Reassert Masculinity.* Rogers and Terry indicate that many boy victims attempt to reassert their masculinity by way of aggressive behavior and posit that this may be the most common behavioral reaction of boys. These researchers view this dynamic as indicative of a compensatory overidentification with the masculine stereotype. Manifestations of aggression include fights; bullying; destruction of property; and confrontational, defiant, or disobedient behavior.

3. *Recapitulation of the Victimizing Experience.* Rogers and Terry note the likelihood that a boy victim will "recreate [a] scenario similar to his own victimization, with modes of inducing compliance, specific sexual acts, and even age differences being patterned after the original incident"

(p. 97). They view this dynamic as an extension of inappropriate attempts to reassert masculinity. Thus, the cycle of victimization, in their view, derives from the boy victim's efforts to reassure himself of his masculinity, which has been taken from him by his own victimization experience. The victimized child, according to Rogers and Terry, may have a worldview that encompasses only two choices: abuser or victim; he chooses the former to escape the latter.

Several studies of sexually abused boys have found concerns about sexuality or sexual orientation (Johnson & Shrier, 1987; Sebold, 1987; Shrier & Johnson, 1988; Zaphiris, 1986). In a series of studies of male adolescents in an out-patient medical clinic, Johnson and Shrier (1985, 1987; Shrier & Johnson, 1988) indicated that more abused than non-abused males presented to the clinic due to sexually related psychosocial problems. Of the abused adolescents, 22.5%—versus 7.5% of nonabused adolescents—sought assistance with sexual issues, including confusion about sexual orientation, difficulties with interpersonal relationships, and problems with sexual performance.

Numerous studies indicate that a characteristic response of boys to their sexual abuse is the sexual victimization of others (Friedrich et al., 1987, 1988; Friedrich & Luecke, 1988; Friedrich et al., 1986; Groth, 1977; Kohan et al., 1987; Ramsey-Klawsnik, 1990b; Zaphiris, 1986). In Ramsey-Klawsnik's (1990b) study, 51% of abused boys sexually offended against other children. More than half of these had been actively and directly trained to assault others sexually by their adult offenders as part of their abuse. Friedrich and Luecke (1988) found that of 14 boys identified as sexually aggressive, 11 were known to have been sexually victimized.

Friedrich et al. (1987, 1988; Friedrich et al., 1986) found that sexually abused boys were more sexualized than both clinical and nonclinical comparison groups, with increased masturbatory activity and interest in their mother's body and clothing. More than half of the parents reported that their children "played with sex parts too much" and "thought about sex too much," and 15% said their children demonstrated behavior or expressed a desire to be like the opposite sex. Findings based on parental reports may, however, say as much about the parents as about their children. A number of other studies provide additional evidence for increased sexual behavior, such as masturbation and use of sexual language, in abused boys (Froning & Mayman, 1990; Kohan et al., 1987;

Table 5.4 Initial Effects: Sexual Problems and Concerns

Symptom	*Study*
Concerns about sexuality/ sexual orientation	Froning & Mayman (1990); Johnson & Shrier (1987); Rogers & Terry (1984); Sebold (1987); Zaphiris (1986)
Sexual victimization of others	Cantwell (1988); Friedrich et al. (1986); Friedrich et al. (1987, 1988); Friedrich & Luecke (1988); Groth (1977); Johnson (1988); Kohan et al. (1987); Ramsey-Klawsnik (1990b); Rogers & Terry (1984); Zaphiris (1986)
Sexualized behavior	Friedrich et al. (1986); Friedrich et al. (1987, 1988); Froning & Mayman (1990); Kohan et al. (1987); Zaphiris (1986)

Zaphiris, 1986). Sexual problems and concerns displayed by boy victims of sexual abuse are displayed in Table 5.4.

Long-Term Effects

Most of the remainder of this chapter explores the sequelae in adult men of childhood sexual abuse. Included in this section are symptoms and responses related to emotional and psychological distress, relationship difficulties, sexual problems and sexual orientation concerns, addictive behaviors, and cyclical victimization (recapitulation of the victimization experience). Grayson (1990) provides a summary of these issues for male survivors. The caveat that preceded the section on initial effects applies here as well: The creation of these categories is artificial. All are interrelated in the experiences of the survivors. Before turning to these domains, Kelly and Gonzalez's (1990) study in progress, which cuts across categories, is reviewed.

Kelly and Gonzalez (1990) assessed the symptomatology of men who wished to join an out-patient treatment group for male survivors of sexual abuse. Severely disturbed men and those who reported being attracted to or having molested children were excluded from the groups and, therefore, from their study. Their study represents an integration of two conceptual frameworks for understanding the impact of sexual abuse—the psychiatric model, which is an extension of research on post-traumatic stress disorder (Briere & Runtz, 1989), and Finkelhor and Browne's (1986) model of the four traumagenic dynamics of child sexual abuse. Two checklists were used for data collection: the Trauma Symptom

Checklist (Briere & Runtz, 1989), and an original measure based on Finkelhor and Browne's (1986) theory. The problems or symptoms were then placed in one of Finkelhor and Browne's four traumagenic categories. A complete list of the items, the traumagenic dynamics under which they are subsumed, and preliminary data on the percentages of men indicating previous or current difficulties in each area is presented in Table 5.5. Kelly and Gonzalez also analyzed Minnesota Multiphasic Personality Inventory (Dahlstrom & Welsh, 1960) data from the first 38 men in their study and found that most profiles included multiple clinically significant elevations. Twenty-nine profiles (78%) had three or more clinical scales elevated, with 22 profiles (59%) having five or more elevated scales. The most frequently elevated scales in this sample were Masculinity-Femininity, Depression, Psychopathic-Deviate, and Schizophrenia. Twenty-nine percent of the men met DSM-III-R (American Psychiatric Association, 1987) criteria for post-traumatic stress disorder.

Kelly and Gonzalez (1990) conclude that male survivors, like their female counterparts, experience the dynamics of betrayal, powerlessness, stigmatization, and traumatic sexualization identified by Finkelhor and Browne (1986). They suggest that the psychological impact of these dynamics may be different because of the very different socialization process males undergo, and call for further research on the gender-specific effects of sexual abuse, which they hope can then be incorporated into gender-specific clinical interventions.

EMOTIONAL AND PSYCHOLOGICAL DISTRESS

In the past several years a number of studies have been conducted with adult male survivors of child sexual abuse. These studies indicate a broad range of emotional and psychological difficulties. Briere, Evans, Runtz, and Wall (1988) found that abused males reported a greater degree of psychiatric symptomatology, including dissociation, anxiety, depression, and sleep disturbance, than a comparison sample of nonabused men.

Fromuth and Burkhart (1987, 1989) administered extensive questionnaires to male undergraduates at two universities, one in the Midwestern United States and the other in the Southeast. They found small but statistically significant correlations between sexual abuse and negative psychological adjustment in the Midwestern sample (1989). Significant correlations were found between childhood sexual activity with older

Table 5.5 Symptomatology of Sexually Abused Males (from Kelly and Gonzalez, 1990)

Symptom	Percentage of Men Reporting Symptom
Traumatic sexualization	
Confusion about sexual identity	63%
Aversion to sexual intimacy	44%
Sexual dysfunction	44%
Sexual preoccupations	75%
Compulsive sexual behaviors	44%
Aggressive sexual behaviors	13%
Stigmatization	
Extreme guilt	69%
Extreme shame	69%
Sense of being different than others	94%
Lowered self-esteem	100%
Feelings of isolation	88%
Substance abuse	
Eating problems	44%
Drug or alcohol abuse	38%
Betrayal	
Depression	88%
Suicidal thoughts	81%
Suicide attempts	13%
Extreme dependency	50%
Impaired ability to trust others	
To trust men	81%
To trust women	50%
Discomfort in intimate relationships	81%
Marital problems	100%
Family problems	75%
Difficulty with male friendships	75%
Difficulty with female friendships	31%
Difficulty establishing romantic relationships	63%
Difficulty maintaining romantic relationships	56%
Powerlessness	
Extreme anxiety	69%
Flashbacks	81%
Nightmares	63%
Sleeping problems	63%
Extreme anger	56%
Employment problems	44%
Self-injurious behaviors	31%
Aggressive behaviors	13%
Criminal involvement	13%

people and Obsessive Compulsiveness, Interpersonal Sensitivity, Depression, Hostility, Paranoid Ideation, and Psychoticism, as assessed by the SCL-90, a psychiatric symptom checklist (Derogatis et al., 1973). These findings are particularly relevant because they demonstrate that such interactions need not be construed negatively or as abusive in order to produce deleterious effects. The Midwestern sample in Fromuth and Burkhart's study reported predominantly female perpetrators (78%) and 60% of those who indicated a history of sexual interaction in childhood stated that they experienced the interactions with interest and pleasure. Nonetheless, sexual interaction is negatively associated with later psychological adjustment.[1]

Peter Olson (1990) conducted a study of 44 sexually abused men who received treatment at an out-patient clinic and a 25-man clinical out-patient control group. He administered five scales of the Minnesota Multiphasic Personality Inventory (Dahlstrom & Welsh, 1960), which he hypothesized would distinguish abused and nonabused males, and found that the victim group indicated significantly more pathology than the clinical control group on all five scales and in terms of overall adjustment. The scales used by Olson were masculinity-femininity, which suggests nonsubscription to traditional sex roles and/or passivity; psychopathic deviance, which measures level of rebelliousness or conflict, with higher scores indicating more overt struggle, an intense level of conflict with society and, possibly, criminal behavior, compulsions, or other antisocial characteristics; schizophrenia, which measures disturbances in thinking, mental confusion, thinking disorders, a lack of logic, and possible chronic disorientation; paranoia, which indicates a higher sensitivity, paranoia, or suspiciousness of others; and psychasthenia, which refers to a long-term trait of anxiety and may include such attributes as a sense of dread, omnipotence, fear of falling, limited productivity, low self-confidence, and moodiness.

Olson also administered a symptom checklist and found significant differences between victims and nonvictims in terms of numerous problems. Compared to the nonabused out-patient sample, sexually abused men displayed a greater degree of substance abuse; compulsive behaviors including sexual behaviors, overworking, spending, and overeating; rage; criminal behavior and arrest history; self-mutilation; involvement with abusive partners; and school truancy.

Bruckner and Johnson (1987) compared their experience conducting groups for male survivors of sexual abuse with those they had facilitated with females. They found that intense anger, often including fantasies of retribution, were seen much more frequently in men. Compared to women, men were more outwardly aggressive and tended to display anger rather than depression or guilt. Men were more action oriented and focused more often and more quickly upon confrontation. They often sought confrontation with the perpetrator(s). Bruckner and Johnson also note that men displayed a greater willingness and desire to make their childhood abuse and its impact public. After an initial dread of disclosure akin to that of women in their groups, men were more eager to educate others. Finally, they found that men were more assertive in taking steps to reverse the dynamics of their situation and retake control of their lives.

Several researchers and clinicians have noted that a history of child sexual abuse is correlated with decreased self-esteem (Bruckner & Johnson, 1987; Finkelhor, 1981; Hunter, 1993; Lew, 1990b; Kelly & Gonzalez, 1990). Hunter (1993) views shame as a prominent outcome of abuse and asserts that male survivors often assume that their abuse occurred because they were bad and that it will not continue or reoccur if only they are good enough. Urquiza and Crowley (1986) administered the Tennessee Self-Concept Scale (TSCS) to abused men and a matched comparison group. They found that the abused group had poorer self-concepts on seven of eight scales: identity, self-satisfaction, behavioral self, physical self, moral-ethical self, personal self, and family self. Other common sequelae of sexual abuse of boys include suicidality (Briere et al., 1988; Kelly & Gonzalez, 1990); depression (Krug, 1989; Stein, Golding, Siegel, Burnam, & Sorenson, 1988; Urquiza & Crowley, 1986); and rage (Bruckner & Johnson, 1987; Fromuth & Burkhart, 1989; Lew, 1990b). Krug (1989) found that seven of eight men in his clinical sample who had been sexually abused by their mothers in childhood reported depression. In his opinion, their depression was characterized by anger turned in against the self because anger or rage against the mother was seen as inappropriate or intolerable. Psychological and emotional sequelae of sexual abuse are summarized in Table 5.6.

RELATIONSHIP DIFFICULTIES

Several researchers have noted disturbances in the relationships of men who had been sexually abused as children (Bruckner & Johnson, 1987; Dimock, 1988; Kelly & Gonzalez, 1990; Krug, 1989; Lew, 1990b; Olson, 1990; Steele & Alexander, 1981; Urquiza, 1993; Woods & Dean,

Table 5.6 Long-Term Effects: Emotional and Psychological Distress

Symptom	Study
Anger	Bruckner & Johnson (1987); Carmen et al. (1984); Freeman-Longo (1986); Fromuth & Burkhart (1987); Kelly (1989); Krug (1989); Lew (1990b); Olson (1990); Summit (1983); Woods & Dean (1984)
Self-concept/self-esteem problems	Bruckner & Johnson (1987); Carmen et al. (1984); Finkelhor (1981); Hunter (1993); Kelly (1989); Lew (1990b); Myers (1989); Urquiza & Crowley (1986)
Relationship problems	Bruckner & Johnson (1987); Dimock (1988); Krug (1989); Lew (1990b); Olson (1990); Steele & Alexander (1981); Woods and Dean (1984)
Suicidality	Adams-Tucker (1982); Briere et al. (1988); Dixon et al. (1978); Kelly (1989)
Depression	Fromuth & Burkhart (1987); Kelly & Gonzalez (1990); Krug (1989); Stein et al. (1987); Urquiza & Crowley (1986)

1984). Lew (1990b) and Dimock (1988) view difficulties with intimate relationships as hallmarks of sexual abuse. Bruckner and Johnson (1987) state that abused men tend to have a great deal of emotional constriction and to find it hard to talk about feelings. Men in their groups frequently reported problems establishing and maintaining intimate relationships or trusting others. They had particular difficulty establishing friendships with men.

Several of these researchers assert that sexually abused men are likely to have difficulty maintaining intimate relationships and are often unfaithful to partners, promiscuous, and/or maintain multiple concurrent partners (Krug, 1989; Steele & Alexander, 1981; Urquiza, 1993; Woods & Dean, 1984). Krug (1989) notes that all of the men in his clinical sample had difficulties maintaining intimate relationships. He connects this with their experience of having parented their own parent or parents in childhood, a pattern that characterized seven of the eight men he treated and that left them incapable of meeting their own needs within a relationship. Urquiza (1993) found that sexually abused men were more likely to have "one-night stands" and less likely to have "best-friend" relationships. He administered Hazan and Shaver's (1987) measure of adult attachment and found that abuse survivors had fewer secure attachments and more avoidant attachments than men who had not experienced childhood sexual victimization.

Dimock (1988) interviewed 25 adult male survivors of child sexual abuse and concluded that relationship dysfunction was one of three characteristic sequelae of childhood sexual abuse among males (the other two response patterns—compulsive sexual behavior and masculine identity confusion—will be discussed in the section on sexuality below). The relational problems he found include difficulty maintaining stability in intimate relationships and inability to form supportive friendships with men. Several of the men reported involvement in abusive relationships in adulthood that mirrored their victimization experiences in childhood. Relationships were often characterized by intense involvement followed by abrupt withdrawal and isolation. In ongoing relationships this pattern often becomes repetitive, with both partners frequently threatening to leave the unstable relationship. Coping mechanisms that had been learned in childhood—such as "turning off" or "checking out" during sexual encounters—were applied maladaptively to later relationships.

SEXUALITY AND SEXUAL PROBLEMS

Difficulties with, and concerns about, sexuality have been a recurrent finding in studies of adult survivors of child sexual abuse, including men. Finkelhor (1981) noted that this population was often dissatisfied with their sexual interactions in adulthood. He devised a 6-item questionnaire to assess what he called sexual self-esteem and found that abuse survivors were especially likely to endorse the following statement: "After sexual experiences, I often feel dissatisfied" (p. 81). Bruckner and Johnson (1987) state that male survivors are often plagued with doubts about their independence and masculinity and attempt to prove their self-worth and adequacy strictly through sexual activity; conversely, survivors of childhood sexual abuse may avoid sexual activity entirely due to their fears and insecurity about sexuality. Woods and Dean (1984) also note that sexual dissatisfaction is common among male survivors.

Dimock (1988) identified compulsive sexual behavior as one of three common characteristics of male survivors, along with relationship dysfunction and masculine identity confusion. Dimock found that men who had been sexually victimized in childhood frequently display compulsive sexuality, which includes preoccupation with sexual thoughts, fascination with pornography, compulsive masturbation, sexual interactions in places such as rest rooms and pornographic bookstores, and frequent and multiple sex partners.

Several other authors identified sexual compulsiveness or preoccupation as a frequent aftereffect of sexual abuse in males (Carlson, Dimock, Driggs, & Westly, 1987; Hunter, 1987; Kelly & Gonzalez, 1990; Urquiza, 1993; Woods & Dean, 1984). Carlson et al.'s study found that 37% of sexually compulsive men reported childhood sexual abuse. Janus et al. (1984) found that 39% of young male prostitutes in their sample had been incestuously abused, and 86% reported a coercive sexual experience prior to becoming prostitutes. Using "coercive sexual experience" as a criterion for sexual abuse is a very narrow, restrictive definition and the incidence of sexual abuse among boy prostitutes may be even higher. Ginsburg (1967) and Coombs (1974) also view prostitution as a frequent outcome of sexual abuse of boys.

Sexual dysfunction has been noted by several researchers (Fromuth & Burkhart, 1989; Johnson & Shrier, 1985, 1987; Sarrel & Masters, 1982; Woods & Dean, 1984). Fromuth and Burkhart's (1989) study of two undergraduate samples found that sexual abuse during childhood was correlated in one sample with premature ejaculation and in the other sample with difficulties maintaining an erection. Of Johnson and Shrier's (1987) sample of abused males, 22% reported sexual dysfunctions compared to 7.5% of controls.

Sarrel and Masters (1982) conducted an intriguing study of 11 men molested by women. They use the term *molestation* to encompass both sexual assault ("undesired sexual activity under threat of physical violence") and sexual abuse (undesired sexual activity as a result of being "overwhelmed by female psychosocial dominance or sexual seduction," pp. 117-118). Their study includes four cases of forced assault; two cases of "baby-sitter abuse," the seduction of a boy by an older female, which may involve direct or implied threats if the incident is reported; two cases of incestuous abuse;[2] and three cases of "dominant woman abuse," an aggressive sexual approach to an adult male that intimidates or terrifies the victim. Even though only 4 of the 11 men in their clinical report correspond to the population studied here (because the other 7 were adults at the time of their victimization experience), Sarrel and Masters found that a consistent pattern of difficulties was displayed by the men in their study. They conclude that the response pattern of these men to their sexual victimization represents a post-sexual assault syndrome analogous to the post-rape trauma syndrome identified by Burgess and Holmstrom (1974) with respect to women. This characteristic response pattern included depression, sexual aversion, and sexual dysfunction. The specific sexual problems reported in this sample include primary impotence, secondary impotence, ejaculatory incompetence, sexual aversion, rapid ejaculation, and inhibited sexual desire. Perhaps the most significant finding of this study is that only 1 of the 11 men sought help because of the molestation experience; the remaining 10 requested treatment because of sexual dysfunctions that they did not consciously associate with the sexual victimization. This finding provides additional support for the hypothesis that sexual abuse of males is only likely to come to light via the emergence of problems secondary to the abuse itself.

SEXUAL ORIENTATION

Most explorations of the long-term effects of sexual abuse upon males have found these experiences to have had a considerable impact in the area of sexual orientation. The third response pattern Dimock (1988) found to be characteristic of male survivors of childhood sexual abuse is masculine identity confusion, which encompasses both sexual orientation and stereotypical male roles. Sixteen of the 25 abused men in his study were classified as confused with respect to their sexual orientation. Confusion was operationally defined as (1) having sexual relations with a partner who is of the sex opposite to one's stated sexual orientation; (2) being unable to state one's sexual orientation; or (3) expressing conscious doubts about sexual orientation that the respondent under-stands to be connected with the abuse experience. Many of the abused men indicated severe doubts about their own masculinity and often saw themselves as failures as men. They used attributes such as "gay" or "wimp" to describe themselves and struggled with their inability to protect themselves from their abuse and what this weakness and vulner-ability signified for them as men.

Several researchers have found higher rates of sexual abuse among homosexual than heterosexual populations or higher rates of homosexual orientation among those who report childhood sexual abuse than among the general population (Bell et al., 1981a, 1981b; Finkelhor, 1984; Johnson & Shrier, 1987; Simari & Baskin, 1981). A number of additional studies indicate that male sexual abuse survivors often express serious concerns about or confusion regarding sexual orientation (Bolton et al., 1989; Bruckner & Johnson, 1987; Dimock, 1988; Hunter, 1990a; Lew, 1990b; Olson, 1990).

Johnson and Shrier's (1985, 1987) studies of adolescents in an outpatient medical clinic indicate that homosexual identification is seven times greater and bisexual identification six times greater for victimized males than for a comparison group of nonabused adolescent boys. In their second study, Johnson and Shrier (1987) compared the 11 adolescents molested by females with the 14 adolescents victimized by males and found that the sexual orientation effect was specific to the male-molested group. Those abused by females were no more likely to identify themselves as homosexual than nonabused controls. Approximately one half of those abused by males identified themselves as homosexual and often linked homosexuality to sexual victimization.

Simari and Baskin (1982) found a very high rate of incest in the childhoods of homosexuals they interviewed. Incestuous experiences were reported by 46% of male homosexuals, with approximately two thirds (64%) of this involving the extended family and one third (36%) involving the nuclear family. The most frequent partners in incest were brothers (32%) and male first cousins (60%). Simari and Baskin report that 96% of their respondents indicated that "they identified themselves as actively homosexual before the occurrence of the incestuous event" (p. 334). In light of the fact that incestuous activity was primarily with brothers and first cousins of the respondents and occurred in early adolescence or just prior to adolescence, these occurrences may have represented consensual acts. Nonetheless, that almost one half of homosexual males report childhood incestuous activity is certainly a striking finding.

Other studies that address the connection between sexual orientation and sexual abuse have yielded mixed results. Fromuth and Burkhart's (1989) study, which looked at a broader range of sexual activities, found no correlation between abuse and homosexual activity. Woods and Dean (1984) state that 12% of the abused males in their nonclinical sample reported sexual experiences with males in the past year, a result that is in line with the oft-cited 10% estimate of homosexuals within the general population. In Bell et al.'s (1981a, 1981b) study, twice as many homosexuals as heterosexuals reported sexual activity in childhood. However, both the rate for homosexuals (5%) and that for heterosexuals (2.5%) are significantly lower than the rate of sexual abuse of males found in most prevalence studies.

Finkelhor (1981) found that men sexually abused as children by older men were four times as likely to engage in homosexual activity in later years. He considers two possible sources for this finding. First, these boys may have already been predisposed to a homosexual orientation. Their predisposition may have made them more vulnerable to abuse by placing them in closer proximity to abusive men and leaving them more responsive to sexual overtures. Abused men did not report higher incidences of homosexual interactions with peers in childhood, however, so Finkelhor views this first possibility as less likely than a second hypothesis—"that the victimization itself spawned the later interest in homosexual activity. A child who has had a homosexual experience may be likely to feel stigmatized by it and may come to label himself as a homosexual" (p. 82).

Gonsiorek (1993) and Lew (1990a) argue for variations of the first hypothesis: that boys who will later self-identify as homosexuals possess certain characteristics or attributes that leave them vulnerable to the predation of sexual offenders. Gonsiorek focuses upon the narcissistic injury that comes from having a sense of oneself as different along with a recognition that this difference is negatively valued. In his view, narcissistic injuries of various sorts create vulnerabilities to sexual assault. Lew argues that such individuals are likely to be or to appear passive, girlish, bookish, or unathletic, which may make them vulnerable to abuse. In the light of research strongly suggestive of an early childhood or even genetic basis for sexual orientation, such explanations would appear to be more likely than a theory in which sexual abuse causes homosexuality. The possibility that there is more than one pathway toward homosexuality should not be ruled out, however.

It appears from Finkelhor's (1981), Johnson and Shrier's (1985, 1987), and Simari and Baskin's (1982) studies that childhood sexual activity between males is a significant predictor of homosexual orientation. The precise nature of the interrelationship between these two variables is much less clear, however. This issue will be discussed in greater depth in Chapter 8. More research is needed in order to identify the relationship between sexual abuse and sexual orientation. Findings related to the long-term impact of sexual abuse upon sexuality are listed in Table 5.7.

Table 5.7 Long-Term Effects: Sexuality and Sexual Problems

Symptom	Study
Concerns about sexuality/ sexual orientation	Bolton et al. (1989); Bruckner & Johnson (1987); Dimock (1988); Hunter (1990a); Lew (1990b); Myers (1989); Olson (1990)
Sexual dissatisfaction	Finkelhor (1981); Woods & Dean (1984)
Compulsive sexual behavior	Carlson et al. (1987); Dimock (1988); Hunter (1987); Urquiza (1993); Woods & Dean (1984)
Prostitution	Coombs (1974); Ginsburg (1967); Janus et al. (1984)
Sexual dysfunction	Fromuth & Burkhart (1987); Johnson & Shrier (1987); Sarrel & Masters (1982); Woods & Dean (1984)
Homosexuality	Bell et al. (1981a, 1981b); Finkelhor (1984); Johnson & Shrier (1987); Simari & Baskin (1981)

ADDICTIVE BEHAVIORS

Addictions and compulsive behaviors appear to be among the most common long-term sequelae of childhood sexual abuse. High rates of substance abuse has been noted by Bruckner and Johnson (1987), Dimock (1988), Krug (1989), Olson (1990), Stein et al. (1988), and Urquiza (1993; Urquiza & Crowley, 1986). Olson found significant differences between abused men and a nonabused clinical control group in terms of chemical dependence and alcohol/drug abuse. He emphasized the prevalence of addictions and compulsions other than to drugs. His study also found significant differences between victims and nonvictims in compulsive overworking, compulsive overeating, and compulsive spending. Finally, in recent years, sexuality has begun to be recognized as an area in which addictions and compulsions may be displayed, as is evidenced by the emergence of 12-step groups, based on the model of Alcoholics Anonymous, for Sex Addicts Anonymous. Thus, many of the compulsive sexual behaviors noted by Dimock (1988) and others as common among adult male survivors of sexual abuse, including preoccupation with sexual thoughts, compulsive masturbation, and frequent and multiple sexual partners, may reflect a sexual addiction. Olson's study (1990) indicated that abused men were also significantly more likely to report compulsive sexual behavior and compulsive relationships.

CYCLICAL VICTIMIZATION

Perhaps the most well-known consequence of childhood sexual abuse is the perpetuation or recapitulation of the abuse. Numerous researchers working with a variety of populations have found high rates of sexual abuse in the backgrounds of sex offenders and incest perpetrators (Ballard et al., 1990; Gelinas, 1983; Gerber, 1990; Groth, 1979b; Groth et al., 1982; Serrill, 1974). It seems clear that sexual victimization in childhood is a critical risk factor for later sexual offenses, including sexual child abuse. It is by no means inevitable that a victim of abuse will go on to perpetrate, however; in fact, the most thorough examination of this topic (Kaufman & Zigler, 1987) indicates that about 70% of families in which parents experienced abuse in the previous generation do not "transmit" the abuse to their children (this statistic refers to various forms of child maltreatment, including neglect, physical abuse, and sexual abuse). This point is especially important because the notion that one is destined to repeat one's abuse is internalized by many male survivors. Bruckner and Johnson (1987) assert that this is an enormous concern of adult male survivors who have not offended. Many even decide not to have children in order to avoid perpetrating. There is a great need for further research into protective factors—aspects of victims' lives that may have helped them to avoid becoming perpetrators. Some likely possibilities include the presence of positive relationships with supportive figures during childhood; modeling of appropriate coping mechanisms for dealing with psychological distress; access to alternate means of expressing or venting anger; and therapy.

Several investigators (Carlson, cited in Kasl, 1990; Condy et al., 1987; Freeman-Longo, 1986; Groth, 1979b; Petrovich & Templer, 1984; Serrill, 1974) have interviewed convicted sex offenders and found high rates of sexual abuse in their histories. Percentages of men reporting such victimization range from 32% (Groth, 1979b) to 70% to 90% (Carlson, cited in Kasl, 1990; Serrill, 1974; Groth, 1979). Very high rates of sexual victimization have also been found in studies of adolescent sex offenders and sexually aggressive children (Becker, 1988; Becker, Kaplan, Cunningham-Rathner, & Kavoussi, 1986; Cantwell, 1988; Fehrenbach, Smith, Monastersky, & Deisher, 1986; Friedrich & Luecke, 1988; Gomes-Schwartz, Horowitz, & Sauzier, 1985; Groth, 1977).

A number of researchers have pondered the issue of cyclical victimization and offered analyses of its sources. Rogers and Terry (1984), as described in the section on initial effects of sexual abuse above, assert that the victim's worldview often encompasses only two positions, victim and perpetrator. Sexually aggressive behavior is an outgrowth of inappropriate attempts to reassert one's masculine identity, which has been damaged and made fragile by the abuse. The victim attempts to gain mastery by overidentifying with the offender and modeling his behavior. Similarly, Lew (1990b), based on his work with adult male survivors of sexual abuse, states that they characteristically have a great deal of confusion over their masculinity and regarding power and abusiveness. He asserts that they have three primary ways of dealing with their confusion: identifying with the perpetrator, continuing to be a victim, or becoming a protector. In the third pattern, the abuse survivor deals with and attempts to master his abuse experience by protecting others from similar occurrences or helping them in their recovery process. In his view, this accounts for the high proportions of sexual abuse survivors in the helping professions.

Briere and Smiljanich (1993) administered Koss and Oros's Sexual Experiences Survey (1982) and found that sexually abused men were significantly more likely than nonabused men to report having had sexual intercourse with a woman against her will either because they "became so sexually aroused [they] could not stop [themselves]" or "by pressuring her with continual arguments." Briere and Smiljanich reason that their childhood experiences modeled aggression in sexual relationships and conditioned sexual arousal to coercive or aggressive behavior. (It seems reasonable to suspect that childhood sexual abuse would also model a lack of impulse control and ability to delay or deny gratification.) Briere and Smiljanich also noted that those who experienced their own abuse as something they had minimal control over were most likely to be sexually aggressive. They view rape and other sexual offenses as a maladaptive attempt to master or gain control over the trauma. They argue that men do not have good ways of dealing with anger and emotional distress and that they tend to externalize their "abuse-related dysphoria" via sex crimes or other forms of aggressive acting out (or, it might be added, via substance abuse or other compulsive behaviors).

It should be made very clear that the sexual orientation of the offender is not the mediating factor in the perpetuation of sexual abuse. That is, the high rate of homosexuality among abused men does not appear to contribute to the incidence of cyclical victimization. In fact, the converse may even be true. In a study of convicted male child molesters, Groth and Birnbaum (1978) found that

> all regressed offenders, whether their victims were male or female children, were heterosexual in their adult orientation. . . . The possibility emerges that homosexuality and homosexual pedophilia may be mutually exclusive and that the adult heterosexual male constitutes a greater risk to the underage child than does the adult homosexual male. (p. 175)

In other words, at least in that study, it is heterosexual rather than homosexual men who molest children, regardless of the gender of the child. For this reason, Hunter (1993) argues that we should use the term *same-sex* rather than *homosexual* to refer to male-male sexual abuse.

Freeman-Longo (1986) focused on connections between sexual abuse and later sexually abusive or aggressive behavior. Based on his work with sexually abused sex offenders, he argues that

> 1) the offender's offense(s) are a replication of what happened in his sexual victimization; 2) the offender's offense(s) are an anger reaction to his sexual victimization; or 3) the offender's offense(s) are a modeling of his sexual victimization because his personal and/or misinterpreted view(s) of his victimization are that it was not that harmful to him, that there were pleasurable aspects of it, and in some cases it is thought of as sexually arousing. (p. 412)

Freeman-Longo emphasizes the enormous amounts of anger, pain, and frustration experienced by the men he studied. He states that they are unable to deal with feelings for fear of becoming vulnerable to others. They often possess tremendous hatred toward their abuser and a desire to retaliate against him or her. At the same time they feel vulnerable to their abuser and may feel in his or her control. They tend to experience themselves as having a lack of power and control in their lives; powerlessness is among the most dominant features of their psychology. Sexual assaults are attempts to regain power and control by sexually abusing others.

Freeman-Longo found two features to be critical risk factors for the repetition of sexual abuse: (1) victimization by more than one perpetrator on separate occasions; and (2) abuse that occurs repeatedly over a long

Table 5.8 Other Long-Term Effects

Symptom	Study
Addictions	Bruckner & Johnson (1987); Dimock (1988); Krug (1989); Olson (1990); Stein et al. (1988); Urquiza & Crowley (1986)
Sexual victimization of others	Becker (1988); Becker et al. (1986); Briere & Smiljanich (1993); Condy et al. (1987); Fehrenbach et al. (1986); Freeman-Longo (1986); Gomes-Schwartz (1984); Groth (1979b); Johnson & Shrier (1988); Petrovich & Templer (1984); Serrill (1974)

period of time. His theory, that the offender's offenses replicate his own victimization, gains some support from the findings of other studies of convicted sex offenders. Groth (1979b) found that rapists (of women) are more likely to have been victimized by females in childhood, whereas child molesters were more often abused by males. Petrovich and Templer (1984) found that 59% of convicted rapists had been molested by females during childhood and that the majority of this abuse was quite severe. Briere and Smiljanich (1993) found that 80% of sexually abused men who reported sexually aggressive behavior toward women had themselves been sexually abused by women during childhood. Summit (1983) also sees the perpetuation of child molestation and rape as part of the sexually abused boy's legacy of rage.

Sebold (1987) discusses the cycle of victimization and calls for earlier intervention with boys to break that cycle. The implication of the research on the recapitulation of sexual victimization is that we must recognize males as victims in order to reduce the incidence of males as offenders. Table 5.8 presents studies that have found cyclical victimization and addictive behaviors to be common consequences of childhood sexual abuse among males.

Effects by Type of Abuse

The remainder of this chapter addresses the impact of various characteristics of sexual abuse, including age at time of abuse, duration and frequency of abuse, gender of the perpetrator, relationship between perpetrator and victim, the use of force or violence, and the severity of the sexual act. In their review of the impact of sexual abuse, with primary reference to female victims, Browne and Finkelhor (1986) noted that, "only a few studies on the effects of sexual abuse have had enough cases and been sophisticated enough methodologically to look at these questions empirically" (p. 72). Not surprisingly, because the study of male victims is still in its infancy, there is an even more severe paucity of studies related to the effects of various types of sexual abuse on males. Factors such as early onset of abuse, long duration of abuse, high severity of abuse, and closeness of relationship between perpetrator and victim, which have been found with some regularity to correlate with later psychological disturbance in studies of female survivors (e.g., Browne & Finkelhor, 1986; Herman et al., 1986; Tsai et al., 1979), have yet to be assessed adequately with respect to male survivors. To date, only Kelly and Gonzalez's (1990) study in progress has undertaken a systematic assessment of the relationships between various factors associated with the abuse and long-term outcome for men.

In their study of men in out-patient therapy groups for survivors of sexual abuse, Kelly and Gonzalez (1990) assessed differences in outcome depending on the presence of physical abuse, whether the respondent's father and/or mother was an alcoholic, whether the abuse was intra- or extrafamilial, whether the abuse included intercourse, whether a female was involved in the perpetration, the sexual orientation of the respondent, the duration of the abuse, and the respondent's age at the onset of the abuse. They used the following outcome measures: total symptomatology, interpersonal problems, sexual problems, self-fragmentation/depersonalization, acting-out/aggressive behaviors, and self-destructive behaviors.

They found that physical abuse was associated with negative outcome for all measures except for sexual and interpersonal problems. Father's alcoholism predicted depersonalization and self-destructive behaviors. Mother's alcoholism was not significantly correlated with any outcome measure. Severity of abuse was not predictive of greater symptomatology on any of the scales. Intrafamilial abuse was not correlated at a statistically significant level with any of the outcome measures, though the relationship with self-destructive behaviors approached significance. The only statistically significant variation by sexual orientation of the respondent was that heterosexuals had a greater degree of overall symptomatology.

Abuse prior to the age of five was associated with a greater degree of overall symptomatology, sexual problems, depersonalization, and self-destructive behaviors. Thus, abuse that began at an early age, and the presence of physical abuse along with the sexual maltreatment, appear to be the strongest predictors of negative outcome in their study. Female perpetration (a female was the sole perpetrator in 5% of cases; abuse included a female perpetrator in 26% of cases) was associated with greater symptomatology on all measures. Kelly and Gonzalez conclude that this difference is due to several other factors rather than female perpetration itself. Abuse that includes a female perpetrator tended to begin at a younger age and to continue for a longer period, and in intrafamilial cases that include a female (as well as a male) perpetrator, the child victim lacks a supportive parent who can act as a "counterweight" to the abuse.

Williams (1991) conducted a study of 61 male victims of sexual abuse and concluded that the most important factors in predicting negative outcome, as assessed by the display of PTSD symptoms and responses to a questionnaire, were maximum intrusiveness of abuse; the use of force; longer duration and greater frequency of abuse; earlier age at onset of abuse; bizarre acts conducted as part of the abuse; and greater number of abusers. As already noted, Freeman-Longo (1986) found that the existence of multiple perpetrators was one of two main risk factors for later sexual offenses.

Urquiza and Capra (1990), in their review of the impact of sexual abuse upon males, state that there is no conclusive relationship between age at onset of abuse and the impact of abuse. Two studies have examined this factor and failed to find a significant relationship (Friedrich et al., 1988; Urquiza, 1988). Rogers and Terry (1984) assert that older boys face a more difficult adjustment to their victimization. With respect to female victims, early onset of abuse has been found to predict negative outcome (Herman et al., 1986). Several studies (Friedrich et al., 1986; Rogers & Terry, 1984; Urquiza, 1988) have found that abuse that continues over time is associated with greater severity of behavioral and emotional problems. As noted above, Freeman-Longo (1986) views long duration as one of the two primary predictors of later sexual offenses.

Briere et al. (1988), in a study of abused and nonabused men and women, rated the severity of abuse by self-report, giving a score of 1 to "fondling only," 2 to "genital contact but no penetration," and 3 to "penetration." They found that men had been abused less severely than women, with the mean severity score for women = 2.95 and the mean for male = 2.45, but displayed a comparable degree of pathology. Within their sample, severity of abuse was not associated with degree of symptomatology. Briere et al. see this as providing some counterindication to the notion that severity of abuse is a negative prognostic indicator.

Urquiza (1988) found the use of force and aggression to be the most important predictor of poor self-concept and psychophysiological symptomatology. Other studies have also indicated that the use of force is associated with negative psychological adjustment. The Tufts Medical School Study (Tufts New England Medical Center, 1984) found this factor to correlate positively with hostility and fear of aggressive behavior. Friedrich et al. (1986) found forceful and violent abuse to be predictive of greater internalizing and externalizing behavior, as measured by the Child Behavior Checklist. Rogers and Terry (1984) also found the use or threat of force to be associated with greater adjustment problems.

Urquiza and Capra's (1990) review found no studies that assessed the impact of sexual abuse by gender of perpetrator. One exception is Johnson and Shrier's (1987) study, which indicates that male-molested adolescents are significantly more likely to identify themselves as homosexual or bisexual than either female-molested adolescents or nonmolested controls. Johnson and Shrier interviewed 25 sexually abused adolescent males whom they had identified through intake questions at an out-patient medical clinic. Of these, 65% viewed the sexual abuse as having had a significant impact on their lives. Fourteen had been abused by males; the perpetrator was female in 11 cases. The female-molested group viewed the impact of the abuse as slightly more severe than the male-molested group: 73% of those abused by females rated the immediate impact of abuse as strong or devastating versus 64% of those abused by males; 54% of female-molested adolescents versus 50% of male-molested adolescents rated the current impact as strong or devastating. As discussed above, several researchers have found correlations between abuse by a female perpetrator and later sexual aggression against women (Briere & Smiljanich, 1993; Groth, 1979b; Petrovich & Templer, 1984).

Blair and Rita Justice (Justice & Justice, 1979) considered the impact of father-son and mother-son incest separately. They concluded that any form of parent-child incest severely impedes the child's social development, but that the specific impact varies depending on which parent perpetrates the incest. Based on their clinical experience and their review of the sparse literature on the topic they concluded that father-son incest causes acute anxiety and is enormously threatening to the boy's sense of masculinity. It is a risk factor for drug abuse, loss of contact with reality, somatic problems, and prostitution. Mother-son incest is seen as even more profoundly detrimental to social development. Boy victims of this type of abuse tend to be emotionally immature and may be incapable of developing sexual relationships with others. These boys are likely to be extremely mistrustful and display low self-esteem and severe guilt.

Several studies (Friedrich, 1988; Friedrich et al., 1986; Friedrich et al., 1988; Rogers & Terry, 1984) found that closeness of relationship between perpetrator and victim correlated with the extent of behavioral and emotional problems. Friedrich et al. (1986) assert that with closer relationships, behavior problems are more likely to become internalized and long term rather than transient. Urquiza (1988) concluded that the relationship with the perpetrator is an important predictor of adult self-concept and psychosomatic symptomatology.

The present study examines the variation in impact upon male survivors of several characteristics of childhood sexual abuse. These include the duration of the abuse, the respondent's age when the abuse began, the severity of the abuse, the number of abusers, the relationship between perpetrator and victim, the gender of the perpetrator, the presence of physical abuse, and the use of alcohol or other drugs by the perpetrator at the time of abuse. Findings of this study are presented in Chapter 8.

The remaining portions of this work describe a study of a clinical sample of 121 sexually abused men. The study is based on the questionnaire responses of these men and semi-structured interviews conducted with a subsample of 9 men. Chapter 6 outlines the method used in the study. Chapter 7 describes the demographic characteristics, psychiatric histories, abuse histories, and current psychosocial functioning of the questionnaire respondents. Chapter 8 examines the impact of various characteristics of the sexual abuse and proposes avenues for further research. Chapter 9 discusses the interviews, describes issues of particular salience to male survivors, and suggests some implications for treatment interventions.

Notes

1. Unfortunately, Fromuth and Burkhart (1989) did not indicate whether there were any differences in terms of outcome measures between those who experienced their sexual interactions benignly or positively and those who saw them as traumatic events. It is therefore possible that the finding of negative psychological adjustment is primarily related to the latter group of men.

2. Sarrel and Masters (1982) note that "there are on record at the [Yale Human Sexuality Program and the Masters and Johnson Institute] seven cases of incestuous relationships that have resulted in adult sexual dysfunction or disorder for boys sexually abused by mothers or by older sisters" (p. 123).

Ben's Story

Ben is a 53-year-old homosexual physician. His childhood experiences constituted "emotional incest" (Love, 1990) and did not include any overtly sexual contact, to the best of his recollection. Emotional incest, as both Love (1990) and Ben explain it, refers to a parent relating to a child as if he or she were a marital partner and turning to the child to meet the parent's needs. The full spectrum of incest, within this perspective, may include overt, physical incest with varying degrees of contact, or it may consist of covert, emotional incest. Ben indicated that his mother was emotionally dependent upon him, with the result that he was unable to be a child himself or to seek gratification of his needs. Ben's upbringing fits the family systems' construct of the enmeshed family (e.g., Hoffman, 1981) and Herman's (1981) notion of the incest-possible family, in which the dynamics characteristic of abuse are present but in which overt incest does not occur. In response to my queries about the concept of emotional incest, Ben indicated that if there are no boundaries and enmeshment exists, this constitutes incest. Put most succinctly, if a parent does not relate to a child as a child then incest is occurring, according to this view.

During the interview Ben discussed the differences between emotional and physical incest and complained that people, including professionals, do not recognize that the existence of sexual contact makes no difference, that the psychological damage is caused by the violation of boundaries and selfhood that occur in emotional incest as well. I think that Ben's point is an important one. Not enough is known about which particular factors within abusive or incestuous upbringings are prognostic of later difficulties. Studies comparing individuals who have experienced overt incest with those whose family environments are similar but in which sexual contact does not occur would be very valuable. It appears that the dynamics and sequelae of Ben's upbringing are in many ways consistent with those reported by other respondents.

Nonetheless, Ben's childhood, in the absence of overt or covert *sexual* activity, appears to represent a set of experiences distinct from those of the remainder of the population studied here. Including relationships of emotional dependency and enmeshment would broaden the frame of sexual abuse considerably and would appear to dilute the concept. Moreover, because such relationships are not commonly understood to constitute sexual abuse, men with such backgrounds are unlikely to have sought inclusion in this study. Therefore, I elected to ally myself with professionals who perceive a difference between sexual activity in child-hood and relationships in which a parent is enmeshed with or dependent upon his or her child.[1]

Ben is the middle of five children, with two sisters and two brothers. He stated that he doubts the existence of physical, sexual contact during childhood, though he recalls some "low-level," nonsexual physical abusiveness by his mother, including hugging very tight and tickling. There was an incident during infancy when he was colicky, and the remedy applied by his mother was to rub his belly while placing her finger in his rectum. Although he does not see the remedy itself as inappropriate, he stated that he knows that period in his mother's life to have been an unhappy and stressful one and therefore suspects that he would have experienced this incident as assaultive. He says that others, including therapists, have strongly suspected the existence of physical sexual abuse, and that he has spent much of his life agonizing over whether such contact occurred. Only recently has he understood that the impact of emotional incest is the same and that the quest to recover memories of physical incest is a futile endeavor.

From the time he was in junior high school, his mother began to use him as a confidant, gaining support from him that she did not get from his alcoholic father, and telling him about their marital problems. He felt that his mother kept him "close to her apron strings." His relationship with his mother was extremely enmeshed, and he reports a lack of clear boundaries between the two of them throughout his life. He continues to feel very emotionally conflicted about his mother, missing her and at the same time harboring considerable anger toward her. He has had a difficult time in recent weeks connected with the upcoming anniversary of her death 4 years previously.

Ben's sense of himself within his family was of "a child in the middle of a boisterous, supposedly loving family, with no one there for (him)." He saw his father as completely selfish and unavailable, devoted primarily to his drinking. Many of the dynamics Ben describes as outgrowths of his upbringing are those characteristic of adult children of alcoholics and he does not feel that it is possible to distinguish the impact of the emotionally incestuous relationship between himself and his mother from the effects of growing up with an alcoholic father. He believes that each of the children in his family have problems with addictions, including food, alcohol, and relationship addictions. Ben himself is a recovering alcoholic, approaching the fifth anniversary of his sobriety. He is currently attempting to quit a smoking habit of 25-years duration and reports having a tendency toward food addictions and a pattern of addictive relationships. He has participated in extensive psychotherapy. He estimated that he has had 10 different therapists, which includes a 14-year psychoanalysis.

The primary legacy of Ben's upbringing is difficulty maintaining appropriate boundaries between himself and others, and consequent problems with intimacy and interpersonal relatedness. He stated that he does not know how to be close without becoming engulfed. He feels that he is not close unless he is in an enmeshed relationship. For him, being intimate has always entailed a loss of boundaries. He has, therefore, both longed for and feared closeness. He tends to scare others off with his all-consuming way of relating. The other person becomes the be-all and end-all of Ben's life when in a relationship, and he has difficulty expressing his needs or even allowing himself to have needs. His entire sense of self becomes entangled in the other person, as was once the case in his relationship with his mother. He was involved in a long-term relationship viewed both by him and his partner as a marriage. He described feeling within this relationship that, "if he ever left me, I would die, cease to exist. I was willing to do almost anything he wanted me to do. I measured what I did according to his standards and values, and adopted these for my own. I didn't have my own self. The boundaries were so blurred, just like they were with my mom." Ben also reports a great deal of difficulty "letting go" in relationships. He perceives his relationship with his mother as involving a loss of self. He fears that letting go sexually, not being in control in a sexual situation, or giving in to feelings of attraction, will elicit a similar loss of self.

Ben's feelings toward and attitudes about both men and women have been strongly affected by his childhood experiences. In "gay situations" he is more comfortable with men than women, but in "non-gay situations" this pattern is reversed. He feels most uncomfortable with straight men. There are, however, certain triggers specific to women that he connects with his relationship with his mother. He has realized that despite often feeling that he is closer to and shares more similarities with women, he fears them. If he is touched in the wrong way by a woman (from behind, or by surprise) this elicits a strong fear response. He also experiences a great deal of anger toward women and becomes more angry with women than with men. He has feelings of repulsion toward the female body, which he connects with the enmeshment with his mother. This repulsion is centered in the female pelvis, which is a powerful metaphorical image for him, conveying the sense of a male child trapped in a cage-like vagina, as he had experienced himself in childhood.

Ben feels that men cannot be trusted, that they will ignore him or fail to be there for him. He recognizes that this sense stems from his father's unavailability during his childhood. The theme of needs being met or left unmet is a pervasive theme for Ben. He sees himself as a classic example of an adult child of an alcoholic, parentified from an early age and responsible for the needs of others but unable to meet or express his own. The concept of codependency also pervades his world. He stated that he is more angry at his father than his mother for the emotional incest, because he feels that his father could have stopped it but did not; he blames his mother primarily for his father's drinking, because he sees her as able but unwilling to put a halt to that. Thus, he blames each parent primarily for the misdeeds of the other. He stated that his father had also been a womanizer, and that his mother wouldn't tolerate that, but supported his drinking. Similarly, he harbors anger toward both his mother and his former partner for not stopping his own alcoholism. He indicated that he is far more angry at his father than at his mother, "because he was never there for me at all." He said that he would never be able to forgive him for that and has not spoken to his father in 3 years. He views his mother, by way of contrast, as a good, but sick and codependent woman. He feels that his mother did not mean harm and was unaware that she was doing something detrimental to his well-being. He cannot exonerate his father's behavior in the same manner, because he sees his alcoholism as an active wrong.

An additional perceived consequence of Ben's incestuous and alcoholic family upbringing is a lack of sense of "proprietorship" over his own body. He stated that until recently he had never felt that he had the right to say no or to determine who does what to his body. He feels that his lack of ownership over his body has also resulted in him not taking good care of himself. This was manifested in his substance abuse, in poor diet and physical exercise, and in promiscuity. Finally, Ben sees his career as a physician, which he hates, as a response to his upbringing. He sees the choice of a helping profession as an inevitable adaptation to his role as the responsible, caretaking child. His sense that there was no one there to help him in his time of need further fuels his tendency to attempt to help others. The particular choice of medicine was motivated by his self-esteem issues and his effort to compensate for his low sense of self-worth. These same issues have also led him to be a perfectionist in everything he does, and to be unable to tolerate mediocre grades in school. Once ensconced in his medical position, his tenuous self-esteem led him to feel that he was not good enough to execute his responsibilities. He became convinced that he was an imposter and living a lie. This reached the point where he reports having been delusional about his ability to perform and suffering panic attacks. He left medicine for a period of about 2 years and has recently returned. He feels that his sense of self is less dependent upon his job than it had been previously, but he remains quite dissatisfied with his career direction.

Note

1. It should be noted that the 121 participants in this study whose responses were included in the data analysis indicated the presence of physical sexual abuse during childhood. Ben's questionnaire responses, along with those of two other men who did not indicate clear sexual abuse, were not included in the data analysis.

6 An Original Study of Sexually Abused Males

Methodology

This study is an effort to increase the knowledge-base about male survivors of child sexual abuse. A multimethod approach was utilized. One hundred twenty-four men who identified themselves as having experienced sexual abuse in childhood completed questionnaires about their abuse experiences and about various other aspects of their lives. Questionnaires included both standardized and original measures. A subsample of 9 men participated in face-to-face semi-structured interviews intended to shed further light upon the impact of child sexual abuse upon men. Both the questionnaire and the guidelines for the interview are described in detail in the Measures section below.

Subjects

Participants in this study were contacted via therapists who identified themselves as working with male survivors of child sexual abuse. This method of obtaining access to the sample was utilized for three reasons:

first, as a convenient means of notifying male survivors of the existence of the study; second, in order to enable men who wished to participate anonymously to do so; and third, so that respondents would have appropriate resources in the event that they found completing the questionnaire to be stressful. Descriptions of the study were sent to approximately 300 therapists, whose names I had obtained from three sources. I attended two professional workshops on the topic of male survivors—a presentation by Mike Lew in Ann Arbor, MI, in January 1990, and a national conference in Tucson, AZ, in November 1990—and obtained attendance lists of each. The third source for therapists working in this area was a resource list published by P.L.E.A., a national organization of male abuse survivors, which is unfortunately now defunct. A letter informed the therapists that their clients would receive a $10 stipend for their participation.

Therapists notified their clients of the study, then returned a stamped self-addressed postcard that had been included along with each letter, indicating how many questionnaires they wished to receive. That number of packets was then sent to the therapist for distribution to his or her clients. Approximately 350 packets were mailed. Each packet contained a questionnaire with informed consent form attached and a stamped, self-addressed envelope. The initial page of the questionnaire described its contents and indicated that completion and return of the questionnaire would be understood to indicate informed consent for participation in the study. The final page of the questionnaire contained information about returning the questionnaire to me and obtaining payment. Respondents had three options. A participant could give the questionnaire to the therapist to return to me, in which case payment would be sent to the therapist to distribute; he could provide his name and address, in which case I would send payment directly to him; or he could return the questionnaire anonymously to me, in which case I would send the $10 to P.L.E.A., in lieu of payment (29 men returned the questionnaire anonymously or requested that I donate the stipend to P.L.E.A.). The final page of the questionnaire also included a box that respondents could check to indicate if they were willing to be contacted in the future for a face-to-face interview. The page with identifying information was separated from the questionnaire upon receipt for the purposes of confidentiality. One hundred twenty-four men completed questionnaires.

Nine of the men who had indicated that they would be willing to participate in the face-to-face interview were then contacted. Interviews were conducted in their homes or offices. Interviewees signed an informed consent form and were asked if they would be willing to have the sessions audio-recorded; a second signature was then obtained to give consent for audio-recording. All interviewees agreed to the audio-recording. Interviewees were paid a stipend of $25. The interview was open-ended and did not follow a strict question-and-answer format. Instead, I referred to a checklist of topics related to the abuse and its impact, which I used as prompts as needed. A summary of these topics is provided in the section headed Interview, below.

Definition of Abuse

Wyatt and Peters (1986b) and Fromuth and Burkhart (1987) have discussed the importance of definitional issues in estimating the prevalence of child sexual abuse. Each study concludes that much of the broad range of prevalence estimates stems from the use of different criteria for abuse. Less restrictive criteria yield higher estimates; more restrictive criteria yield lower estimates. Fromuth and Burkhart (1987) identify an additional factor that appears to have particular relevance to male victims. Looking only at incidents that are defined by the boy victim or adult male survivor as abusive is likely vastly to underestimate the true incidence of sexual activity between adults and boys. This appears to be the case especially with incidents involving older females, which males are less likely to construe as abusive. (See the section on prevalence in Chapter 3 above for a detailed discussion of this issue.)

The current study was not intended to provide an estimate of the prevalence of sexual abuse among males nor among male clinical populations. Instead, it is an examination of sexual abuse within a clinical population of men who have identified themselves as sexual abuse survivors. Therefore, the criteria used to define abuse do not have as far-reaching methodological implications for this study as for those concerned with the prevalence or incidence of sexual abuse. This study reached men who had identified themselves as having experienced childhood sexual abuse and who had sought treatment, often for assistance with difficulties related to their abuse. Thus, this was a self-selected clinical sample.

Within the questionnaire, several questions were asked regarding childhood sexual interactions. This made it possible to conduct analyses of subsamples that meet more restrictive definitions of abuse. Respondents were asked to consider a number of different relationships— with mother, father, sibling(s), aunt(s) and uncles(s), grandparents(s), stranger(s), and "anyone else"—and to indicate whether anything sexual occurred with that person before the respondent reached the age of 16. The term *sexual* was operationally defined in the instructions given to the respondent as including "a broad range of activities, anything from 'playing doctor' to sexual intercourse—in fact, anything that seemed 'sexual' to you." This provides the least restrictive criteria for abuse. For each relationship regarding which the respondent indicates sexual activity, several additional questions are asked. One of these concerns whether the respondent construes the sexual activity as abusive: for example, if he indicates that there was sexual activity between him and a grandparent, he is then asked, "Were you sexually abused by your (grandparent)?"

Looking only at those activities considered by the respondent to be abusive would yield a somewhat smaller sample.[1] Finally, respondents are asked to indicate which specific sexual acts occurred. Statistical analyses could then be conducted, for example, only with those who were subjected to intercourse, or only those who experienced "contact offenses" (Bolton et al., 1989). For the purposes of this study, all men who indicated sexual activity in childhood were included in statistical analyses.[2] Because this sample consisted entirely of men who have identified themselves as sexual abuse survivors, each has experienced at least one incident that he defines as abusive. For example, though 30% of those reporting sexual activity with a sibling do not consider this activity to be abusive, each reported at least one other sexual interaction that he construed as abuse.

Measures

The questionnaire included three standardized measures along with several items taken from a fourth, demographic questions about the respondent, questions about his psychiatric history, items pertaining to childhood physical abuse, and a detailed measure of his childhood sexual experiences.

STANDARDIZED MEASURES

The Trauma Symptom Checklist (TSC; Briere & Runtz, 1989) is a 33-item self-report psychiatric symptom checklist. It represents the ongoing efforts of Briere and his colleagues to identify the particular symptoms that best distinguish adult survivors of childhood abuse from other clinical and nonclinical populations. The resultant 33-item scale comprises five subscales: *Dissociation, Anxiety, Depression, Sleep Disturbance, and Post-Sexual Abuse Trauma-Hypothesized (PSAT-h)*, and a Total Scale Score. The PSAT-h includes the six items that Briere and his colleagues have found to discriminate most reliably between abuse survivors and those who have not experienced childhood abuse.

Respondents to the TSC are presented with a list of symptoms and asked to indicate "how often [they] have experienced each of the following in the last two months." For each, respondents circle a number between 0 and 3, representing occurrences of the symptoms ranging from "never" to "very often." Briere and his colleagues continue to fine-tune the TSC. Briere and Runtz (1989) proposed an additional seven experimental items. Two of these were to be added to the extant Sleep Disturbance Scale, and five were intended to create a new "Sexual Problems" scale. An adaptation of the TSC-33 was included in the current study. The two items related to sleep disturbance were included in this study, whereas those related to sexual problems were not, because each was covered elsewhere in the questionnaire. The response choices were expanded to include a fifth option, "always," in order to provide a broader, more well-balanced range of responses. One adaptation was made to the subscales derived from the TSC. Briere et al.'s Post-Sexual Abuse Trauma scale (see Briere & Runtz, 1989) includes "Fear of Men," which is presumably associated with male perpetration. Because the literature on the sexual abuse of boys suggests a much higher incidence of female perpetration than had previously been assumed (Fromuth & Burkhart, 1989; Risin & Koss, 1987) the item "Fear of Women" is also included in a new, PSAT-Revised subscale, which is calculated along with the five subscales created by Briere and Runtz. The TSC comprises 34 questions in the questionnaire used in the current study.

Janoff-Bulman (1989) developed the World Assumptions Scale (WAS) in order to assess individuals' beliefs and attributions about the world. The WAS comprises three categories of assumptions: perceived *benevolence of the world; meaningfulness of the world;* and *worthiness of the self.* These are further divided into particular assumptions, which result in eight subscales, each based on four statements that respondents rate on a 6-point scale from "strongly disagree" to "strongly agree." Benevolence of the World comprises attributions of the *benevolence of the impersonal world* and the *benevolence of people.* Meaningfulness of the World includes conceptions of *justice*—whether outcomes are distributed according to principles of justice and deservingness; *controllability*—whether outcomes correspond to a person's behavior, rather than to his or her character; and *chance* or randomness—whether it is possible to make sense of why particular events happen to particular people. Finally, the component parts of the worthiness of the self category are *self-worth; self-controllability*—the extent to which the individual sees him- or herself as exercising appropriate precautions to leave him or her minimally vulnerable in a controllable world; and *luck*—whether the individual perceives him- or herself to be lucky or unlucky. These constructs are considered to be orthogonal; therefore, no total score is derived.

Janoff-Bulman (1989) found two of these factors—benevolence of the impersonal world and perceived self-worth—to discriminate most reliably between victims and nonvictims. Only these two subscales have been analyzed. The current questionnaire includes the 31 questions from the World Assumptions Scale.

This questionnaire included a number of items about current sexual functioning and sexual attitudes. Several of these were taken from the Brief Sexual Function Questionnaire for Men (BSFQ: Reynolds et al., 1988). Much of the BSFQ concerns physiological sexual response, which was not assessed in the current study. Topics covered in this study include sexual orientation, frequency of various types of sexual activity, and sexual satisfaction.[3]

ORIGINAL MEASURES

The bulk of the questionnaire used in the current study consists of questions related to the respondents' abuse history. The format and content of sexual abuse questions are patterned after Finkelhor's (1979) study and incorporate some of Fromuth and Burkhart's (1987, 1989) revisions of his survey. Each respondent was asked whether "anything sexual occurred" between himself and his mother, father, sibling(s), aunt(s) and/or uncle(s), grandparent(s), stranger(s), or other people. For each relationship regarding which the respondent indicated that something sexual occurred, several additional questions were asked, including which specific sexual acts occurred; the respondent's age at the onset of the sexual activity; its duration; its frequency; the respondent's emotional reaction; whether drugs or alcohol were involved; and whether the respondent considers the sexual activity to constitute sexual abuse. Additional items were included pertaining to respondents' experiences of physical abuse.

A number of demographic questions were asked regarding the respondent's age, ethnic status, marital status, educational level attained, and several variables related to his family of origin. Questions were also included concerning the respondent's psychiatric history, including psychiatric hospitalizations, psychotropic medication, psychotherapy, and suicidality.

Interview

Nine men participated in a semi-structured face-to-face clinical interview. The interview was intended as a means of gaining greater insight into men's perceptions of their childhood sexually abusive experiences and the impact these experiences have had upon their lives. The interview was conducted in a fairly informal manner and participants were encouraged to discuss issues related to their abuse as comprehensively as they felt comfortable doing. Interviews lasted between 1½ and 3 hours. The format and purpose of the interview was first explained, and a consent form was provided for signature. The first portion of the interview referred to the questionnaire, and the respondent's reactions to completing the questionnaire were discussed. Any inconsistencies or unclear aspects of his questionnaire responses were explored. Following this review some additional information about the participant's family background was obtained. A number of questions regarding the participant's current circumstances were then asked.

The remainder of the interview pertained to the respondent's understanding of the effects of his childhood sexual experiences upon his life. Typically, by this point in the interview, the participant had already discussed a number of consequences of his abuse. He was told that the rest of the interview concerns the impact of the abuse upon various areas of his life and was handed a card covering the following life-domains: intimate relationships, friendships, career, education, parenting (if applicable), leisure-time pursuits, substance use or abuse, sense of self and self-esteem, sense of self as a man, feelings about women, feelings about men, physical health, and sex and sexuality. If they reported physical as well as sexual abuse, they were also asked to consider how their lives might have been different had only one of these forms of abuse occurred. The content and format of the interview are loosely based upon a clinical interview conducted by Gold-Steinberg (1991).

Notes

1. Depending on the relationship, between 70% and 94% of sexual activity is construed as abusive, with interactions with siblings least likely to be considered to be victimizing. These findings will be discussed in greater detail in Chapter 7.

2. The questionnaire responses of three men were excluded from statistical analysis. These men did not indicate the occurrence of any sexual activity per se during childhood, overt or covert, but rather described "emotionally incestuous" relationships (Love, 1990). Emotional incest refers to a parent turning to his or her child to meet the parent's emotional needs. The child is treated as a spouse or even as a parent to his or her parent. This relationship may or may not evolve into sexual activity. In the case of these three particular respondents, it did not. The concept of emotional incest is closely related to the family systems construct of the enmeshed family (see, for example, Hoffman, 1981; Minuchin, 1967) and to Herman's (1981) notion of seductive relationships, in which dynamics characteristic of incest are present, but in which incest does not develop. It is a very intriguing concept and one that is certainly worthy of further research. It appears, however, that in the absence of sexual activity—overt or covert—the experiences of these men are distinct enough from those of the rest of the population in this study to warrant exclusion from the statistical analyses. One of these three men was interviewed. His childhood experiences and the impact he perceives them to have had upon his life are presented as "Ben's Story."

3. A portion of the Bell Object Relations and Reality Testing Inventory (BORRTI; Bell, 1989; Bell, Billington, & Becker, 1986), comprising four object relations subscales— *Alienation, Insecure Attachment, Egocentricity,* and *Social Incompetence*—was also administered but has not been analyzed.

7 The Men and Their Abuse Experience

This chapter and Chapter 8 outline the findings of the questionnaire portion of this study and discuss the meanings and implications of these findings. The present chapter presents the men who participated in the study and describes their demographic characteristics, psychiatric histories, current psychosocial functioning, and the characteristics of the abuse they experienced. Chapter 8 examines the relationship between these abuse characteristics and adult psychosocial functioning. All results, regardless of statistical significance, are presented in data tables throughout the next two chapters.

Chapter 9, the final chapter of this book, aims to bring a "human face" to the topic, looking at the men themselves and attempting to understand their experience: What have been the effects of their childhood sexual victimization? How do they view these events and make sense of them? How do they cope with them or overcome them? The emphasis in the final chapter is upon the clinical interview portion of this study.

Demographic Characteristics of the Sample

One hundred twenty-four men completed questionnaires. The responses of 3 men were excluded from statistical analyses because their developmental histories did not include clear instances of sexual abuse. Thus, there was a statistical sample of 121 men. Men from 21 states and four Canadian provinces participated in this study. The average age of the respondents was 36 years, with a range of 18 to 60 years. Approximately 75% of the sample was between 25 and 45 years of age. Respondents tended to come from fairly large families, with a mean number of siblings of more than three. Thirty percent of the sample came from families of divorce, though it is not possible to determine whether divorce occurred during the respondents' childhood or at a later time.

Of the respondents, 92% were white, 3% Hispanic, 2% African American, 2% Native American, and 1% Asian. Respondents were predominately highly educated—30% of the men had completed a graduate or professional program, 61% had received a baccalaureate degree, and 95% had completed high school. Sixty percent of the respondents indicated that they were mainly or entirely heterosexual, and 36% identified themselves as mainly or entirely homosexual. Clearly, the proportion of homosexual respondents in this study is far higher than in the general population. Implications of this finding will be discussed in Chapter 9, in the section on sexual orientation. Demographic data are presented in Table 7.1.

Psychiatric History and
Current Psychosocial Functioning

As would be predicted on the basis of the prevalence of abuse characteristics found in numerous studies to be predictive of later disturbance (which are outlined below), the men in this sample displayed multiple indications of psychological dysfunction. The sample is characterized by extensive psychiatric histories. Access to participants in this study was obtained through out-patient therapists; therefore, a large majority (90%) were receiving therapy at the time of participation in this study. The average lifetime duration of psychotherapy for the men in this sample was approximately 5 years. Twenty percent had participated in psycho-

Table 7.1 Demographic Characteristics

Age	Mean = 36; Range = 18 to 60	
Marital Status	41%	Single, never married
	21%	Married
	22%	Separated or divorced
	13%	Unmarried, in long-term relationship
Ethnicity	92%	white
	3%	Hispanic
	2%	African American
	2%	Native American
	1%	Asian
Education	30%	Completed graduate/professional school
	61%	Completed college
	95%	Completed high school
Sexual orientation	60%	Mainly or entirely heterosexual
	36%	Mainly or entirely homosexual

therapy one time only, whereas 29% had been in therapy twice, 15% three times, and 35% four or more times. Twenty-one percent (25 men) had been hospitalized for psychiatric purposes; 56% of these had been hospitalized once, 28% hospitalized twice, and 16% three or more times.

Psychotropic medication had been prescribed for 45% of the sample (54 men). The most frequently identified categories of medication were antidepressants (51 men) and tranquilizers/antianxiety medication (21 men). Seven men had received antipsychotic medications, 3 had received Ritalin, and 4 were prescribed Lithium.

Thirty-nine men (32% of the sample) had attempted suicide. Of these, 55% had made one attempt, 26% had attempted suicide twice, and 18% had made three or more attempts. The most frequently reported method was medication overdose (23 men), followed by self-stabbings or slashings (16 men), gunshots (5 men), hanging (5 men), jumping off buildings (3 men), and drug or alcohol abuse (3 men). Six men attempted suicide by stepping in front of cars or by way of intentional car "accidents." Fifteen men reported suicide attempts prior to the age of 18. The youngest reported attempt was at age five. The modal age for suicide attempt was between 16 and 23. Data related to psychiatric history are summarized in Table 7.2.

In addition to the psychiatric indices just cited (history of psychiatric hospitalization, psychotropic medication, and/or suicide attempts), the

Table 7.2 Psychiatric History

	Percentage of Sample	Number of Experiences	
Psychiatric hospitalization	21% have been hospitalized	1:	14 men
		2:	7 men
		≥ 3:	4 men
Psychotropic medication	45% have received medication	1:	31 men
		2:	9 men
		≥ 3:	12 men
Suicide attempt	32% have attempted suicide	1:	21 men
		2:	10 men
		≥ 3:	7 men
Duration of psychotherapy	Mean duration in psychotherapy is approximately 5 years		

outcome measures used in this study include the extent of psychiatric symptomatology as assessed by the Trauma Symptom Checklist (TSC; Briere & Runtz, 1989); two scales from the World Assumptions Scale (WAS; Janoff-Bulman, 1989), one measuring beliefs about the benevolence or malevolence of the world and the other assessing the respondent's sense of self-worth; and self-ratings of sexual satisfaction, sexual adjustment, and sexual orientation. A composite outcome variable, The Composite Index of Functioning (CIF), was created to provide a global assessment of functioning. It is based on the means of the TSC, the Benevolence and Self-Worth scales of the WAS, and the self-report of sexual adjustment. (Because high scores on the TSC indicate greater disturbance, unlike the other three measures, the TSC was reverse coded to create the CIF.) There were extremely high correlations between the overall Trauma Symptom Checklist and its component scales indicating that the component scales are not independent measures. Therefore, only the overall Trauma Symptom scale was used. These correlations are displayed in Table 7.3.

Most respondents considered themselves to be below average in terms of sexual adjustment. The Trauma Symptom Checklist, a 5-point symptom rating scale, yielded a mean score of 2.6, indicating that respondents report that they experience symptoms, on average, between "sometimes" and "very often." The means on the Benevolence and Self-Worth scales of 3.94 and 3.36, respectively, were among the lowest of any study

Table 7.3 Correlations Between the Trauma Symptom Checklist and
                Component Scales

Dissociation	.8796
Anxiety	.9124
Depression	.9260
Sleep disturbances	.8292
Post Sexual Abuse Trauma-Hypothesized (PSAT-h)	.9256
PSAT-h (Revised)	.9396

utilizing these measures, according to Ronnie Janoff-Bulman (personal communication, spring 1992), indicating that these men felt quite poorly about themselves and viewed the world in which they lived as a very malevolent, hurtful place. Table 7.4 displays the sample means for all outcome measures.

The Characteristics of Abuse

As discussed in Chapter 3, official case reports of sexually abused boys and the retrospective self-reports of adult males appear to represent relatively discrete databases. Reported cases consist primarily of severe abuse perpetrated by males. Most of the victimized boys in such studies are quite young. Retrospective self-report studies reveal a broader range of sexual activity—including mild as well as severe acts, by female as well as male perpetrators—that continues into adolescence. Multiple perpetrators are common in both databases.

The picture of childhood sexual abuse that emerges from the current study is an amalgam of that of case-report and self-report studies. Multiple perpetration was the norm in this sample, with a mean number of abusers of 2.34. Approximately one third of the sample reported three or more abusers. This is consistent with the findings of several earlier studies that indicate that boys are more likely than girls to be abused by more than one person (Dixon et al., 1978; Faller, 1989; Farber et al., 1984; Finkelhor, 1984; Neilsen, 1983; Pierce & Pierce, 1985; Spencer & Dunklee, 1986). This finding has implications for all the other findings of this study; that is, each respondent was likely to report childhood sexual interactions beginning at various ages, by a variety of perpetrators,

Table 7.4 Description of Outcome Measures for the Entire Sample

Scale	Mean	Comments
Trauma Symptom Checklist	2.6100	• 35 symptoms rated for frequency from 1 to 5. Higher scores indicate greater symptomatology. Mean of 2.61 indicates that symptoms are, on average, experienced between "sometimes" and "very often."
Benevolence	3.9421	• 4 statements rated from 1 to 6. Higher scores indicate a more benevolent worldview.
Self-worth	3.3636	• 4 statements rated from 1 to 6. Higher scores indicate more positive self-worth.
Sexual satisfaction	4.7731	• Self-rating of satisfaction with sex-life from 1 to 7. Lower score indicates greater satisfaction.
Sexual adjustment	2.3109	• Self-rating of overall sexual adjustment from 1 to 5. Higher score indicates better adjustment.

and of varying severity and duration. The broad range of sexual activity found in this study resembles that described in retrospective studies.

The sexual activities experienced by the respondents during childhood were divided into three levels: Severe, Moderate, and Mild. Severe abuse comprised anal, oral, and/or vaginal intercourse. Moderate abuse consisted of genital contact and fondling that did not result in intercourse. Mild abuse include such acts as exhibitionism, voyeurism, exposure to pornography, sexual invitations or requests, and kissing or hugging in a sexual manner. Three percent of the sample (4 men) experienced only mild sexual abuse. The most severe abuse experienced by 20% of the sample (24 men) was moderate, and 77% of the sample (93 men) were subjected to severe abuse.

Data about age at onset of abuse, duration of abuse, severity of abuse, emotional reaction to abuse, and the involvement of drugs along with the abuse, are organized by relationship between respondent and perpetrator in Table 7.5. Sexual activity with mothers was significantly less severe than that with other perpetrators. In all other relationships, the modal severity was severe: Penetration occurred in the majority of cases involving each category of perpetrator, with the exception of mothers. Sexual activity with mothers was most often moderate, indicating the presence of fondling or genital contact without penetration.

Table 7.5 Variations in Abuse by Perpetrator

		Mother (N = 50)	Father (N = 48)	Sibling (N = 51)	Aunt/Uncle (N = 21)	Grandparent (N = 16)	Stranger (N = 56)	Other (N = 56)	Total* (N = 121)
Severity (% by category, Mode in bold)	Mild	22%	11%	18%	9%	18%	6%	4%	3%
	Moderate	54%	17%	25%	24%	37%	24%	37%	20%
	Severe	24%	72%	57%	66%	44%	70%	59%	77%
Age of onset (Mean in years)		4.3	4.6	8.8	5.6	4.4	8.4	9.4	5.5
Duration of abuse (Mean in years)		6.6	5.8	3.2	4.9	3.1	1.8	2.6	6.0
Incidence of drug use by perpetrator		20%	43%	23%	37%	38%	16%	18%	37%
Common emotional responses (Descending order of frequency)**		Fear Pleasure Interest Shock Surprise Revulsion Terror Shame	Fear Shock Surprise Interest Pleasure Terror — —	Fear Pleasure Interest Surprise Shock Anger Curiosity —	Fear Pleasure Interest Surprise Shock — — —	Fear Shock Interest Surprise Pleasure Shame — —	Fear Interest Shock Surprise Pleasure Shame — —	Fear Pleasure Shock Surprise Interest Shame Terror Numbness	— — — — — — — —
Mean number of abusers									2.34

NOTES: * Figures in the Total column refer to the most severe abuse, the earliest age of onset, and the longest duration of abuse experienced by each respondent.
** The following attributes—fear, pleasure, interest, shock, and surprise—were provided for the respondents to circle. They were also asked to describe any other feelings they may have experienced.

Looking only at the abuse of greatest severity and duration and earliest onset reported by each respondent reveals abuse histories similar to those found in case reports. The average age of earliest sexual experience in the sample was 5.5 years. This varied considerably by relationship between perpetrator and victim, with parental and grandparental abuse beginning, on average, between the ages of four and five, and sexual activity with non-family members and siblings beginning at age eight or nine. The average duration of the longest abusive experience reported by each respondent was 6 years. Average duration of abuse ranged from 1.8 years for nonrelatives to 5.8 and 6.6 years for fathers and mothers, respectively. Forty-five men (37% of the sample) reported that a perpetrator was drunk or on other drugs at the time of the abuse.

PHYSICAL ABUSE

Physical abuse by a parent or parental figure was reported by 70 men (61%); 52 men (43%) reported physical abuse by mothers, and 62 men (52%) stating that they were physically abused by fathers. The most common physically abusive behaviors reported of the mothers (in descending order of frequency) were slapping, pulling hair, hitting with objects, throwing objects at the respondent, hitting with the back of the hand across the face, and kicking. The most common behaviors reported of the fathers were backhanding, slapping, hitting with objects, punching, kicking, pulling hair, hitting with a belt or whip, and throwing objects at the respondent. Open-ended questions yielded brutal behaviors by parents, including sewing a respondent's hand into a sewing machine, attempting to run a respondent over with a car, lowering a respondent into a septic tank, and shooting a respondent in the face with a pellet gun.

"SEXUAL ACTIVITY" VERSUS "SEXUAL ABUSE"

A large majority of all sexual interactions reported in this study were considered abusive by the respondent. Childhood sexual interactions were considered to be abusive at somewhat different rates, however, depending on the relationship with the perpetrator. Sexual activity with a sibling was least likely to be seen as abusive, whereas sexual activity with a father was most often construed as such. These data are displayed in Table 7.6. Milder sexual activity was somewhat less likely to be viewed

Table 7.6 Percentage Who Consider Sexual Interaction to Be Abusive: Variations by Relationship

	Mother	Father	Sibling	Aunt/Uncle	Grandparent	Stranger
Number of cases of sexual interaction	50	48	56	21	16	56
Number of cases considered abusive	43	43	39	18	13	49
Percentage of cases considered abusive	86%	90%	70%	86%	81%	87%

as abusive. There were exceptions, however: Two cases of sexual interactions with parents (one with father, one with mother) that included penetration were not considered to be abusive. Five cases of moderate sexual activity and five cases of severe sexual activity with siblings were not interpreted as abuse. (Chapter 8 includes a discussion of the implications of utilizing all childhood sexual activity versus utilizing only such activity that is construed as abusive when examining the impact of sexual abuse.)

RELATIONSHIP BETWEEN PERPETRATOR AND VICTIM

Complete data on the relationship between respondent and perpetrator are presented in Table 7.7. Childhood sexual interactions were reported with a variety of perpetrators. Because of the frequency of multiple perpetration, most respondents indicated several abusers. Seventy-seven percent of the sample report sexual activity with a member of their immediate family, 29% reported sexual interactions with a relative outside of the immediate family, and 67% report sexual interactions with a nonrelative. This finding diverges from case-report studies that indicate primarily extrafamilial abuse. There was also a much higher incidence of female perpetration in this study than most case-report studies have indicated. Sixty percent of the sample reported childhood sexual activity with females, and 88% reported sexual interactions with males. Forty-six percent of the sample reported sexual activity with both males and females, 14% indicated interactions with females only, and 42% stated that they experienced sexual interactions only with males during childhood. Less than half of those reporting sexual interaction with both males and females state that there was sexual activity with both mother and father, indicating that a minority of abuse by males and females consisted of mothers and fathers acting in unison. Twenty-one percent of the sample reported sexual activity with mother only, 18% reported sexual activity with father only, and 21% reported activity with both parents. These findings differ from those of Faller (1987), Mathews et al. (1990), McCarty (1986), and Wolfe (1985), who found that female perpetrators tended to act in conjunction with or under the coercion of male partners. The most frequently reported perpetrators were mothers (41% of the sample), followed by fathers (39%), male strangers (31%), and brothers (30%).

These findings—the high incidence of intrafamilial abuse and of female perpetration—appear to confirm a central hypothesis of Chapters 2 and 3: Cases of sexual abuse of boys that are reported to police or protective services are not representative of the true nature of the phenomenon. Reported cases primarily involve unrelated adult male perpetrators. In "real life" much or most of the sexual victimization of boys is incestuous. Although men abuse more frequently than do women, female perpetration is a far more common occurrence than it is generally considered to be. What we notice, what we report, and how we respond are all profoundly influenced by our expectations and beliefs. The more prepared we are to recognize and accommodate the experiences of boys who are abused by a family member and/or by a woman, the better able we will be to serve them. Because approaches to understanding the impact of sexual abuse and formulating treatment interventions are based upon a male perpetrator-female victim paradigm, relatively little is known about the experiences of victims and survivors who do not meet these criteria. The psychological impact of childhood sexual victimization by a female is likely to be qualitatively different than abuse by a male, but there are minimal data about the lives of men who have had such experiences. Further research aimed at understanding incestuously abused males and, particularly, those abused by females would be extremely beneficial.

The characteristics of the abuse histories of the men in this sample provide support both for the parameters of abuse found in the surveys of such researchers as Fromuth and Burkhart (1987, 1989) and Risin and Koss (1987) and for the work of investigators like Browne and Finkelhor (1986) and Herman et al. (1986) on trauma-predictive factors associated with the abuse. The broad range of childhood sexual activity, varying in

Table 7.7 Relationship Between Respondent and Perpetrator

Perpetrator	Percentage of Sample Reporting Sexual Interaction With This Perpetrator
Male only	42%
Female only	14%
Both	46%
Immediate family	77%
Other relative	29%
Non-Relative	67%
Parent	60%
Mother	41%
Father	39%
Mother only	21%
Father only	18%
Both	21%
Sibling	42%
Male sibling	30%
Female sibling	12%
Both	0%
Aunt/Uncle	17%
Aunt only	3%
Uncle only	11%
Both	2%
Grandparent	13%
Grandfather only	6%
Grandmother only	6%
Both	2%
Stranger	46%
Male only	31%
Female only	5%
Both	10%
Other perpetrator*	46%

NOTE: * Other perpetrators most frequently mentioned were neighbors (17 cases), family friends (11 cases), priests/ministers (7 cases), cousins (6 cases), and teachers (4 cases). Cases involving cousins as perpetrators were included in the "other relative" category.

degree of severity, duration, age at onset, and with a high incidence of female perpetration, closely resembles the profile of men in Fromuth and Burkhart's and Risin and Koss's nonclinical samples. The men in the current study differed from the college samples assessed in those studies, however, by virtue of the preponderance of severe abuse (including penetration) and the prevalence of sexual activity beginning at a very early age and continuing over several years. There was also a high incidence of sexual interactions with parents and other close relatives in the present sample, unlike in the college surveys. Numerous researchers investigating factors associated with the abuse have identified long duration, early onset, severity of abuse, and close relationship between victim and perpetrator as predictors of later disturbance (Browne & Finkelhor, 1986; Herman et al., 1986; Tsai et al., 1979). I would speculate that the presence of these factors distinguishes the men in this sample from nonclinical populations and plays a large part in giving rise to the difficulties for which they seek treatment. The relationships between each of these factors and outcome measures will be discussed in the following chapter.

Three other factors that have less often been investigated as predictors of later disturbance were also assessed. These include number of perpetrators, substance use by perpetrators, and the presence of physical abuse. As previously noted, the majority of the sample indicated multiple perpetrators, with an average of 2.34 perpetrators reported. There was a high incidence of drug and/or alcohol use by perpetrators at the time of abuse. Respondents indicated that 37% of perpetrators were under the influence of alcohol or other drugs at the time of abuse. Fathers, grandparents, aunts, and uncles were approximately twice as likely to combine substance and sexual abuse than were mothers, siblings, and nonrelatives. Sixty-one percent of the total sample indicated physical abuse by a parent, with 43% reporting that their mothers had been physically abusive to them and 51% stating that their fathers had physically abused them. The relationships between these factors and outcome indices will be discussed in Chapter 8.

There are, I believe, powerful implications of these findings. Sexual abuse must not be viewed in a vacuum; much, perhaps most, sexual abuse occurs in multiply-dysfunctional families, with physical and/or substance abuse present in addition to the sexual abuse. The traumagenic impact of sexual abuse is likely to increase dramatically with the coexistence of other forms of dysfunction and abuse within the family. Sexual abuse by both parents may be more likely to occur within such families, and there may be a decreased likelihood of a supportive parent to provide a counterweight to the abusive caregiver (Kelly & Gonzalez, 1990). The presence of substance abuse is itself associated with later disturbance (Payne & Zuber, 1991; Whitfield, 1987; Wood, 1987) as is physical abuse (Kempe & Kempe, 1978). Further research on the relationships among these various forms of dysfunction and abuse and their impact on doubly and triply jeopardized children would be very valuable. (See Black [1990], Briere [1988], Payne & Zuber [1991], and Yeary [1982] for examples of research on this topic.)

Generalizability of the Current Study

The primary limitations of the current study concern the capacity to generalize from this sample to broader populations. Virtually all of the men assessed in this study had participated in psychotherapy, most for a duration of several years or more. The characteristics of childhood sexual experiences and the extent and specific nature of psychological disturbance of clinical and nonclinical populations of male sexual abuse survivors may differ. For example, although perpetrators were not excluded from this study, a considerable proportion of the therapists who referred their clients to this study screen perpetrators out of their groups. The psychological profile of the men in this study may differ significantly from that of populations consisting largely of perpetrators. In other ways, conversely, such as age and geography, the sample in the present study comes from a broader, more diverse population than the undergraduate or geographically limited samples from which much of our information on childhood sexual activity derives. Nonetheless, considerable caution should be exercised in extrapolating from the results of this study to nonclinical populations of abused men.

Several aspects of the demographic characteristics of this sample raise questions regarding the extent to which it is representative of the general population of sexually abused men. First, the present sample is predominantly white. Second, the level of educational attainment in the current study was extremely high. Educational level is highly correlated with socioeconomic status, so the sample studied here is probably not representative of the full SES spectrum; of course, nor are undergraduate samples. Third, most respondents had participated in extensive psychotherapy, with an average duration in therapy of approximately 5 years. The argument could be made that white sexually abused men of high socioeconomic status, who have been in psychotherapy for long periods of time, were more likely to have completed and returned questionnaires. To the extent that this hypothesis is accurate, the ability to generalize from this sample to the overall clinical population of sexually abused men is weakened.

There are several ways of addressing these potential limitations and assessing the generalizability of this study. First, the psychological profile of the men in this study can be compared with the picture that emerges from the literature on sexual abuse survivors. An objection that could be raised regarding a sample such as this with an unusually high level of educational attainment is that it may represent one extreme of the spectrum of psychological health. That is, the men who completed questionnaires may be among the most healthy of sexual abuse survivors—those who, despite their abuse, were able to reach high levels of educational and professional development. A number of the men interviewed held prestigious positions in the helping professions. Several, however, identified their educational and professional achievements as compensatory reactions to their childhood abuse, whether in an effort to ameliorate poor self-esteem or through helping others as a means of mastering their own helplessness and victimization. Thus, high educational attainment may be one pattern of response to abuse rather than an indication that one has escaped its ill effects (see also Lew, 1990b).

Educational achievement notwithstanding, respondents to this study reported considerable psychological distress and dysfunction, as indicated by the extremely low mean scores on the Benevolence and Self-Worth scales (Janoff-Bulman, 1989), and high rates of psychiatric hospitalization, psychotropic medication, and suicidality. The finding of a long average duration in psychotherapy is itself likely to be indicative of a high degree of emotional distress on the part of participants in this research. Each of the men interviewed described profound and pervasive psychosocial disturbance. The specific areas of concern raised during the interviews meshed with Finkelhor and Browne's (1985) model of the four traumagenic dynamics of the impact of sexual abuse—traumatic sexualization, betrayal, powerlessness, and stigmatization. The difficulty with trust and intimacy and the confusion around interpersonal boundaries mentioned by several men as critical issues have been cited in the literature as common sequelae of childhood sexual abuse. In sum, it appears that the psychological profile of the men in the current study is consistent with the literature on sexual abuse survivors. Information is not available regarding substance use or abuse by respondents or sexual offenses perpetrated by the respondents. Such data, and the use of standardized measures that tap experiences of shame and powerlessness, would represent significant additions to our understanding of these men.

A second means of addressing the question of generalizability is to examine the impact of demographic characteristics within the current sample: Does educational level or duration in psychotherapy predict a higher or lower level of psychosocial functioning? The ability to extrapolate from this sample to those of lower socioeconomic status, for example, is strengthened if socioeconomic status is not correlated at a statistically significant level with the various outcome measures utilized in this study. These statistical tests were not conducted as part of the current study, but would be a valuable addition to this research.

Third, it would be useful to know more about the men who did *not* return questionnaires. Approximately 350 questionnaires were mailed. A number of therapists requested and received numerous questionnaires for distribution to their clients. One hundred twenty-four questionnaires were completed and returned. Thus, this was partially a self-selected sample, with men electing whether or not to participate after learning of the study from their therapists. Data are not available regarding similarities and differences between the 124 respondents and those who chose not to participate in this study. One avenue for future research would be to request from therapists who received multiple questionnaires anonymous descriptions of aggregate characteristics of their clientele, such as age, ethnicity, educational level, duration in psychotherapy, and characteristics of the abuse. The ability to generalize from this study to broader clinical populations of sexually abused men would be strengthened to the extent that the 124 men who completed questionnaires are representative of the clientele of the therapists who received questionnaires.

Fourth, several interesting and important studies could be conducted comparing the present sample with other populations. Comparison groups could include nonclinical populations of sexually abused men, including samples of perpetrators; clinical samples of non-sexually abused men; and clinical samples of sexually abused women. Replications of these findings in other samples would strengthen the confidence with which implications may be drawn from the results of this study. It is my sincere hope that despite the limitations in generalizability discussed here, the findings of this study will shed light on the phenomenon of male sexual victimization and the impact of sexual abuse on men.

Chris's Story

Chris is a 44-year-old married, heterosexual, self-employed handyman. He is the youngest of five, with four older sisters. He reported sexual abuse by several different perpetrators. As was characteristic of the men in this sample, his focus was upon the sexual activity that occurred within his own family, despite the fact that in his case more severe abuse took place with a nonrelative. He indicated that sexual activity occurred with one of his sisters, who is 5 years older than he is. His sister played with his penis and tried to get him to insert it in her anus. This activity took place over approximately a 2-month period when Chris was 7 years old. He also described his mother lying down with him when he was six and placing his leg between hers and his head on her breast. He recalls feeling uncomfortable about this and generally being anxious about her hugs. When Chris was 9 years old he was sodomized by an older boy in the neighborhood. During his recent therapy, he discussed his abuse with his sister and described the abuse by the neighbor boy as well. She stated that this boy had also had anal intercourse with her, and Chris realized that this was where his sister had gotten the idea.

During the interview, Chris focused upon being the only male in his family and the inferior light in which males were cast in his family. Chris's father had died when Chris was three. He grew up with his mother and his four sisters, who were 20, 10, 5, and 4 years older than him. (Chris's oldest sister was actually the daughter of his father's first wife, and the next sister was a half sister from his father's previous marriage, facts that Chris did not know during childhood.) He shared a room with the two sisters closest to him in age, and recalls them laughing at his penis. His mother and his sisters made fun of him for being a boy and teased him about his voice changing. His sisters constantly walked in on him without knocking while he was changing. He also recalled his mother saying things that made him very confused about sexuality—referring, for example, to "when (she) was a little boy." He grew up believing that women had all the power and authority; that he, as a male, was inherently inferior; and that a man was not a good or desirable thing to be. In addition, he has realized in therapy that he had considerable unconscious apprehension about the capacity of women to damage men. He referred during the interview to "growing up with five women who emasculated (him)."

He indicated that his mother was a very unhappy woman, who constantly complained about her life. Two of his sisters (the one 10 years older than him, and the one 5 years older who had abused him) also complained about having to take care of him and how much better their lives would be if they did not need to do so. The sister closest to Chris in age, with whom he had the best relationship ("she didn't resent spending time with me"), was hospitalized at age 15 and diagnosed as a paranoid schizophrenic. She committed suicide when Chris was about 30. Chris's characteristic response to the anger and negativity of his mother and sisters was to withdraw, hide, and sulk. As a teenager, he was extremely depressed. He reported presenting an outward facade of the "happy-go-lucky guy," but inside he felt terrified and depressed. He often thought about death and suicide. This culminated in a pivotal event in his life when, at age 21, he purchased a gun, which he loaded, cocked, and held to his head. He reported an epiphanic experience at this point, as he realized that he "had never really lived, never felt like a live human being, like (he) was just watching someone else go through the paces of being alive." He decided he needed to die or to start living. Thus, he feels that his thoughts of suicide had the effect of reviving his life. He stated that he has not considered suicide since that point.

Chris has participated in extensive psychotherapy and indicated that his responses to the questionnaire were quite different now than they would have been prior to therapy. Much of what he described in the interview as sequelae to the childhood abuse are no longer true for him. For example, prior to therapy he felt that bad things inevitably happened to him, but now he is able to recognize his role in eliciting negative outcomes. He stated that he used constantly to keep his guard up and mistrust others. He indicated that it remains an effort to keep his past and the emotions linked to his childhood trauma from getting the better of him. He had not discussed the sexual abuse with anyone during his childhood and indicated that he didn't communicate with his family about anything, much less an issue of such importance and emotional impact. He also stated that he did not recall much of his childhood, including the sexual activity, until beginning psychotherapy.

His childhood experiences have had a profound impact upon his sexual life. He reported feeling isolated and very insecure as an adolescent and not being involved in dating relationships. His first sexual experience, at age 22, reinforced his sense of inadequacy. He reported that the woman requested that he not call her again, because he was so bad in bed. He had no further sexual contact until age 27. He felt extremely intimidated by women and reported suppressing any sexual thoughts because of how painful these were for him. He said that it was not until he was about 40 that he began to consider sex as a natural and positive aspect of relationships with women. He had been married for 6 months at age 29 and stated that there was no sexual intercourse during this marriage. He described a constant state of tension and said that he had not realized that it was possible to disagree about something and still have sex. He has been married for 1½ years now and stated that this is the first relationship in which he has been able to have sexual intercourse without enormous anxiety.

Chris sees the relational matrix in which he was brought up as having significant consequences for his later relationships. He said that he was virtually incapable of trusting other people and had no sense of appropriate boundaries between individuals. As a child, boundaries were constantly violated, as exemplified by the recurrent instances of his sisters walking in on him while he was dressing. He indicated that a double standard existed with regard to anger. His sisters often hit him, but there were no outlets for his anger. If he hit his sisters in return he was punished.

He felt powerless as a result and learned to suppress and store his anger. He stated that his sisters and mother frequently acted impulsively and without explanation.

Chris had long assumed that this was an inevitable aspect of relationships and involved himself with women who mistreated him and lashed out at him without apparent cause or explanation. The unconscious fantasy that guided him in these relationships was that if he were only better, nicer, or tried harder, they would be kind to him in return. Only recently has he recognized that he continually recreated the environment of his childhood relationships with his mother and sisters. Chris stated that unhappy women were familiar and comfortable to him and he realizes now that he sought them out as surrogate mothers. He stated that his relationships had largely consisted of efforts on his part to rescue women from their unhappiness by his patience and support. He would then become frustrated by his inability to make them happier. Anger and disappointment were, until recent years, the only emotions in Chris's repertoire. As he stated, "if I didn't feel anger and disappointment, I wouldn't know what to feel. They were the only ones I was familiar with."

Chris sees his life and the process of recovery that he has undertaken as much like that of an alcoholic or drug addict or, perhaps most accurately, like that of an adult child of an alcoholic family. He had always assumed that life is disappointing and painful. He has lived with the guiding belief that everyone else has the problems and that his role is to help or rescue them. He had not, until recently, recognized his own contribution to his pain and suffering. It was not until he lost everything (including his house) as a result of an abusive relationship that he began to ask himself why this sort of relationship constituted a recurrent pattern in his life. He indicated that he has been able to have some satisfying close friendships with both men and women. His friendships with women have in part stemmed from his fear of sexual intimacy. He feels that as a result of his avoidance of sexual contact, he was able to develop other aspects of relationships with women. He also recognizes that he sought out friendships with women rather than men because of his sense that men were inferior and unlikable. He has recently become better able to befriend and trust men. Chris stated that as a result of not developing self-esteem and confidence in childhood, he seeks that in his career. He left a lucrative career as an engineer because he felt that he was unable to identify with his work in an emotional sense. His current career, which involves painting and working with his hands, feels to him far more creative and emotionally fulfilling. He had been told in his earlier job that he had risen as far as he could and experienced this information as akin to the childhood message that he did not matter.

When asked about the impact of his childhood abuse upon his parenting, Chris provided an answer characteristic of the men in this sample. He stated that he had always viewed himself as incapable of competent parenting. He had seen childhood as inevitably painful and was not about to inflict that upon someone else. By the time he felt capable of adequate parenting, he was 40 years old and thought that this was too late to begin planning a family.

At the conclusion of the interview Chris summarized the impact he feels his sexual abuse has had upon his life. "Incest and sexual abuse are so offensive because they go so far beyond all boundaries—body, spiritual, emotional—all are violated. How is it possible to understand limits, respect them, or have yours respected?"

8 Understanding the Impact of Sexual Abuse on Males

Though clinical reports of boy victims appeared as early as 1937 (Bender & Blau), male sexual victimization remains a relatively unexplored topic for research. The past few years have seen an increase in studies on the prevalence and descriptive characteristics of abuse, but very little is known about the long-term effects of childhood sexual abuse on males. Empirical studies of clinical samples of adult men abused during childhood are especially rare (Kelly & Gonzalez, 1990; Olson, 1990). To date, the present study represents the largest clinical sample of sexually abused men. Only Kelly and Gonzalez (1990) have analyzed differences in outcome by variations in the characteristics of the sexual abuse in order to assess the impact of such factors upon the male victim. Therefore, a central focus of the present study is the relationship between various abuse characteristics and adult psychosocial functioning.

Relationships Between Abuse
Characteristics and Outcome

This study assesses variations in outcome dependent on specific features of the abuse. The relationships between various factors associated with the abuse and multiple measures of psychosocial functioning were examined. Independent variables include duration of abuse; severity of abuse; number of perpetrators; age of respondent at onset of abuse; presence of physical abuse; drug use by perpetrator; gender of the perpetrator; intra- versus extrafamilial abuse; and sexual interactions with mother, with father, and with a sibling.

"SEXUAL ACTIVITY"
VERSUS "SEXUAL ABUSE"

An issue of both practical and theoretical import is whether to consider all childhood sexual activity or only activity interpreted by the respondent as abusive in assessing variations in outcome measures. Research utilizing the latter definition (e.g., Cameron et al., 1986; Finkelhor, 1979; Finkelhor et al., 1990) results in a more narrow range of sexual activity and a lower incidence of female perpetration than research that includes all childhood sexual activity (Fromuth & Burkhart, 1987, 1989; Risin & Koss, 1987). It is an empirical issue, with insufficient data at this time, whether all sexual activity or only sexual activity construed as abuse is associated with later psychological disturbance. In the present study, therefore, as in Fromuth and Burkhart's (1987) study, both the "sexual activity" and "sexual abuse" criteria were utilized as independent variables. Respondents were asked whether childhood sexual activity had occurred. If they indicated that it had, they were also asked whether they considered the activity to have been sexually abusive. (It should be kept in mind that each man in this study had experienced at least one incident of sexual activity that he considered to be abusive, because this was the explicit basis for inclusion in the study.)

Seventy percent of sexual activity with siblings was considered abusive, which is a considerably lower frequency than that found in any other relationship. Between 80% and 90% of sexual activity was considered abusive in all other relationships. With respect to childhood sexual activity between siblings, the sexual abuse criterion, but not the sexual activity criterion, was associated with several negative outcomes. It appears that consensual sexual activity between siblings is not highly pathogenic, at least for this sample. Sexual activity between parents and children, conversely, was associated with multiple negative outcomes regardless of whether it is considered abusive. In summary, it appears that childhood sexual activity, even if not considered abusive, may have pathological sequelae. Both "sexual activity" and "sexual activity considered to be abusive" are valid criteria for assessing the long-term effects of sexual abuse. The multiple-definition method pioneered by Fromuth and Burkhart (1987) appears to be the most appropriate means of assessing this aspect of the impact of childhood sexual activity. Again, all of the men in this study had experienced at least one incident that they considered to be abusive. It was therefore not possible to assess differences between men whose childhood sexual activity is seen as consensual and those who view their sexual activity as abuse. (It was only possible to do such comparisons between, for example, those who viewed their sexual activity with a sibling as abusive versus those who did not view their sexual activity with a sibling as abusive.) This would be a valuable avenue for future research and could shed light on the role of the individual's construction and interpretation of his life experiences in determining the impact of these experiences.

Complete data on the correlations between outcome measures and these variables (both "sexual activity" and "sexual abuse") are displayed in Table 8.1. Sexual activity with mother predicted trauma symptoms. Sexual activity with father was correlated with trauma symptoms, malevolent worldview, duration of psychotherapy, sexual maladjustment, psychiatric medication, and poor overall functioning as assessed by the CIF. Sexual activity with sibling predicted sexual dissatisfaction. Using the sexual abuse criterion with mothers resulted in significant correlations with duration of psychotherapy and sexual dissatisfaction, which were not significant when the sexual activity criterion was used instead. The sexual activity, but not the sexual abuse, criterion was correlated at a significance level of $p < .10$ with heterosexual orientation and with receiving psychiatric medication. When the men who consider their childhood sexual activity with their mothers to be abusive were compared directly to those who do not, two statistically significant differences emerged. Men in the former group were more likely to be homosexual and to be dissatisfied with their sex lives.

Table 8.1 Comparisons in Outcome Variables Between All Sexual Activity and Sexual Activity Construed as Abuse

Outcome Variables	Predictor Variables					
	Sexual Activity with Mother (N = 50)	Sexual Abuse by Mother (N = 43)	Sexual Activity with Father (N = 48)	Sexual Abuse by Father (N = 43)	Sexual Activity with Sibling (N = 56)	Sexual Abuse by Sibling (N = 38)
Trauma symptoms	**.0442**	**.0490**	**.0010**	**.0013**	.2627	**.0091**
Malevolent worldview	.1652	.4759	**.0024**	**.0028**	.1113	**.0089**
Low self-worth	.3008	.5136	.0595	**.0261**	.0925	.0902
Duration of psychotherapy	.0750	**.0188**	**.0361**	.2964	.2297	.7747
Low sexual satisfaction	.3920	**.0260**	.2396	.1719	**.0221**	**.0362**
Sexual orientation (hetero- or homosexual)	.0774 (heterosexual)	.6760 (heterosexual)	.4911 (homosexual)	.5671 (homosexual)	.1677 (homosexual)	.0716 (homosexual)
Poor sexual adjustment	.1953	.0766	**.0097**	**.0018**	.2272	.0522
Poor functioning (Composite Index)	.0639	.1103	**.0004**	**.0002**	.0691	**.0042**
Psychiatric hospitalization	.3570	.3261	.0748	.1495	.9155	.1651
Psychotropic medication	.0666	.8570	**.0126**	**.0126**	.1910	.1439
Suicide attempts	.5091	.4978	.7283	.7901	.0902	**.0060**

NOTE: Numbers are p values indicating significance of association: Values of $p < .05$ are in boldface type.

Using the sexual abuse rather than the sexual activity criterion with respect to fathers resulted in a significant correlation with poor self-worth. (The sexual activity criterion had yielded a correlation with $p <$ .10.) The sexual activity criterion, but not the sexual abuse criterion, yielded a significant correlation with duration of psychotherapy and a correlation of $p <$ .10 with psychiatric hospitalization. A relatively low percentage (70%) of those reporting sexual activity with a sibling viewed this activity as abusive. Using the criterion of sexual activity construed as abuse resulted in much higher correlations with indices of disturbance than including all sexual activity. Sexual activity with a sibling was a statistically significant predictor only of sexual dissatisfaction. Sexual activity with a sibling that is interpreted as abusive was also correlated with trauma symptoms, a malevolent worldview, suicide attempts, and overall psychological dysfunction as assessed by the CIF. It would appear that using the criterion of sexual activity understood as abuse rather than all sexual activity provides a better predictor of later disturbance with respect to childhood sexual interactions with siblings.

Sexual Orientation

Respondents were asked to categorize their sexual experiences and desires on a 7-point scale ranging from exclusively homosexual to exclusively heterosexual.[1] Sixty percent of the respondents indicated that they were mainly or entirely heterosexual, and 36% identified themselves as mainly or entirely homosexual. Clearly, the proportion of homosexual respondents in this study is far higher than in the general population. Sexual orientation was used as an outcome measure and the relationships between characteristics of the abuse and sexual orientation were assessed.[2] In order to ensure that the apparent predictive relationships between abuse characteristics and outcome measures were not due to differences between homosexual and heterosexual men, sexual orientation was also considered as an independent variable and the relationships between it and the various outcome measures were examined. These relationships are displayed in Table 8.2.

There were no significant differences between homosexuals and heterosexuals in terms of traumatic symptomatology, overall functioning as assessed by the CIF, self-worth, sexual adjustment, or sexual satisfaction.

Table 8.2 Relationship Between Sexual Orientation and Outcome Variables

Outcome Variable	Heterosexual (N = 72)	Homosexual (N = 43)	Significance
Trauma symptoms	2.5669	2.6855	.3422
Benevolent worldview	3.7581	4.2713	.0214
Self-worth	3.3611	3.3895	.9146
Duration of psychotherapy (in months)	41.912	82.631	.0040
Sexual satisfaction (high numbers = dissatisfaction)	4.5429	5.1395	.1334
Sexual adjustment	2.3803	2.2619	.6188
Psychiatric hospitalization (21% of sample have been hospitalized)	22%	16%	.4356
Psychiatric medication (45% of sample have received medication)	37%	56%	.0558
Suicide attempt (33% of sample have attempted suicide)	25%	42%	.0680
Composite Index of Functioning			.7796*

NOTES: * As a composite variable, the CIF cannot meaningfully be expressed as a mean. There were no significant differences in overall functioning between homosexuals and heterosexuals, as assessed by the CIF.
Values are means or percentages. Percentages are indicated by %; p values < .05 are in boldface type.

This finding is itself certainly noteworthy. Two statistically significant differences did emerge. Homosexual men had a more benevolent view of the world than did heterosexuals, and they participated in much more extensive psychotherapy. The average duration of psychotherapy for homosexuals was almost exactly twice that of heterosexuals (6 years, 11 months compared to 3 years, 6 months). There were, in addition, two statistical trends (p < .10): Homosexuals were more likely to have received psychotropic medication and to have attempted suicide, at levels approaching statistical significance.

It is interesting that despite a level of psychological functioning comparable to heterosexuals, homosexuals attempted suicide and received medication more frequently and participated in therapy for a much longer duration than heterosexuals. It is likely that these findings are due in large part to the difficulties inherent in being gay in our society. The majority of suicide attempts occurred between the ages of 16 and 23, and a large percentage of hospitalizations and medications occurred during these life-stages. This is a life-stage during which the struggle for identity is central (Erikson, 1963). It is likely to be particularly difficult and wrought with psychic pain for young homosexuals who must, on top of the identity struggles that characterize all adolescents, come to terms with a sexual identity different from the norm in a society often unaccepting of such difference. They must navigate this while at the same time struggling to cope with their sexual victimization. It may be that the extensive psychotherapy these individuals have received has resulted in marked psychological growth and recovery since those times. The source of the difference between homosexuals and heterosexuals in terms of perceived benevolence of the world is unclear, though this is certainly a striking finding. It is possible that these findings are related and that psychotherapeutic experiences may have contributed to a more benevolent worldview. That is, interacting over a long period of time with a therapist or therapists who are benign, supportive, and invested in one's growth and well-being may alter the abuse survivor's outlook on the world so that he sees it as a more friendly, benevolent place.

The relationship between factors associated with childhood sexual abuse and sexual orientation is complex and controversial. The views of the psychological and medical fields with respect to the etiology of sexual orientation have swung between the poles of nature and nurture. The results of several studies have been published thus far in the 1990s documenting differences in brain structure and genetic markers between homosexual and heterosexual men (Hamer, Hu, Magnuson, Hu, & Pattatucci, 1993; LeVay, 1991; Swaab & Hofman, 1990). Studies in the area of child sexual abuse have repeatedly found a higher incidence of victimization among homosexual than heterosexual men (Bell et al., 1981a, 1981b; Finkelhor, 1984; Simari & Baskin, 1982). Similarly, in the current clinical sample of sexually abused men, 34% identified themselves as primarily or exclusively homosexual. This is considerably higher than the 10% (or less) commonly cited as an estimate of the proportion of homosexuality in the population. Other than the finding of higher rates of sexual abuse among homosexual men, little is known about the relationships among abuse characteristics and sexual orientation.

In the current study, factors related to the gender of the perpetrator were the main predictors of sexual orientation. Specifically, men sexually abused during childhood by males were much more likely to identify themselves as homosexual than were men abused by females. The strongest statistical correlation was that between childhood sexual interactions with a brother and homosexual orientation. Men reporting sexual activity with mothers were more likely to be heterosexual, at a level approaching statistical significance. Those abused more severely were more likely to be homosexual. This last finding appears to be the result of the more severe abuse typical of male abusers, however, as regressions indicate only gender of perpetrator independently predicts sexual orientation.

The significant correlations between gender of perpetrator and sexual orientation are striking. They should not, however, be taken to indicate that sexual abuse, sexual abuse by males, or any other environmental variable causes homosexuality. The dictum that correlation does not imply causality should be kept in mind. Several alternate explanations have been suggested for the finding of the high rate of sexual abuse among homosexual men, each of which offers insight into the relationship between abuse by males and homosexual orientation. Simari and Baskin (1982), in discussing their finding that 64% of homosexual men in their study reported sexual activity with a relative during childhood, noted that most of these men indicated that they were already aware of their homosexual orientation at the time of the sexual interaction. In other words, sexual orientation preceded the childhood sexual activity rather than arising out of it. There are several differences between the Simari and Baskin study and the current one. Sexual interactions in their study consisted largely of consensual activity between siblings or cousins that was not perceived by the respondents as abusive, either at the time or in retrospect. Age at the time of sexual activity ranged from 9 to 16 years, which is considerably older than the age reported by men in the current study. In short, Simari and Baskin's study examined the childhood sexual activity of homosexual men and found very high rates of homosexual interaction in the preadolescent and early adolescent years. Though it appears that their research involved a population distinct from that of this study, it is relevant in that the present study found that childhood sexual activity with a brother is the single best predictor of homosexual orientation and that such activity is considered abusive at a relatively low rate. Thus, a large portion of the correlation between same-sex sexual interaction in childhood and adult homosexual orientation may stem from consensual sexual activity among boys, as was the case in Simari and Baskin's study.

Mike Lew (1990a) noted that his clinical practice with sexually abused men includes a high proportion of homosexuals. He speculated that during childhood, even if the victims themselves have not yet identified themselves as homosexuals, they may have discernible characteristics that make them vulnerable to sexual abuse. These features may include such qualities as passivity, a girlish appearance or demeanor, bookishness, and a lack of interest in stereotypically masculine interests such as athletics. In his view, such features are risk factors for sexual abuse and are also disproportionately represented in homosexual populations. Thus these characteristics are predictive of both sexual abuse and homosexuality, rather than the former causing the latter.

Gonsiorek (1993) proposes an explanation similar to that of Lew's, based upon the predatory nature of perpetrators. He argues that child abusers seek out vulnerable children. A child in an abusive or neglectful home or in a substance-abusing family would be vulnerable, as would a child with some sort of narcissistic injury. Gonsiorek asserts that children who later identify themselves as homosexual are aware from an early age (by about the beginning of latency) that they are different in some way from most of their peers and, moreover, that this difference is negatively valued. This sense leads to considerable self-disparagement, or what Gonsiorek terms "internalized homophobia," and leaves the child vulnerable to the sexual offender's predation.

A fourth perspective on the relationship between sexual abuse and sexual orientation was proposed by Finkelhor (1984), who found a four times greater incidence of sexual abuse among homosexuals than among heterosexuals. His view comes closest to being a causal model of homosexuality. Finkelhor argues that the experiences of sexual victimization cause the victimized boy to doubt and to question his masculinity and his sexual orientation. He wonders whether the fact of being victimized, helpless, and passive means that he is gay or feminine. If, as in the studies reviewed by Finkelhor, the perpetrator was male, the victim may conclude that he was chosen for the abuse because of some attribute that signified to the perpetrator that he was gay and thus susceptible to sexual advances. In the wake of the abuse, the victim makes attributions about himself—"I must have wanted it; he must have known I was gay; I'm not a 'real man' "—that contribute to a later identification as homosexual. In addition, the tendency of males to attribute to themselves desire and willing participation in all sexual activity—what Gerber (1990) termed "the myth of complicity"—may also contribute to the victim's assumption that if sexual activity with a male occurred, he must ipso facto be gay.

It is doubtful whether cognitive attributions such as those proposed by Finkelhor are sufficient to explain the etiology of sexual orientation. Recent biomedical research seems persuasive in demonstrating that there is at least a significant physiological component in the development of homosexuality—that nature plays a major role. Moreover, most research on sexual orientation indicates that it is set in place by the beginning of latency, whereas sexual abuse typically does not begin until later (Gonsiorek, 1993). Finkelhor's discussion of the thought processes of sexually abused men is consistent, however, with the comments of the men interviewed here and with the writings of numerous clinicians in this area who find that their clientele almost uniformly express doubts and concerns about the implications of their abuse for their sexual orientation (Bolton et al., 1989; Bruckner & Johnson, 1987; Dimock, 1988; Lew, 1990b). Thus, regardless of whether one identifies oneself as a homosexual or heterosexual, the experience of childhood sexual victimization, particularly by a male perpetrator, is likely to raise profound issues regarding sexual orientation. It is not possible to determine the precise relationship between sexual abuse and sexual orientation on the basis of the present study or with currently available data. Further research on the relationships between childhood sexual abuse and adult sexual orientation would be extremely valuable.

Statistical Relationships Between Predictors and Outcomes

Table 8.3 lists the independent variables that were correlated with each of the outcome measures.[3] As may be seen in this table, there were numerous predictors of most of the outcome measures. Each outcome variable was associated with a different set of predictive variables; different independent variables were most accurate in predicting various dependent variables. For example, of all the independent variables, abuse of long duration had the highest correlation with psychiatric hospitalization and duration of psychotherapy. The most accurate predictors of traumatic symptoms were drug use by perpetrator and abuse by males. A malevolent worldview was most highly correlated with the early onset of abuse, and the best predictor of poor self-worth was drug use by perpetrator. The existence of physical abuse, especially by the father, along with the sexual abuse was the most accurate predictor of suicidality. Sexual orientation was associated with the gender of perpetrator, with those abused by females more likely to be heterosexual and those abused by males more likely to be homosexual. Sexual interaction with a brother was the best statistical predictor of homosexual orientation. Abuse of greater severity was also correlated with homosexual orientation, though this appears to have been an artifact of the greater severity of abuse by males. The best predictors of the global measure of functioning (CIF) were abuse by males and drug use by perpetrator. In addition to the independent variables already mentioned, severity of abuse, number of abusers, abuse by a member of the immediate family, sexual activity with father and/or mother, and sexual abuse by a sibling were all associated with multiple negative outcomes.

CONTINUOUS PREDICTOR VARIABLES
AND OUTCOME VARIABLES

Tables 8.4 through 8.6 provide complete data on the relationships between predictor and outcome variables. Tables 8.4 and 8.5 display the relationships between continuous predictor variables—number of abusers, duration of abuse, age at onset of abuse, and severity of abuse—and dichotomous and continuous outcome variables, respectively. For all outcome variables, early onset of abuse, abuse of long duration, more severe abuse, and higher number of abusers were associated with greater disturbance. The Composite Index of Functioning (CIF) was correlated at a statistically significant level ($p < .05$) with each of these four independent variables. Other statistically significant correlations with the continuous predictor variables are as follows: Age at onset of abuse was correlated with malevolent worldview, psychiatric hospitalization, and psychiatric medication. (Again, early onset of abuse predicts poor outcome on each variable.) Number of abusers predicted traumatic symptomatology, malevolent worldview, poor self-worth, poor sexual adjustment, sexual dissatisfaction, and psychiatric medication. Severity of abuse was correlated with traumatic symptomatology, poor self-worth, homosexual orientation, and sexual maladjustment. Duration of abuse was correlated with poor self-worth, duration of psychotherapy, psychiatric hospitalization, and psychotropic medication.

Table 8.3 Statistically Significant Predictors of Each Outcome Variable

Outcome Variable	Predictor Variables	Significance
Trauma symptoms	Sexual activity with parent(s)	.0052
	Sexual activity with father	.0010
	Sexual abuse by father	.0013
	Sexual activity with mother	.0442
	Sexual abuse by mother	.0490
	Sexual abuse by sibling	.0091
	Abuse by both male and female	.0002
	Abuse by male	.0001
	Severity of abuse	.0022
	Number of abusers	.0089
	Physical abuse by father	.0008
	Physical abuse by mother	.0043
	Drug use by perpetrator	.0001
	Abuse by immediate family member	.0080
Malevolent worldview	Sexual activity with parent(s)	.0194
	Sexual activity with father	.0024
	Sexual abuse by father	.0028
	Sexual abuse by sibling	.0089
	Abuse by male	.0056
	Early onset of abuse	.0011
	Number of abusers	.0223
	Physical abuse by father	.0176
	Abuse by immediate family member	.0016
Poor self-worth	Abuse by both male and female	.0201
	Abuse by male	.0012
	Sexual abuse by father	.0261
	Severity of abuse	.0480
	Number of abusers	.0217
	Duration of abuse	.0126
	Drug use by perpetrator	.0007
Duration of psychotherapy	Abuse by both male and female	.0386
	Sexual abuse by mother	.0188
	Sexual activity with father	.0361
	Duration of abuse	.0057
Poor sexual satisfaction	Abuse by both male and female	.0040
	Abuse by male	.0017
	Sexual abuse by mother	.0260
	Sexual activity with sibling	.0221
	Sexual abuse by sibling	.0362
	Number of abusers	.0176
Sexual orientation (correlation with homosexual orientation)	Sexual activity with brother	.0017
	Abuse by male	.0153
	Severity of abuse	.0227

Table 8.3 Continued

Outcome Variable	Predictor Variables	Significance
Sexual maladjustment	Abuse by both male and female	.0125
	Abuse by male	.0001
	Sexual activity with father	.0097
	Sexual abuse by father	.0018
	Drug use by perpetrator	.0014
	Abuse by immediate family member	.0123
Psychiatric hospitalization	Duration of abuse	.0019
	Early onset of abuse	.0532
	Physical abuse by father	.0501
Psychotropic medication	Sexual activity with parent(s)	.0152
	Abuse by both male and female	.0009
	Abuse by male	.0002
	Sexual activity with father	.0126
	Sexual abuse by father	.0126
	Physical abuse	.0238
	Abuse by immediate family member	.0148
	Duration of abuse	.0010
	Early onset of abuse	.0285
	Number of abusers	.0470
Suicide attempt	Physical abuse by father	.0041
	Physical abuse	.0104
	Sexual abuse by sibling	.0060
Composite Index of Functioning	Abuse by male	.0001
	Abuse by immediate family member	.0088
	Physical abuse by father	.0031
	Sexual activity with father	.0049
	Sexual abuse by father	.0016
	Abuse by both male and female	.0042
	Abuse by parent	.0332
	Drug use by perpetrator	.0009

NOTE: All predictor variables with $p < .05$ are listed.

DICHOTOMOUS PREDICTOR VARIABLES
AND OUTCOME VARIABLES

Table 8.6 displays the relationships between dichotomous predictor variables and the outcome variables. Predictor variables include childhood sexual activity with a member of immediate family, physical abuse by mother and father, and drug use by perpetrator. Each of these variables was associated with multiple indications of disturbance. The experience

Table 8.4 Correlations Between Continuous Predictor and Continuous
         Outcome Variables

Continuous Outcome Variables	Continuous Predictor Variables			
	Duration	Age of Onset	Severity	Number of Abusers
Trauma symptoms	.1493	−.1383	.2755***	.2367**
Benevolent worldview	−.1251	.2954****	−.0291	−.2076*
Self-worth	−.2319*	.1102	−.1802*	−.2086*
Duration in psychotherapy	.2653**	−.1735ᵗ	.0658	.1643ᵗ
Sexual satisfaction	−.1464	.1189	−.0705	−.2173*
Homosexual orientation	.0046	−.0181	.2070*	.1459ᵗ
Sexual adjustment	−.1755ᵗ	.1595ᵗ	−.1846*	−.2285*
Composite Index of Functioning	−.2227*	.2274*	−.2164*	.2839**

NOTES: Number in each box indicates correlation.
p value for significance is indicated by *
The most accurate predictor of each outcome variable is in boldface type.
$t = p < .10$; * $= p < .05$; ** $= p < .01$; *** $= p < .005$; **** $= p < .001$.

Table 8.5 Correlations Between Continuous Predictor and Dichotomous
         Outcome Variables

Dichotomous Outcome Variables	Continuous Predictor Variables			
	Severity	Duration	Age of Onset	Number of Abusers
Psychiatric hospitalization	.5453	.0019	.0532	.3977
Psychiatric medication	.2434	.0010	.0285	.0470
Suicide attempt	.0955	.6001	.6791	.5710

NOTE: Age is inversely correlated with each of the outcome variables; early onset of abuse predicts poor outcome.
Numbers listed are p values for significance of association; p values $< .05$ are in boldface type.

of physical abuse was significantly correlated with trauma symptoms, psychiatric medication, and suicidality. In addition to those outcomes, physical abuse specifically by father predicted a malevolent worldview, psychiatric hospitalization, and low scores on the CIF. The use of alcohol or other drugs by a perpetrator at the time of abuse was correlated with the following outcome variables: trauma symptoms, poor self-worth, sexual maladjustment, and poor overall functioning. Abuse by a member

Table 8.6 Correlations Between Dichotomous Predictor Variables and All
Outcome Variables

Outcome Variables	Physical Abuse (N = 74)	Physical Abuse by Mother (N = 52)	Physical Abuse by Father (N = 62)	Drug Use by Perpetrator (N = 45)	Abuse by Immediate Family Member (N = 93)
Trauma symptoms	.0106	.0043	.0008	.0001	.0080
Malevolent worldview	.0535	.4406	.0176	.2888	.0016
Low self-worth	.4134	.5443	.0605	.0007	.1958
Duration of psychotherapy	.7090	.9327	.5003	.3938	.0823
Low sexual satisfaction	.5461	.3603	.1616	.2213	.2177
Sexual orientation (hetero- or homosexual)	.6725	.5588	.6140	.2857	.8001
Poor sexual adjustment	.6736	.6267	.1735	.0014	.0123
Psychiatric hospitalization	.2041	.6561	.0501	.0896	.3266
Psychiatric medication	.0238	.1174	.0674	.9751	.0148
Suicide attempts	.0104	.0779	.0041	.4933	.9632
Poor functioning (Composite Index)	.0632	.1263	.0035	.0001	.0018

NOTE: Numbers are p values indicating significance of association: Values of $p < .05$ are in boldface type.

of the immediate family was associated with trauma symptoms, malevolent worldview, sexual maladjustment, psychotropic medication, and low scores on the CIF.

DIFFERENTIATING BETWEEN EXTREMES IN OUTCOME

Post hoc analyses were conducted in order to determine which of the predictor variables were capable of discriminating most accurately between opposite extremes of the outcome measures. Five outcome indices were used: trauma symptoms, benevolent/malevolent worldview, self-worth, sexual adjustment, and the Composite Index of Functioning. The predictor variables that discriminated between the highest 20 and lowest 20 scores on each measure at a significance level of $p < .05$ are displayed in Table 8.7. Several independent variables discriminated between the highest and lowest scores on each outcome measure. Inclusion in the bottom group on the global measure (CIF), which is based on the means

Table 8.7 Predictor Variables That Discriminate Most Accurately Between
Extremes on Outcome Variables

Outcome Variable	Predictor Variables	Significance
Trauma symptoms	Severity	.0097
	Number of abusers	.0496
	Abuse by immediate family member	.0390
	Physical abuse	.0293
	Physical abuse by mother	.0239
	Physical abuse by father	.0107
	Sexual activity/abuse with father	.0049
	Gender of perpetrator	.0006
	Parental abuse	.0149
	Drug use by perpetrator	.0016
	Sexual abuse by sibling	.0095
Benevolent/malevolent	Age at onset	.0207
worldview	Abuse by immediate family member	.0038
	Sexual orientation	.0565
	Sexual abuse by sibling	.0272
	Abuse by male	.0032
Self-worth	Severity	.0194
	Duration of abuse	.0335
	Abuse by male	.0088
	Physical abuse by father	.0530
	Sexual activity with sibling	.0083
	Sexual abuse by sibling	.0050
	Drug use by perpetrator	.0016
Sexual adjustment	Abuse by male	.0052
	Drug use by perpetrator	.0043
Composite Index of	Abuse by male	.0001
Functioning	Abuse by immediate family member	.0088
	Physical abuse by father	.0031
	Sexual activity with father	.0049
	Sexual abuse by father	.0016
	Gender of perpetrator	.0042
	Parental abuse	.0332
	Drug use by perpetrator	.0009
	Sexual abuse by sibling	.0009

NOTE: All predictor variables with $p < .05$ are listed.
Predictor variables listed are associated with poor functioning on the outcome variable.

of the other four measures, was associated with the following variables:
abuse by male, abuse by a member of the immediate family, physical abuse
by father, sexual interaction with father, sexual interaction with both

Table 8.8 Stepwise Logistical Regressions (Dichotomous Outcome Variables)

Outcome Variable	Predictor Variable	Coefficient	Coefficient/ Standard Error
Psychiatric hospitalization	Duration of abuse	0.67432	2.517
Psychotropic medication	Abuse by male and female	2.82100	3.214
	Duration of abuse	0.13007	2.952
	Abuse by male	1.81820	2.083
	Drug use by perpetrator	−0.84882	−1.830
Attempted suicide	Abuse by sibling	1.44060	2.969
	Physical abuse	1.28870	2.674
	Abuse by member of immediate family	−1.10060	−1.900

NOTE: Absolute values of coefficient/standard error > 2.000 are statistically significant.

mother and father, gender of perpetrator (abuse by both male and female), drug use by perpetrator, and abuse by sibling.

Regression Analyses

Tables 8.8 and 8.9 display the results of the stepwise logistical and linear regressions, respectively. The following independent variables were entered into each regression equation on the basis of their associations with negative outcomes on the bivariate statistical tests: duration of abuse, age at onset of abuse, severity of abuse, sexual interaction with both male and female, sexual interaction with a male, sexual interaction with a member of the immediate family, sexual interaction with both father and mother, sexual interaction with father, sexual interaction with mother, sexual abuse by sibling, number of abusers, physical abuse, and drug use by perpetrator. Depending on which outcome measure was used, between one and five variables emerged as significant independent predictors of that measure.

Approximately 17% of the total variance in trauma symptomatology could be accounted for by two factors, sexual interactions with both male and female and drug use by a perpetrator. With these factors held constant, sexual activity with mother was correlated with the presence of fewer symptoms, at a level approaching statistical significance. The

Table 8.9 Stepwise Linear Regressions (Continuous Outcome Variables)

Outcome Variable	Predictor Variable	R^2	Coefficient	Significance
Trauma symptoms	Drug use by perpetrator	—	0.38779	.0011
	Abuse by both male and female	.19438	0.35280	.0028
	Sexual activity with mother	—	-0.26192	.0637
Malevolent worldview	Early onset of abuse	.09562	0.10822	.0011
Low self-worth	Drug use by perpetrator	.10738	0.66036	.0103
	Duration of abuse	—	0.25034	.0742
Duration of psychotherapy	Duration of abuse	—	0.21152	.0076
	Abuse by both male and female	.15397	37.13300	.0103
	Drug use by perpetrator	—	-27.52900	.0594
Sexual maladjustment	Abuse by immediate family member	—	0.81301	.0037
	Drug use by perpetrator	.15468	0.56456	.0124
	Physical abuse	—	-0.38690	.0958
Sexual orientation (correlation with homosexuality)	Abuse by male	.09943	2.74440	.0012
	Abuse by both male and female	—	1.88520	.0222
Poor functioning (Composite Index)	Abuse by immediate family member	.15079	0.46330	.0081
	Drug use by perpetrator	—	0.37175	.0103

reference group for this variable consists of men not abused by either parent and those abused by both males and females, indicating that the level of functioning of men abused by their mothers is higher than the aggregate of this group. A malevolent view of the world was predicted by early onset of abuse, which accounts for approximately 10% of the total variance. The sole statistically significant independent predictor of low self-worth was drug use by perpetrator. This variable, along with duration of abuse, was responsible for approximately 11% of the variance in outcome. Duration of abuse and abuse by both male and female contributed independently to long duration of psychotherapy, accounting for about 12% of the variance. With these factors held constant, drug use by perpetrator was predictive of shorter duration of psychotherapy, at a level approaching statistical significance. Sexual interaction with a member of the immediate family and drug use by perpetrator were statistically significant independent predictors of sexual maladjustment and were responsible for about 13% of its variance. With these factors held constant, physical abuse was predictive of better adjustment, at a level approaching statistical significance. Homosexual orientation was independently correlated with childhood sexual interactions with males and with sexual interactions with both males and females. These two factors accounted for about 10% of the variance in this outcome variable. Low scores on the Composite Index of Functioning were associated independently with sexual activity with a member of the immediate family and drug use by perpetrator. These two factors were responsible for about 15% of the total variance in this global measure of functioning.

A history of psychiatric hospitalization was associated solely with abuse of long duration. Sexual activity with both males and females, sexual activity with males, and abuse of long duration contributed independently to receiving psychotropic medications. With these variables held constant, those who reported drug use by a perpetrator were less likely to have received psychotropic medications, at a level approaching significance. Abuse by a sibling and physical abuse were statistically significant independent predictors of suicidality. With these variables held constant, those who reported sexual activity with a member of their immediate family were less likely to have attempted suicide, at a level approaching significance.

Implications of Statistical Findings

Results of statistical tests of association indicate that each of the independent variables was predictive, at statistically significant levels, of several indices of negative outcome. This replicates in a clinical sample of men the findings of Herman et al. (1986) that closer relationships between perpetrator and victim, longer duration and greater severity of abuse, and early age at onset of abuse predict later disturbance in survivors of childhood sexual abuse. The results of the present study were also consistent with the preliminary findings of Kelly and Gonzalez (1990) that the presence of physical abuse and drug or alcohol abuse by parents are associated with a greater degree of later pathology.

Closer examination of the results reveals that no independent measure was predictive of poor outcome on all of the measures used; each outcome measure was associated with a different set of predictor variables. This demonstrates that one can go beyond simply concluding that certain factors are associated with poor functioning. It seems to me that all too often conclusions remain too general to do much practical good: "Those abused from an early age are less healthy than those whose abuse begins later." Greater precision may be attained with respect to understanding the impact of abuse characteristics and their relationships with psychosocial functioning. Furthermore, greater precision in understanding these relationships allows for increased attunement in treatment interventions. More data on men who were raised in substance-abusing households and who were sexually abused by males over long periods of time, for example, may alert clinicians to the specific areas likely to be problematic for these particular men. An example of the potential utility of this greater degree of specificity emerged from this study. A strong, unexpected correlation was found between physical abuse and suicidality. Men who were subjected to physical abuse as well as sexual abuse were far more likely to report a history of suicide attempts than were men who did not experience physical abuse. Thus, it is probably prudent to be especially watchful when working with such doubly abused men. This finding is discussed in greater detail below.

In the following pages, the relationships with the highest level of statistical significance between each of the independent variables and the outcome measures are presented. For each measure, several factors associated with the abuse predicted negative outcome. The complete list of statistically significant relationships is presented above in Table 8.3. This discussion focuses upon the highest correlations and those that are shown by the stepwise regressions to be independent predictors at $p \le .05$.

SEVERITY, AGE AT ONSET, AND DURATION OF ABUSE

Increased severity of abuse was correlated with extent of psychiatric symptomatology and poor self-worth. Abuse of long duration was associated with poor self-worth, duration of psychotherapy, psychiatric hospitalization, and receiving psychotropic medication. Early onset predicted a malevolent worldview, psychiatric hospitalization, and psychotropic medication. None of these three variables was associated at statistically significant levels with indices of sexual adjustment or sexual satisfaction. Number of perpetrators was a highly significant predictor of several outcome measures, with level of disturbance tending to increase with number of abusers. This factor was associated with psychiatric symptomatology, a malevolent view of the world, low self-worth, sexual dissatisfaction, and psychotropic medication.

Interestingly, severity of abuse, duration of abuse, and age at onset of abuse, which are among the most commonly studied trauma predictors, were each correlated with poor functioning on one—and only one—of the three standardized outcome measures used in this study. Severity of abuse predicted traumatic symptomatology, long duration predicted poor self-worth, and early onset predicted malevolence of worldview. This is testament to the kind of specificity that is possible and the greater understanding that can come from such specificity. I would speculate that abuse from a very early age influences the victim to perceive the people around him and the world in general as malevolent forces. Abuse of long duration acts to erode the self-esteem of the individual. Severe abuse most closely resembles the types of trauma regarding which the literature on post-traumatic stress disorder developed. Abuse of this type results in considerable symptomatology associated with post-traumatic stress.

RELATIONSHIP BETWEEN PERPETRATOR AND VICTIM

The relationship between perpetrator and victim was a highly significant factor in contributing to later disturbance. Sexual activity with a member of the immediate family was correlated with trauma symptomatology, malevolent worldview, sexual maladjustment, and psychotropic medication. Sexual interactions with a parent was associated with trauma symptoms, malevolent worldview, and psychotropic medication. Sexual activity with fathers, specifically, predicted negative outcome on these three measures as well as duration of psychotherapy and sexual maladjustment. Using the criterion of sexual abuse by father, rather than all sexual activity with fathers, resulted in a significant correlation with poor self-worth. Sexual activity with mothers was predictive only of trauma symptoms, whereas assessing only those men who considered their sexual interactions with their mothers to be abusive resulted in statistically significant correlations with duration of psychotherapy and sexual dissatisfaction as well. Sexual interactions with a sibling were associated at a statistically significant level only with sexual dissatisfaction, whereas sexually abusive activity was correlated with sexual dissatisfaction, trauma symptoms, a malevolent view of the world, and suicidality. The vast majority of the men in the current study were abused by an immediate family member, which diverges from the findings of studies reviewed by Finkelhor (1990; Browne & Finkelhor, 1986), in which most boys were victimized outside the home. Abuse by a member of one's immediate family was associated with greater disturbance. For male survivors, like their female counterparts in earlier research (e.g., Browne & Finkelhor, 1986; Herman et al., 1986), sexual abuse by a close relative appears to be far more damaging than extrafamilial sexual abuse. Sexual activity with a member of the immediate family was among the most powerful predictors of psychological disturbance of all the predictor variables examined in this study. It was correlated at a statistically significant level with trauma symptoms, malevolent worldview, sexual maladjustment, and psychotropic medication.

There are several plausible reasons for the greater impact of intrafamilial abuse. In terms of Finkelhor and Browne's (1985) traumagenic model of the impact of sexual abuse, sexual interactions with a family member, particularly a parent, are likely to be experienced as a profound betrayal and a violation of the caretaking role. Such abuse is likely to hamper severely the victim's ability to enlist trust in others and to develop or maintain intimacy in relationships. Sexual abuse by a nonrelative may be more easily experienced as a transient or anomalous event in the life of the victim, rather than as a pervasive and paradigmatic occurrence.

Although detailed information was not obtained on the families of origin of the men in this study, it is also likely that men abused by a member of their immediate family were raised amid a greater degree of family dysfunction than were those abused only by a nonrelative. The incidence of physical abuse and substance abuse are likely to have been higher in incestuous families than in the families of men abused outside the home. This hypothesis is supported by the finding that relatives—particularly fathers, grandparents, aunts, and uncles—were considerably more likely to have used drugs at the time of the abuse than were nonrelatives. Finally, intrafamilial abuse tends to begin when the victim is younger and continue for a longer period than extrafamilial abuse. Both of these factors have been found to predict later disturbance. The negative impact of abuse by a family member does not appear to be reducible to early onset and long duration, however. Results of the statistical regressions indicate that intrafamilial abuse was the most significant independent predictor of poor functioning, as assessed by the Composite Index of Functioning, an outcome measure built upon the means of trauma symptoms, malevolence of worldview, poor self-worth, and sexual maladjustment.

GENDER OF PERPETRATOR

Gender of perpetrator was also a highly significant predictor of multiple negative outcomes. The patterns of association with respect to abuse by males, by females, and by both; and with respect to abuse by fathers, by mothers, and by both, were perhaps the most consistent to emerge from this study. As noted earlier, for each outcome measure, those abused by both males and females fared most poorly, followed by those abused by males only, with those abused by females only reporting the highest level of psychological functioning. Similarly with respect to parental abuse, abuse by both parents was associated with the highest level of disturbance, followed by abuse by fathers only. At the other end of the spectrum, those who were not abused by either parent appeared to be most healthy, followed by those abused only by their mothers. The only variations in this pattern were three outcome measures (suicidality, psychiatric medication, and self-worth) on which those abused by fathers only displayed a greater degree of disturbance than did those abused by both parents, which is certainly an intriguing finding. Sexual dissatisfaction and sexual maladjustment—which were not predicted by age at onset, severity of abuse, or duration of abuse—were associated with abuse by males. Findings regarding the impact of gender of perpetrator are presented in Table 8.10.

There are two implications of these patterns of findings. First, abuse by both males and females or by both parents is more traumatic than abuse by only one of the two. A portion of this result is likely due to the associated increase in number of abusers that, as previously discussed, is correlated with negative outcome. However, number of abusers was associated with several of the outcome variables that did not correlate significantly with gender of perpetrator or parental abuse variables and vice versa; number of abusers and abuse by both males and females emerged as independent predictors of psychotropic medication. These results indicate that the effect of abuse by both parents or both genders is not reducible to the increase in number of perpetrators. Those abused by both males and females may, with good reason, make more globally negative attributions about the world. They cannot simply ascribe their abuse to the particular nature of a certain individual; nor can they attribute the evil around them solely to men (or women, or mothers, or fathers). Instead, they are likely to see the world around them, and the people who inhabit it, as malevolent. They are also more likely to view themselves as bad or deficient than someone who is able to see his victimization as an anomalous occurrence.

The second aspect of results related to gender of perpetrator is that abuse by males was highly predictive of later disturbance. In other words, as assessed by the outcome measures utilized in the current study, men abused during childhood by males reported a lower level of psychosocial functioning than did men abused by females. This replicates and extends the findings of Finkelhor (1979) and Herman et al. (1986). Earlier research was primarily conducted on female survivors. It is noteworthy, then, that gender of perpetrator—specifically, abuse by males—appears to be a powerful trauma predictor for male survivors of childhood sexual abuse.

The greater extent of negative sequelae of abuse by males may derive from two sources. First, in the present study, abuse by male perpetrators was more severe, on average, than that perpetrated by females. This finding is consistent with the majority of previous research on the topic (Finkelhor, 1979; Fromuth & Burkhart, 1987, 1989; Kasl, 1990) but diverges from a number of studies that found high incidences of severe

Table 8.10 Analysis of Variance Between Gender of Perpetrator and Parental Abuse and Outcome Variables

| | Predictor Variables | | | | | | | | |
| | Gender of Perpetrator | | | | Parental Abuse | | | | |
Outcome Variables	Both (N = 55)	Male Only (N = 50)	Female Only (N = 14)	Significance	Both (N = 25)	Father Only (N = 22)	Mother Only (N = 25)	Neither (N = 46)	Significance
Trauma symptoms	2.8358	2.5289	2.1061	.0002	2.9600	2.7033	2.5312	2.4130	.0052
Benevolent worldview	3.7152	4.0383	4.3929	.1094	3.5033	3.5568	4.0300	4.2808	.0194
Self-worth	3.1227	3.3550	4.2321	.0201	3.0800	3.0682	3.3600	3.6304	.2677
Duration of psychotherapy (in months)	80.086	46.924	37.074	.0386	84.883	67.669	64.914	37.116	.0574
Sexual satisfaction (higher numbers = dissatisfaction)	5.3962	4.4400	3.6429	.0040	5.1667	5.0000	4.8000	4.4667	.5473
Sexual orientation (higher numbers = homosexual)	3.2545	3.9600	1.2857	.0012	2.3000	3.5455	2.8800	3.7174	.3517
Sexual adjustment	2.000	2.4600	3.000	.0125	1.9200	2.0000	2.3750	2.6222	.0642
Psychiatric hospitalization (21% of entire sample have been hospitalized)	27%	16%	14%	.2948	28%	27%	20%	13%	.3731
Psychiatric medication (45% of entire sample have received medication)	62%	36%	14%	.0009	56%	59%	52%	26%	.0152
Suicide attempt (33% of entire sample have attempted suicide)	37%	32%	21%	.5150	25%	40%	32%	30%	.7103

NOTE: Numbers listed are means or percentages. Percentages are indicated by %; p values < .05 are in boldface type.

abuse by females (Condy et al., 1986; Petrovich & Templer, 1984; Ramsey-Klawsnik, 1990a, 1990b). In the present study, data are not available on the relative severity of all abuse perpetrated by males and all abuse perpetrated by females. Sexual interactions between fathers and children, however, were considerably more severe than those between mothers and children. On a 3-point scale, with 3 indicating the most severe abuse, sexual activity with mothers averaged 2.02 and sexual activity with fathers averaged 2.61. The modal severity of sexual activity with mothers was "moderate," unlike all other categories of perpetrator, for which the mode was "severe." Only 24% of those reporting sexual interactions with mothers experienced penetration, compared to 72% of those reporting sexual interactions with fathers. Comparing sexual activity with mothers and with fathers among those reporting sexual interactions with both yields a significant difference between the two means ($p < .05$). The mean for mothers was 2.12, and that for fathers was 2.68. Only 2 men reported more severe abuse by their mothers than by their fathers, and 14 reported more severe abuse by their fathers. Because severity of abuse is associated with later disturbance in this sample, as it was in such studies as Herman et al. (1986), the finding that abuse by men predicts poor functioning is likely due in part to the fact that such abuse tends to be more severe. That is, it may not be that the abuse is by men per se that disposes victims to more negative sequelae, but that men tend to commit more severe abuse than do women.

This answer does not appear to be sufficient in accounting for the greater damage that ensues from sexual abuse by men. Abuse by males was predictive of multiple indices of later disturbance and was among the best predictors of low scores on the Composite Index of Functioning (CIF). Abuse by males emerged from the regressions as an independent predictor of several outcome measures including psychotropic medication, duration of psychotherapy, and trauma symptomatology. Severity of abuse, conversely, was not a significant independent predictor of poor outcome on the CIF or on any of the regressions. It appears that the fact that the victim was subjected to abusive sexual contact in childhood by a male makes such contact more traumatic and damaging than comparable contact by a female. I would surmise that much of the greater trauma associated with abuse by males stems from the stigma of homosexuality; the victim's feelings of shame, self-reproach, and disgust; and the concerns raised in the victim regarding his masculinity. As Justice and Justice (1979) note, abuse of boys by male relatives evokes two potent stigmas, incest and homosexuality. These issues will be discussed in greater depth in the following chapter when the clinical interviews are reviewed.

SUBSTANCE USE BY PERPETRATOR

Drug use by perpetrator was a powerful predictor of negative outcome. Regressions indicate that this factor was one of the two independent predictors of overall poor functioning (along with male perpetration), as assessed by the CIF. The use of alcohol or other drugs by a perpetrator at the time of abuse was associated at statistically significant levels with trauma symptoms, low self-worth, and sexual maladjustment. I would speculate that men reporting substance abuse by perpetrators fare more poorly due to the multiple types and greater degree of dysfunction occurring in their families of origin. Men reporting both sexual abuse and substance abuse in their families of origin are doubly jeopardized for later disturbance.

Regression equations suggest an additional source of the impact of this variable. With other variables held constant, drug use by perpetrator was *negatively* correlated with duration of psychotherapy, at a level approaching statistical significance ($p = .0594$). In other words, men who were abused in an environment that also encompassed substance abuse participated in less psychotherapy than men whose victimization did not occur in the context of substance abuse. The fact that substance abuse by perpetrator was associated with both greater disturbance and shorter duration of psychotherapy for the victim may indicate that men in this group are less able to seek out and/or to benefit from psychotherapy. Briefer participation in psychotherapy may be a mediating factor in these men's disturbance. That is, they may be faring more poorly because they are less able to avail themselves of resources for recovery. It is not possible to conclude from the present data why men who were abused by perpetrators on drugs were less likely to continue in psychotherapy. The greater level of dysfunction in such families and the lower self-esteem characteristic of these men may, however, make it more difficult for them to enlist hope and trust in the therapeutic endeavor. Further exploration of the interplay among these factors would certainly be helpful.

PHYSICAL ABUSE

Physical abuse was also predictive of multiple indices of poor functioning. Although both physical abuse by mother and by father were associated with negative outcomes, most of the predictive ability of this variable stemmed from the impact of physical abusiveness by fathers. Abuse by fathers predicted trauma symptoms, malevolent worldview, psychiatric hospitalization and medication, and suicidality, whereas physical abuse by mother was associated at a statistically significant level only with trauma symptoms. The multiple forms of trauma experienced by men both physically and sexually abused appear to result in more severe psychiatric disturbance, as reflected in the greater extent of symptoms and psychiatric interventions (hospitalization and medication). Physical abuse was not associated with any of the outcome measures dealing specifically with sexual issues (sexual satisfaction, sexual orientation, or sexual adjustment). It appears that physical abuse has powerful effects on its victims but does not have specific impact on the development or experience of sexuality.

The correlation between physical abuse and suicidality is striking. A history of suicide attempts was associated with fewer of the independent measures than any other outcome measure. That is, suicidality was the most difficult measure to predict on the basis of characteristics of the abuse. None of the "traditional" predictors of negative outcome—abuse by a parent, early onset of abuse, long duration of abuse, severe abuse, and so forth—were able to predict suicidality at a statistically significant level. The only variables capable of doing so were physical abuse, physical abuse by father, and sexual abuse by a sibling. Although this is highly speculative, I would suspect that the connection between physical abuse and suicidality is related to self-blame, anger turned inward, and the modeling of physical aggression. As will be discussed in the following chapter, male victims tend strongly to hold themselves accountable for their abuse and to rail at themselves for their inability to protect themselves. When physical abuse is added to this equation, a man may be particularly likely to "recreate" the abuse in a different sense. Rather than targeting others with the abuse done to him, as is the case in the inter-generational transmission of abuse, he aims his aggression inward and recapitulates his abuse experiences via suicidal acting-out. If this finding is replicated in other populations, the treatment implications are clear. Professionals working with male victims of sexual abuse should be especially alert to suicidality among those reporting physical abuse as well. Similarly, clinicians should be alert to suicidality among men abused by a sibling.

The Composite Index of Functioning

In an attempt to arrive at a better sense of which abuse characteristics are associated with overall disturbance, the Composite Index of Functioning (CIF) was created based upon the means of four outcome measures—trauma symptoms, malevolent view of the world, poor self-worth, and sexual maladjustment. Using this scale as an outcome measure sacrifices the precision that is gained from examining the specific relationships between predictor and dependent variables; however, it adds to the ability to identify factors associated with global disturbance. The following variables predicted poor functioning as assessed by the CIF: abuse by male, abuse by a member of the immediate family, physical abuse by father, sexual activity with father, abuse by both male and female, abuse by parent, and drug use by perpetrator. Regression analyses indicate that drug use by perpetrator and male perpetration are the two statistically significant independent predictors of poor functioning on the CIF.

The results of this study of trauma-predictive characteristics of abuse both overlap with and diverge from the findings of earlier researchers who have examined these questions with primarily female populations (Browne & Finkelhor, 1986; Conte & Schuerman, 1987; Herman et al., 1986; Tsai et al., 1979). The most powerful predictors of disturbance in the current study were abuse by a male, drug use by perpetrator, physical abuse (especially by father), sexual abuse by father, and abuse by a member of the immediate family. Several of these variables correspond to those identified by previous studies, including abuse by fathers (Browne & Finkelhor, 1986) and abuse by a member of the immediate family (Browne & Finkelhor, 1986; Herman et al., 1986; Tsai et al., 1979). Preliminary data from Kelly and Gonzalez (1990) indicate that physical abuse and drug use by perpetrator may be associated with greater trauma. It is noteworthy that abuse by fathers and abuse by males were associated with negative sequelae in this population of *male* sexual abuse survivors. Previous studies that found these factors to be predictive of poor psychosocial functioning were conducted with predominantly or exclusively female populations. Three of the factors identified by Herman et al. (1986) as particularly damaging to the victim—early onset of abuse, long duration of abuse, and greater severity of abuse—were each predictive of several indices of negative outcome in the current study, but appear to be less pervasively associated with damage than the variables listed above.

Proposals for Future Research

Numerous gaps remain in our knowledge about sexually abused males. Over the course of this chapter, several potentially beneficial avenues for future exploration have been suggested. These are briefly reviewed here, and some additional research is proposed.

First, too often, sexual abuse is examined in a vacuum. In this study a majority of respondents reported physical as well as sexual abuse, and a large proportion came from substance-abusing families. Drug use by a perpetrator was among the most powerful predictors of negative psychosocial functioning. History of physical abuse, although less predictive of most outcome measures, was critically implicated in suicidality. A greater understanding of the interplay among these factors, and the impact of multiple forms of abuse and family dysfunction, would be very valuable. Second, the preponderance of information about sexual abuse involves male perpetrators. Even less is known about female offenders than is known about male victims. Further data regarding the effects upon men of sexual victimization by women—and differences in impact between abuse by males and abuse by females—would add greatly to our understanding of sexual abuse.

Third, the present study briefly assessed differences in outcome depending upon what criterion of abuse was used: childhood sexual activity or only childhood sexual activity that the respondent construed as abusive. Every respondent to this study, however, had experienced at least one incident that he considered to be abuse. It would be useful to compare individuals who report only childhood sexual activity that they experienced as consensual with those reporting sexual abuse. If, moreover, severity of abuse could be held constant between these two groups, then the importance of one's construction and interpretation of childhood sexual experiences would come into much sharper focus. Fourth, research has found with a fair degree of consistency a disproportionate incidence of homosexual orientation among men reporting a history of childhood sexual activity or sexual abuse. Little is known, however, about the relationships between sexual activity or abuse and sexual orientation, and further research on this topic would likely be as valuable as it would be controversial.

A fifth area in which further research would be helpful is protective, as opposed to risk, factors for sexual abuse survivors. What makes some men fare better than others subjected to comparable maltreatment? Such factors were only minimally addressed in the present study, though several of the men indicated that psychotherapy has made an enormous difference in their lives. One direction would be to utilize duration of therapy as an independent variable and examine the relationship between it and the various outcome measures. Several researchers have pointed to the childhood support system and to the response of others to the victim's disclosure as important variables in predicting outcome. Urquiza (1993), for example, noted that the best adaptation is made by those with the most support from their family, peers, and school. (There is, of course, a possible confound there in that those receiving support from family in the wake of abuse are less likely to have been abused by a member of the family. Intrafamilial abuse is among the strongest predictors of negative outcome.)

Two additional lines of potentially fruitful investigation emerged from the interview portion of this study. Sixth, one of the men whose stories is included here, Ben, argues that "emotional incest" can have the same impact as overt sexual abuse. This is discussed in greater depth in the following chapter. Further research aimed at understanding the similarities and differences in outcome between individuals subjected to overt incest and those from analogous family environments who did not experience sexual activity would be helpful. Seventh, a striking aspect of the interviews is that the men had considerable access to feelings of loss, sadness, and vulnerability related to their childhood abuse experiences. This differs from research such as that of Sepler (1990), who argues that male victims, unlike female victims, have access primarily to feelings of anger. This divergence is likely due in part to the extensive therapy participation of the men in this sample. I believe that it may also reflect a critical difference between abused men who perpetrate sexual abuse and those who do not. That is, perpetrating survivors may feel primarily anger regarding their victimization, whereas nonperpetrators may have much greater awareness of loss, sadness, and vulnerability. Studies comparing perpetrating and nonperpetrating male sexual abuse survivors in terms of access to and expression of various effects could shed a great deal of light on this crucial topic. This, too, is discussed in greater depth in the following chapter.

Notes

1. For statistical analyses, *sexual orientation* was defined in terms of desire rather than experience. This decision was made because many men included their childhood abuse when indicating sexual experience. For example, a respondent with exclusively heterosexual consensual contact who was abused during childhood by his father may have identified himself as "mostly heterosexual, with some homosexual experience." Because this is a confound, the question regarding sexual desires was utilized instead. For the purposes of this study, *homosexual* refers to men who report sexual desire primarily or exclusively for men, and *heterosexual* refers to men who report sexual desire primarily or exclusively for women.

2. I would like to make very clear that I do not consider sexual orientation to be an indication of disturbance. The purpose of inclusion of this variable is to assess the relationships between sexual abuse and sexual orientation.

3. All correlations reported in this chapter have a significance level of $p < .05$, unless otherwise noted.

Wayne's Story

Wayne is a 21-year-old heterosexual maintenance person. He is the middle child of three, with an older brother and a younger sister. He has had no contact with his father, a heroin addict, since he left the family when Wayne was three. He describes his mother as emotionally disturbed and said that she had a series of relationships with married men since that time. Both of Wayne's parents were alcoholics, and he indicated that his mother had been severely physically and sexually abused during her childhood. Wayne grew up in a family that was dysfunctional in multiple ways.

Wayne's sexual abuse was by his brother, who is 3 years older than him. The abuse was extreme and terrifying. It began when Wayne was 3 or 4 years old, continued until his brother left the home at age 18, and occurred several times a week. It included oral and anal intercourse and was accompanied by a high level of force and violence. Wayne reported that his brother would drag him across the room by his hair, throw him down the stairs, hit and kick him, cut him with knives, shoot him with a BB gun, and generally terrorize him. He attempted to hide or lock himself in his room, but his brother inevitably found him or kicked in the door to reach him. He indicated that his brother abused their sister in a similar manner.

He stated that his mother and brother ruled the house, and that in his father's absence, his brother had essentially become his mother's husband. As noted above, Wayne's mother had been sexually abused as a child, and Wayne assumes that his brother must have been abused himself, in order to perform such acts of violence and sadism. In addition to the abuse by his brother, Wayne also experienced a single instance of sexual abuse by his maternal grandfather, involving a sexual kiss and an invitation to perform other sexual acts, when he was 5 years old. He suspects that he was sexually abused by his father as well. He recalls vague memories of his father calling down to him in the basement and wanting him to do something. He remembers putting things against the door in an attempt to keep his father out, and his father throwing a hammer through the door. He also recalls his father being removed in a police car but does not know whether these events are connected. He has early memories of observing his father beat his mother and knock her unconscious.

Wayne completed the questionnaire over the course of a number of therapy sessions. Both he and his therapist indicated that this was a very helpful means of discussing his abuse experiences. Wayne stated that he would have had great difficulty completing it by himself but was able to do so in the safe presence of his therapist, whom he trusts. He had discussed his abuse only minimally and superficially until beginning therapy about a year ago. He has "briefly and nonchalantly" referred to it with his sister, who was also abused by their brother, but feels that "it is too much for me to think that I should have protected her as well as myself."

Wayne's abuse has had profound impact upon him in several areas. He stated that he feels "disabled" by it. He said that although he has gotten better as a result of therapy, he has emotional problems, some of which will never go away, as a consequence of the abuse. Wayne used a great deal of drugs until he entered a drug treatment program at the age of 18. He began to smoke marijuana at age eight and was a daily user by 13. He began to drink and use cocaine at age 12 and used both regularly throughout junior high and high school, along with frequently taking LSD. He stated that he used drugs all the time in order to hide from his pain. He sees his substance use entirely as a consequence of the abuse and, in fact, as a necessary and adaptive response to the abuse: "It saved my life. My head would have exploded if I had to deal with all the things going on in my house, but I was high." He finally recognized the extent of his drug problem when he was 18 and entered an in-patient program. He has been completely sober and drug-free since that time. Without the drugs, however, he was unable to dispel the feelings associated with the abuse, and he sought psychotherapy for help in that area.

One year after his discharge from the drug treatment program, Wayne was diagnosed with bipolar disorder and a medication regimen was initiated. He had a severe depressive "crash" about 7 months ago that resulted in a brief hospitalization and an adjustment in dosage. He feels that he is currently on an appropriate medication regimen and sees his bipolar disorder as under control. He believes that the cycles he experiences are connected with feelings stemming from the abuse. He stated that memories of the abuse trigger anxiety that builds over a period of days until he is no longer eating or sleeping and is in a state of panic. Following a few days of this manic period, he becomes filled with overwhelming feelings of sadness, loneliness, loss, and fear, and "crashes" into depression.

Wayne struggles with self-esteem issues. He feels that being happy requires a constant effort to convince or remind himself that he is not a bad person. At one point in the interview, Wayne looked at me and said, "You want to know how this affects me? Right there, I was sure you were going to laugh at me. That's how I think of people. I always think they're going to condemn me." He said that it would be an enormous relief to see people's intentions for what they are rather than in a distorted fashion. Wayne has always looked down on himself and has only recently begun to acknowledge positive attributes. In short, he says that the abuse has destroyed his self-esteem.

He experiences a great deal of shame, guilt, self-blame, and self-hatred associated with the abuse. He stated that, "The abuse tells me that I'm not a man. The way society looks at sleeping with a man, I feel like I've done something wrong." This tendency to view oneself as an active participant in one's abuse—even when it involves such extreme force and violence as in Wayne's case—appears to be characteristic of male survivors. When he does not think about the abuse, Wayne indicated that he feels fairly positively about himself as a man: "I do what I need to do; I don't hurt others; I face what hurts." When feelings and memories of the abuse emerge, however, he is filled with shame and self-loathing. He recalls wanting desperately to be close to someone. He said that his mother never once hugged him, and blamed him for making her life miserable. "I didn't exist as far as my mother was concerned." His father was gone, and his brother was there. He sought closeness and affection from his brother and, therefore, blames himself for bringing the abuse upon himself.

Wayne speculates that if the physical abuse but not the sexual abuse had occurred, he would not feel so ashamed and dirty, and would not feel so conflicted about sexuality. Had only the sexual abuse occurred, he would not be so fearful. He describes flinching if someone moves quickly and feeling as if someone is lurking outside the shower ready to hurt him. He thinks he would feel less "jumpy" but still have the same negative feelings about himself. Wayne feels that on the one hand, the abuse has made him a very sexual person. Sex is very important to him, and he thinks he is close to being addicted to it. He tries to fulfill many needs through sex and sees sex as the primary, often the only, way he has to express care for another person. On the other hand, he is tremendously wary of and fearful about interpersonal contact and intimacy. He said that he fears both men and women and does not want to be around them unless he has to.

He indicated that he has a great deal of difficulty trusting people and that it takes him a long time to get close to another person. He said that, "The abuse was so damaging that it is difficult for me to let myself care about someone." In both friendships and romantic relationships it is hard for him to trust others' motivations or to be close to and supportive of others. He stated that he is very suspicious of others and thinks that they are out to hurt him. Wayne was in a relationship of about a one-year duration, until his hospitalization for bipolar disorder. He said that allowing himself to care about her and to trust her was the hardest thing he has ever done. He sees this relationship as relatively healthy and fulfilling—"amazingly so, considering our backgrounds." He stated that they had both been satisfied with their relationship, but that she was unable to deal with his illness.

Wayne has found a career path that he finds very satisfying. He is self-employed as a maintenance person, which allows him to work by himself for the most part, rather than interacting with others. He is able to work with his hands, which he said he finds very enjoyable, and to be responsible to and for himself. Finally, Wayne indicated that he is so terrified of doing the sort of things that were done to him that he will never have children. He said that he has seen people say that they will be different to their children, then turn around and repeat the abuse. He said that he knows he is fully capable of doing the same and will, therefore, remain childless.

9 The Male Survivor

The aim of this concluding chapter, and of the life stories included throughout the book, is to bring a "human face" to the topic of male sexual victimization. It is hoped that from this work the reader can develop a greater understanding and appreciation of the male survivor and of the impact his abuse has had upon his life. The focus of this chapter is upon the clinical interviews, from which the men's stories are culled. The first portion of the chapter examines issues common to both male and female survivors of childhood sexual abuse. Most of the remainder of the chapter explores concerns of particular salience to male survivors. Finally, this book concludes with a brief discussion of treatment implications of this study. Summaries of the clinical interviews cited are interspersed throughout the book.

Common Issues for Male and Female Survivors

In 1990 David Finkelhor updated the review he and Angela Browne had conducted in 1986 on the impact of childhood sexual abuse. Although the earlier article pertained exclusively to female victims, the emergence in the late 1980s of research on boys who had been sexually abused enabled Finkelhor to address sequelae for males. He writes that, "perhaps the major surprise is the relative similarity of response of boys to that of girls" (p. 325). Similarly, in the current study many of the issues discussed by men in clinical interviews resembled those cited in the literature as common responses of women to sexual abuse.

The men interviewed uniformly perceived their abuse as severely damaging to all or most aspects of their life. One man, Wayne, used the term *disabled* to describe himself in the wake of the abuse. Chris summarized the impact of sexual abuse as follows: "Incest and sexual abuse are so offensive because they go so far beyond all boundaries—body, spiritual, emotional: All are violated. How is it possible to understand limits, respect them, or have yours respected?" Most respondents saw themselves as having made enormous progress through psychotherapy. Several indicated that the traumatic effects they described, which had dominated much of their lives, had now been reduced or relieved. One stated that, "growing up in a dysfunctional family, with sexual abuse, is like putting scales all over your body; . . . therapy has been like removing the scales. It's not that I've changed, but that I've rediscovered who I am."

Issues related to each of the four traumagenic dynamics proposed by Finkelhor and Browne (1985)—stigmatization, betrayal, traumatic sexualization, and powerlessness—were apparent in the present study. Numerous respondents described feeling stigmatized as a result of their abuse. They felt that they were bad, worthless, different from those around them, unable to be "one of the guys," and so forth. Several men cited the lack of societal recognition of the sexual abuse of boys as an additional source of their stigmatization. One said that he believes men are isolated and don't recognize themselves as victims because male sexual abuse isn't talked about in the media and on talk shows. As noted earlier, one of the purposes of this study was to contribute to an atmosphere in which male survivors could feel less isolated.

The importance of this goal was highlighted for me during the research process. The responses of the participants in the study were different from what I had expected. I brought with me something of a notion that I, as a researcher, was intruding on their lives and that they were doing me a favor by assisting me with my research. Instead, I heard and read numerous expressions of gratitude directed toward me for conducting

this research. Several questionnaire respondents, for example, wrote
letters thanking me for doing this study, discussing how important they
felt it was that their experience receive attention, and asking me whether
there was any way they could further assist me in my research. I believe
that the response of the participants in the study attests clearly and
eloquently to the denial and invalidation they have experienced and the
urgency they feel to be heard.

Betrayal was a recurrent theme in the interviews. Unlike the studies
reviewed by Finkelhor (Browne & Finkelhor, 1986; Finkelhor, 1990), in
which a majority of boy victims were abused by someone unrelated to
them, all of the men interviewed as part of the present study experienced
incestuous abuse; most was perpetrated by adults in a caretaking role.
Many asked variations of the question: "How could someone who was
supposed to love me and take care of me abuse me instead?" As David
asked, "How could a mother do that to her child?" There was also
considerable confusion and ambivalence regarding the contamination of
affection by way of the abuse. In several cases, the perpetrator was a
primary, or even solitary, source of warmth and positive interaction. This
was expressed most vividly by Ron, who was abused by his adoptive
father. He indicated that this man, Glen, was the first person to provide
him with any affection or caring. He invested all of his hopes and
yearnings for closeness in Glen. With the abuse, "All my dreams were
stopped." Glen remains for Ron an ambivalent figure, imbued with
positive as well as negative attributes.

Like their female counterparts, male survivors struggle with issues of
trust and intimacy. Ron, like most of the men interviewed, experiences a
great deal of difficulty allowing himself to become close to another human
being. Difficulties with trust and intimacy appear to be an almost inevitable residue of intrafamilial childhood sexual abuse. As Wayne stated,
"You want to know how (the abuse) affects me? Right there, I was sure
you were going to laugh at me. That's how I think of people. I always
think they're going to condemn me."

Traumatic sexualization was prevalent in the lives of these men. One
pattern of response to the abuse appears to be an atrophying of sexual
drive. Two men stated that their abuse had "ruined" sex for them. Pete
said that through therapy he has become able to seek out affection, but
that his capacity for sexual desire is virtually nonexistent. Others indicated, conversely, that sex is the only way they know to achieve human

contact and to express warmth or affection. Wayne, for example, stated that he is "close to addicted" to sex, that he tries to fulfill many needs through sex, and that sex is the only way he has to express care for another person. The notion of the fusion or confusion of sex and affection was a recurrent theme in the interviews.

Powerlessness was also a pervasive issue for the participants in this study. It appears that powerlessness has different meanings for men than for women, due to the socialization of males as powerful and active beings. Therefore, concerns related to power and the meaning of victimization for men will be discussed in greater depth in the following section on issues particularly salient for male survivors.

Another issue frequently mentioned by participants in the current study and commonly cited in literature on female survivors is difficulty establishing and maintaining appropriate interpersonal boundaries. Several men discussed their tendencies to become immersed in or "engulfed by" relationships, once they allow themselves to become emotionally involved. Ben, for example, sees this as the primary legacy of his incest experience. He described feeling within his adult long-term relationship that, "If he ever left me, I would die, cease to exist. I was willing to do almost anything he wanted me to do. I measured what I did according to his standards and values, and adopted these for my own. I didn't have my own self. The boundaries were so blurred, just like they were with my mom." He reported only feeling close to someone when he is in an enmeshed relationship and said he scares others off with his all-consuming way of relating.

A number of men reported always playing the rescuer role in relationships, a carryover from their parentified, caretaking responsibilities in childhood. David, for example, stated that he has always sacrificed his needs and desires for those of others. Chris indicated that his intimate relationships have been founded upon his unsuccessful efforts to rescue women from their unhappiness. Still others, as discussed above, find it inordinately difficult to trust and get close to others.

A striking aspect of the interviews was the emphasis placed by the respondents on intrafamilial abuse. Two men had experienced mild to moderate abuse by members of their family and been anally raped by an unrelated male. In each case, the men presented the rape in a casual, almost offhand manner, while emphasizing the impact of the incestuous sexual interaction. This supports the statistical finding of this study that intrafamilial abuse is more damaging in terms of each outcome measure. It is also consistent with Herman's (1981) argument that the source of the traumatic impact of incest lies in the "corruption of parental love" rather than in the sexual act itself. As noted above, Ben, one of the men whose stories are included here, did not report any sexual activity during childhood. Instead, he stated that he was subjected to "emotional incest," consisting of his mother's emotional dependence upon him. In Ben's view, the impact of such a relationship is the same as overt sexual abuse. He believes that the damage is caused by the violation of boundaries and selfhood that occur in "emotional" as well as physical incest.

It seems to me that Judith Herman; the men in the current study, with their focus on intrafamilial abuse over more severe extrafamilial sexual interaction; and Ben, in his argument that the sexual activity per se is not the damaging factor in incest, are all making similar points. Not enough is known about which of the precise factors within sexually abusive environments are most damaging to their victims.

It remains unclear, too, to what extent the "sexual" aspect of sexual abuse contributes to its traumatic impact. The results of the present study suggest that overtly sexual factors, such as the presence of penetration, are indeed associated with later disturbance. At the same time, however, there is some support for Ben's argument. Intrafamilial abuse was among the most powerful predictors of negative outcome, and familial factors distinct from the sexual abuse itself, such as substance abuse and physical abuse, were associated with greater disturbance. Further research regarding similarities and differences between sexually abused individuals and those from family environments lacking in appropriate boundaries and roles, but in which sexual activity did not occur, would be very valuable.

Issues of Particular Salience for Male Survivors

A number of other concerns and difficulties were raised that appear to be particular to male survivors or to have different meanings and ramifications for males. This is not to suggest that these issues are more important to male survivors than are the difficulties reviewed above. Rather, these responses to childhood abuse appear to be especially characteristic of men, due to differential male and female socialization. These issues may be divided into three overlapping categories: the dissonance between and attempt to integrate the male role-expectation and the experience of victimization; shame and gender-shame; and identification with the perpetrator and fear of continuing the cycle of abuse.

MASCULINITY AND VICTIMIZATION

Virtually all of the men in this study reported struggles integrating their sense of themselves as men with their childhood experiences of victimization. Their schemas of what it is to be male do not incorporate feelings of helplessness and passivity. Wayne put this most succinctly: "The abuse tells me that I'm not a man." Men who have been sexually abused appear to live in a state of dissonance, struggling to find congruence between these conflicting aspects of their lives. They often feel very ambivalent about masculinity and what they perceive to be male attributes. Ron, for example, discussed the conflict between his desire to be strong and assertive and his discomfort surrounding activity and aggression.

The experience of helplessness and being-acted-upon appears to be very threatening to men's sense of themselves as men. Several expressed doubts about their capacity to be masculine in the aftermath of their abuse. Sepler (1990) built her theory upon this fact, arguing that providing male victims with assurances of their blamelessness in the face of abuse (or even using the jargon of victimization) is counterproductive because it evokes men's sense of helplessness, which is their greatest fear. In her view, male victims gravitate toward activity and aggression because they find the state of helplessness and weakness unbearable. The interviews conducted in this study do not appear to support Sepler's theory that men are hurt by efforts to affirm their blamelessness: A number of men indicated gaining psychological relief through accepting that they were not responsible for their abuse. It may be that with the passage of time and the assistance of therapy, however, these men have reached a level of comfort in their masculinity that has enabled them to begin to integrate their victimization. Boys, and younger men, may mobilize a number of defensive mechanisms to distance themselves from their helplessness. The implication for therapy with a male victim is, perhaps, that one must first assist him in affirming his masculinity, strength, and competence before helping him to accept that despite these attributes he was victimized and acted-upon.

Men appear to be very prone to blame themselves and shoulder responsibility for the abuse. As several clinicians who work with male survivors have noted (e.g., Bolton et al., 1989; Dimock, 1988), a man who has been sexually abused often feels like "less of a man" or like a failure as a man by virtue of "permitting" the abuse to occur. Finkelhor (1984) used the term "male ethic of self-reliance" to denote the male trait of seeing oneself as responsible for one's well-being and preservation. A number of men in the current study reported struggling with feelings of failure for being incapable of protecting themselves from the abuse. Wayne, for example, indicated that this was a centerpiece of the lingering trauma of the abuse. He has been unable, moreover, to discuss the abuse with his younger sister, who was also abused by their older brother, because he found it too painful "to think that (he) should have protected her as well."

This appears to represent a divergence from a pattern more characteristic of female survivors. Several writers (e.g., Herman, 1981; Jacobs, 1990) have noted the tendency of female victims to blame their mothers for not protecting or rescuing them from incest by their fathers. This theme—anger at someone else for not protecting them from the abuse—was virtually absent from the interviews. Instead, the failure to protect seems to be almost entirely internalized: men in this study experience themselves as deficient, unmanly, and incompetent because they could not provide themselves with adequate protection against the abuse. The sense of self-blame is exacerbated by the myth that males are constantly and indiscriminately sexually willing. The message to the male victim is not simply that if he was abused he must not be a man, but also that if he is a man he must not have been abused.

Obviously, victim-blaming is not limited to the male victim. Writers such as Herman (1981) and Rush (1980) describe the pervasive cultural myth of the seductive daughter. Such notions are internalized by women, so that female survivors of sexual abuse are also likely to hold themselves accountable for their victimization. I believe, however, that male socialization and societal notions of masculinity make men even more vulnerable to self-blame. The myth of complicity, as Gerber (1990) terms it, and cultural schemas of men as strong, active, and competent militate against men perceiving themselves as victims of sexual abuse.

In addition, there is a societal equation of males with oppressors. The sexually abused male is told, in effect, not only that he is not a victim but that he is, by virtue of membership in the class of males, a perpetrator. Struve (1990) refers to the dissonance of being a victim while a member of an "oppressor class." One man, Ron, enlisted this argument in presenting his theory of the transmission of abuse: "Men can't express their pain and grief because they see themselves as the oppressors rather than the oppressed in society. Therefore, they identify themselves as oppressors and end up as perpetrators. Men lash out in anger because they can't express their pain." In short, the men in this study feel profoundly and, I believe, understandably, that their victimization is unrecognized and invalidated. It is incumbent upon professionals in this area to recognize males as victims both for their sakes and—to the extent that Ron's theory of the transmission of abuse is accurate—for the sake of future generations.

Ron's theory is also consistent with Sepler's (1990) model of male patterns of response to victimization. She asserts that male victims are only, or primarily, in touch with feelings of anger. Helping a victim to obtain access to such feelings, which may be effective with females, is redundant or counterproductive with males, according to Sepler. The interviews conducted here indicate a different pattern. These men had considerable access to feelings of loss, sadness, pain, and vulnerability. In fact, such feelings emerged more prominently in these interviews than did expressions of anger. Again, this discrepancy may be due in part to the extensive therapy experience of the men in this study. As discussed in previous chapters, the high incidence of childhood sexual victimization among sex offenders appears to be well established (Condy et al., 1987; Groth, 1979b; Petrovich & Templer, 1984). I would speculate that a critical distinction between victimized men who go on to perpetrate and those who do not is the ability of the latter to integrate their experience of victimization and access the feelings of pain, loss, and vulnerability associated. Sex offenders, by contrast, may emerge from their childhood victimization primarily experiencing anger, which is expressed via sexually aggressive acts.

Along with doubts about masculinity, childhood sexual abuse also evokes confusion and insecurity regarding sexual orientation. As discussed in the preceding chapter, a very high proportion of the men in this study (34%) characterized themselves as primarily or exclusively homosexual. Several of the interview respondents indicated that they had been concerned about whether the abuse signified that they were gay. Pete, conversely, believes that the abuse caused him to become so distanced from his sexuality that he was unable to recognize that he was gay until years of therapy allowed him access to these feelings. Ron reported that people assume that he is gay because of his gentle nature and lack of sexual aggressiveness. He also feels more comfortable around gay men than around other straight men. Another man (whose story is not included in this book) reported that he has struggled throughout his life with issues related to sexual orientation. He was sexually abused at age five by his father—who, aside from the abuse, was distant—and molested at age 13 by a male family friend. Throughout his adolescence, he felt attracted to men, which he found enormously threatening and upsetting. As a result, he reported blocking off all sexual feelings. He now feels that he misconstrued as sexual his desires for contact and friendship with males. He feels that he longed for interaction with males because of his father's unavailability and sexualized this desire because of the sexualization of the relationship with the father. With these realizations, he now reports having increased sexual interest in women and a new-found ability to develop friendships with men, both of which he finds quite satisfying.

Whatever the specifics, concerns about sexual orientation appear to be fairly ubiquitous among male survivors of childhood sexual abuse. Doubts about masculinity and confusion about sexual orientation have been reported in several studies of male survivors. They represent two of the three constellations of issues—the third being compulsive behaviors—Dimock (1988) found to characterize this population. The relationships between sexual orientation and childhood sexual abuse are discussed in greater depth in the preceding chapter.

SHAME AND GENDER SHAME

Shame related to sexual abuse is a common characteristic of both male and female survivors. Both men and women may experience shame at having been victimized, shame for aspects of the abuse that they found pleasurable, shame for secondary gains accrued due to the sexual interaction (special privileges from a parent, for example), and shame for their perceived complicity or responsibility for the sexual interactions. There appears to be a somewhat different cast to men's shame regarding sexual abuse, however. As described above, men may be particularly vulnerable to viewing themselves as responsible for their childhood sexual activity, which results in increased shame. Another aspect of male shame, already discussed, stems from the lack of societal recognition of male victimization and the consequent stigma experienced by male survivors. Ron discussed his need to keep his "shameful" secret hidden; he likened his first experience of disclosure to that of a "gay man coming out of the closet."

Men who were subjected to sexual abuse experience an additional stratum of shame, which Dimock, Hunter, and Struve (1991) call gender shame. As the term implies, this refers to a sense of shame about oneself as a member of the class "men." It is an example of what Karen (1992) refers to as "class shame," as opposed to the more personal or narcissistic forms of shame described above.

The notion of gender shame is closely tied with the equation of males and oppressors. As one man in the current study said, "I know who men are; they're the ones who abuse you." Male survivors experience a pervasive sense that men are evil, hurtful, and abusive. The sense of class shame is not limited to those abused by men. Chris, who was sexually abused by his sister and by his mother, noted that he grew up assuming that men were inferior and worthless. This, of course, elicits profound ambivalence and confusion in terms of male survivors' identities as men and their identifications with men. A recurrent theme in the interviews was the feeling of not belonging or fitting in. Gender shame may also contribute to the erosion of self-esteem that is characteristic of sexual abuse survivors: Perceiving one's gender as loathsome is not likely to facilitate the development of a positive sense of self. Another outgrowth of this dynamic, which will be discussed in the following section, is the fear that one, as a man, is destined to become a perpetrator. Many men appear to de-identify with all things male, as a means of distancing themselves from what they perceive as an opprobrious class.

Along with shame about being male, many male survivors are ashamed of themselves as males. In other words, they feel that they come up short as men by virtue of having been raped, abused, weak, helpless, passive, victimized, and any other "unmanly" attribute that may be applied to the abuse experience. To repeat Wayne's pithy summary of this issue: "The abuse tells me that I'm not a man." Shame may also lurk beneath a number of other common features of the male sexual abuse survivor. Recent psychological writings on shame (e.g., Kaufman, 1989) view addictive behaviors as rooted in the shame experience. Such behaviors may be seen as efforts to avoid or dull one's sense of shame. Several studies have found

very high rates of addictions and compulsive behaviors among populations of male sexual abuse survivors (Dimock, 1988; Kelly & Gonzalez,
1990; Stein et al., 1988). Stein et al. suggest that substance abuse is
particularly characteristic of male survivors. In their study, female survivors most often displayed affective and anxiety disorders, but men
gravitated to alcohol and drug abuse. As noted above, Dimock (1988)
sees compulsive behaviors as one of the three characteristic responses of
male survivors of sexual abuse. Many of the men in the current study
reported extensive histories of substance abuse. Wayne, for example,
reported heavy use of various drugs until he entered a drug treatment
facility at age 18. He had begun to smoke marijuana at age eight and was
a daily user by 13. He drank and used cocaine, marijuana, and LSD
regularly throughout junior high and high school. He stated that he used
drugs in order to hide from his pain: "It saved my life. My head would
have exploded if I had to deal with all the things going on in my house,
but I was high."

In recent years, compulsive sexual behaviors have begun to be included
among addictions. Sexual compulsivity was quite common in the current
sample. It may be understood in part as an addictive behavior, rooted in
some of the same causes, including shame, as drug or alcohol addiction.
Compulsive sexuality would appear to be multiply-determined, however.
A number of the respondents noted that sex is the only way they have
learned to express affection or to gain intimacy. In addition, as Finkelhor
(1984) noted, sexual activity may be a way for men to reconfirm their
sexual adequacy in the wake of victimization and the consequent damage
to masculine identity. Through sexual activity, such men attempt to undo
what was done to them, proclaiming their virility, potency, and control
over their own bodies and sexuality.

Shame is a core dynamic for the sexual abuse survivor. Karen (1992),
in a recent article on the concept of shame in psychotherapy, argues that
shame has been psychology's neglected "stepchild," shunted aside in favor
of guilt as a basis for emotional disturbance and conflict. He contrasts the
neglect of shame within traditional psychotherapeutic modalities with the
emphasis given it by Alcoholics Anonymous and the other 12-step programs that comprise the "recovery movement." Such programs provide
a group venue of nonjudgmental others attempting to work on the same
problems and a focus on ridding oneself of the shame connected to one's
addiction (in Bradshaw's [1988] terms, "healing the shame that binds

you"). Kaufman (cited in Karen, 1992) asserts that this framework is ideal for helping the individual to overcome what Kaufman calls "secondary shame," the shame attached to the addictive behavior, as opposed to the shame that gave rise to the addiction. Recently, a 12-step group has been formed to deal specifically with incest survivors (Survivors of Incest Anonymous, or SIA). Many of the male survivors with whom I have had contact participate in 12-step groups, whether for the sexual abuse itself or for various addictions. I would speculate that the recovery movement appeals to survivors largely through its attunement to shame dynamics. Other approaches to psychotherapy may be better able to serve this population through increased attention to shame.

IDENTIFICATIONS AND FEAR OF PERPETRATING

Based on his clinical work with male survivors, Mike Lew (1990a, 1990b) asserts that there are three patterns of identification available to a sexually abused man: victim, perpetrator, and rescuer. Each pattern was evident in the interview responses of the men in the current study. A few discussed recurrent victimization, though this did not appear to be as widespread a pattern as it is for female survivors. Chris, for example, who was sexually and physically abused by his mother and older sister, stated that until therapy he had always assumed that impulsive, unexplained violence was an inevitable aspect of relationships. He has been involved in several relationships with women who lashed out at him without apparent cause. He recognizes now that he continually recreated the environment of his childhood and that unhappy and aggressive women felt familiar and comfortable to him. "Rescuers" were very well repre-sented in the current sample. Of the nine men interviewed, three were medical doctors, two social workers, and one a chiropractor. Several of the men drew direct links between their childhood abuse experiences and their career choice. Pete, for example, indicated that becoming a doctor represented a natural evolution of his childhood role as caretaker for his younger siblings. Ben noted that the fact that no one was there to help him during his childhood has fueled his attempts to help others. Ron sees his career as a chiropractor as an adaptive response to the abuse. He feels able to provide others with what he wishes had been provided him—warm, healthy physical contact in the context of safe boundaries. Career choice was also motivated by another dynamic connected to the abuse.

Several men indicated that they felt they had to reach the pinnacle of their field in order to attain self-esteem. They see their career development as compensatory to the diminution of self-worth caused by the abuse.

Perhaps the single most salient issue for the male survivor is the fear of perpetrating. As Bruckner and Johnson (1987) found in their groups with male survivors, the threat of becoming a perpetrator is the male survivor's Sword of Damocles. To the best of my knowledge and clinical judgment, none of the men who participated in interviews had perpetrated sexual abuse. Almost all, however, expressed apprehension about this issue. There is a sense among male survivors, also noted by Bruckner and Johnson (1987), that they are virtually fated to perpetuate the cycle of abuse. Three of the men interviewed stated that they had decided never to have children out of fear that they would do to their children what was done to them. Chris, for example, said that he saw childhood as inevitably painful and had determined "not to inflict childhood upon someone else."

One of the implications of the literature review in Chapter 2 is that we should not assume that male victims inevitably identify with perpetrators, or that female victims remain victims rather than aggressors. For numerous reasons, however, it does appear that men are more likely to gravitate toward the perpetrator rather than the victim role. Sources of this tendency include male socialization as active and aggressive; a trend toward identification with the same-sex parent, thus perpetuating existing sex-differences in rates of perpetration; the need—especially salient for males—to master trauma through identification with the aggressor and thus reassure oneself that one is not weak or helpless; the societal equation of males with oppressors and females with victims; and the lack of resources and outlets available to male victims. The motivation displayed by men in the present study to escape this "destiny" underscores the need to recognize boys as victims. This is necessary for their sake, to assist them on the road to recovery. It is also necessary for children of future generations. By dealing more with boys as victims, we may be free to deal less with men as perpetrators.

Treatment Implications

The final section of this book presents some suggestions for therapeutic interventions with male survivors. These suggestions are based primarily on the themes that emerged from the clinical interviews as particularly salient for male survivors. This book does not purport to be a comprehensive guide to the treatment of this population. Interested readers are referred to Briere (1989), Bruckner and Johnson (1987), Gonsiorek, Bera, and LeTourneau (in press), Hunter (1990b), or Lew (1990b); or, for work with child victims, Friedrich (1990) or Porter (1986). First, it may be helpful or reaffirming to those working with this challenging population to know how vital psychotherapy has been in the lives of these men. Most of the men interviewed saw therapy as fundamentally improving or even saving their lives.

In my view, the ultimate task for the survivor of sexual abuse is to move "beyond survival," to borrow from Briere's (1989) title. A man who has been sexually abused is likely to see himself primarily or even solely in that light: "Abuse Survivor" becomes his identity. For survivors to move beyond this and fully overcome their childhood maltreatment, they need help in understanding that their experience of abuse is not the sum total of who they are. A man who has been abused is not simply a survivor of this abuse, but a human being replete with all the various attributes, strengths, weaknesses, likes, dislikes, quirks, idiosyncracies, worries, foibles, and frailties that make us human.

I believe that an overarching goal in working with male survivors of childhood sexual abuse is to help them integrate their masculinity—their sense of themselves as men—with their experience of victimization. As discussed above, the male survivor often struggles with a sense that he is less of a man by virtue of the fact that he was victimized. He is likely to view himself as passive, helpless, weak, or girlish, all of which are incongruent with his (and societal) notions of what it is to be male. One aspect of this dynamic is the male need to be able to protect oneself. A boy victim or adult male survivor is likely to blame himself for being unable to do so and view the abuse as a reflection of his own shortcoming. The therapist who can assist him in understanding that as a child it is not possible to protect oneself, and that his victimization says nothing about his manhood, does him an enormous service.

In order for the male survivor fully to work through his experience of childhood sexual abuse, it is necessary for him to access, accept, and integrate feelings of helplessness, sadness, pain, and vulnerability. He must be able to recognize that he had such experiences as a child and to integrate this recognition into his sense of himself. This long-term objective may not be feasible as a first-order goal, however. As Sepler (1990) emphasizes, helplessness and vulnerability are enormously threatening to men. Boy victims and adult male survivors may need to feel secure in themselves as strong competent individuals before they can address their own vulnerabilities and weakness. Therefore, it may be necessary for the therapist first to assist the male victim/survivor in affirming his masculinity and capability before he can turn to the task of integrating his experience of victimization. Potentially, therapeutic work with male survivors may benefit from the assertiveness and activity characteristic of men. Bruckner and Johnson (1987), who have conducted survivor groups both with males and with females, indicate that men were more assertive in counteracting the effects of their abuse and retaking control of their lives.

A powerful issue in the interviews and in earlier research on male survivors is their sense that perpetration is their destiny. This is often the most lasting legacy of the abuse, as the survivor channels his energy and resources into his determination not to perpetuate the abuse. The therapist can play a tremendously beneficial role if he or she can help the survivor know that perpetration need not be his fate. Moving beyond survival entails putting this preoccupation to rest in favor of confidence in one's own nonabusiveness. Moreover, there is much the therapist can do to help the survivor take a different track. I believe that access to such feelings as vulnerability, loss, pain, and helplessness; and acceptance and integration of the victimization experience are critical factors differentiating nonperpetrating and perpetrating abuse survivors. Nonperpetrators appear to be able to access painful feelings, to incorporate their childhood victimization into their overall sense of themselves, and to work through this trauma. Perpetrators appear, by contrast, to emerge from their childhood maltreatment experiencing primarily anger. This anger is expressed via sexual aggression. A number of researchers (e.g., Briere & Smiljanich, 1993; Rogers & Terry, 1984) have viewed sexually aggressive behavior as a maladaptive attempt to master or gain control over one's traumatic experience. A central task for the abuse survivor is to find nonabusive means of doing so. Accepting and working through one's victimization, and integrating it with a sense of oneself as a competent man, appears to be the highroad to recovery and nonperpetration.

It is important that therapists working with this population recognize the ubiquitousness of concerns regarding sexual orientation. These appear to be especially salient for men abused by other males but are present among most sexually abused males. Men often assume that they must have done something to invite the abuse, and that the fact that they were abused (or, if the abuse was by a female, the fact that they did not enjoy the contact) must signify that they are gay. The therapist can help by disabusing him of these notions.

It is also important to reflect on the reasons the recovery movement holds so much appeal for abuse survivors. One reason appears to be its attunement to shame dynamics. Increased attention to the issue of shame, and the particular variants of shame that are prominent for male survivors, can help in work with this population.

Hunter (1993) made an important and astute observation—that in several respects the therapy setting mirrors the abuse experience. Both comprise the victim/survivor and an authority figure, behind closed doors, doing something that can be painful, and involving elements of secrecy. There are, I believe, some significant implications of this observation. It is crucial for therapists to be sensitive to these dynamics and to the potential for the therapy situation to evoke feelings related to the client's childhood abuse experience. For the same reason, it is helpful to make very clear to the client the parameters of confidentiality. The survivor/victim in therapy needs to understand that he is free to tell anyone as much as he likes about what goes on in therapy; it is the therapist who will not tell. This is a critical distinction between therapy and earlier circumstances where the client may have been ordered not to tell and threatened with dire consequences should he tell.

I would like to return briefly to some of the findings of the questionnaire portion of this study and outline some treatment implications of these findings. Men who experienced physical abuse along with their sexual abuse were significantly more likely to have attempted suicide than those who were subjected only to sexual abuse. Men who were abused by a sibling were also more likely to have attempted suicide. Therefore, therapists working with these particular populations should be especially alert to suicidality.

Drug use by perpetrator was one of the most powerful predictors of negative outcome for the survivor. Those abused by a substance-user also received less psychotherapy and psychotropic medication. I believe that these two findings are related, and that growing up in a multiply-abusive environment (one including both substance abuse and sexual abuse) makes it very difficult to get the help one needs. Survivors of both substance-abusing families and of sexual abuse may fare more poorly than those whose families of origin did not abuse drugs because they are less able to seek or maintain treatment. One implication of these findings is that there may need to be more outreach to adult children of alcoholics (and of other substance abusers) in order to assist the male survivors of childhood sexual abuse among them. Therapists working with male survivors should also be aware that those who come from such a background may be less likely to remain in treatment. No data was obtained regarding the substance use of the survivors themselves. This may be an additional mediating factor. If men from substance-abusing families are more likely to abuse drugs themselves, this may render them more resistant to therapy and interfere with their ability to benefit from treatment.

Finally, no intervention can proceed without the willingness and openness of helping professionals to recognize male victimization. The most important single step a therapist can take with respect to this population is increased awareness of its existence. The more we are able to recognize and to help boy victims and male survivors, the less we will need to focus upon male perpetrators. Better treatment of male victims/survivors thus benefits both them and future generations. It is my hope that this book has served to increase understanding of male survivors, thus contributing to their recovery.

References

Achenbach, T. M., & Edelbrock, C. S. (1979). The child behavior profile. *Journal of Consulting and Clinical Psychology, 47,* 223-233.

Adams-Tucker, C. (1981). A sociological overview of 28 abused children. *Child Abuse & Neglect, 5,* 361-367.

Alexander, P. C. (1992). Application of attachment theory to the study of sexual abuse. *Journal of Consulting and Clinical Psychology, 60,* 185-195.

Allen, C. M. (1990). Women as perpetrators of child sexual abuse: Recognition barriers. In A. L. Horton, B. L. Johnson, L. M. Roundy, & D. Williams (Eds.), *The incest perpetrator: A family member no one wants to treat* (pp. 108-125). Newbury Park, CA: Sage.

American Association for the Protection of Children. (1987). *Highlights of official child neglect and abuse reporting: 1985.* Denver, CO: American Humane Association.

American Association for the Protection of Children. (1988). *Highlights of child neglect and abuse reporting.* Denver: American Humane Association.

American Humane Association. (1981). *National Study on child neglect and abuse reporting.* Denver, CO: Author.

American Psychiatric Association. (1987). *Diagnostic and statistical manual of mental disorders* (3rd ed., rev.). Washington, DC: Author.

Awad, G. (1976). Father-son incest: A case report. *Journal of Nervous and Mental Diseases, 162,* 135-139.

Baker, A. W. (1985). Child sexual abuse: A study of prevalence in Great Britain. *Child Abuse & Neglect, 9,* 475-467.

217

Ballard, D. T., Blair, G. D., Devereaux, S., Valentine, L. K., Horton, A. L., & Johnson, B. L. (1990). A comparative profile of the incest perpetrator: Background characteristics, abuse history, and use of social skills. In A. L. Horton, B. L. Johnson, L. M. Roundy, & D. Williams (Eds.), *The incest perpetrator: A family member no one wants to treat* (pp. 43-64). Newbury Park, CA: Sage.

Bandura, A. (1977). *Social learning theory.* Englewood Cliffs, NJ: Prentice Hall.

Banning, A. (1989). Mother-son incest: Confronting a prejudice. *Child Abuse & Neglect, 13,* 563-570.

Becker, J. V. (1988). The effects of child sexual abuse on adolescent sexual offenders. In G. E. Wyatt & G. J. Powell (Eds.), *Lasting effects of child sexual abuse* (pp. 193-207). Newbury Park, CA: Sage.

Becker, J. V., Kaplan, M. S., Cunningham-Rathner, J., & Kavoussi, R. (1986). Characteristics of adolescent incest perpetrators: Preliminary findings. *Journal of Family Violence, 1,* 85-97.

Bell, A. P., Weinberg, M. S., & Hammersmith, S. K. (1981a). *Sexual preference: Its development in men and women.* Bloomington: Indiana University Press.

Bell, A. P., Weinberg, M. S., & Hammersmith, S. K. (1981b). *Sexual preference: Statistical appendix.* Bloomington: Indiana University Press.

Bell, M. (1989). *An introduction to the Bell Object Relations Reality Testing Inventory (BORRTI).* Unpublished manuscript. [Address requests to Dr. M. Bell, Psychology Service, West Haven VA Medical Center, West Haven, CT 06516]

Bell, M., Billington, R., & Becker, B. (1986). A scale for the assessment of object relations: Reliability, validity, and factorial invariance. *Journal of Clinical Psychology, 42,* 733-741.

Bender, L., & Blau, A. (1937). The reaction of children to sexual relations with adults. *American Journal of Orthopsychiatry, 7,* 500-518.

Bender, L., & Grugett, A. (1952). A follow-up report on children who had atypical sexual experiences. *American Journal of Orthopsychiatry, 22,* 825-837.

Black, C. (1990). *Double duty.* New York: Ballantine.

Bly, R. (1990). *Iron John: A book about men.* Reading, MA: Addison-Wesley.

Bolton, F. G., Morris, L. A., & MacEachron, A. E. (1989). *Males at risk: The other side of child sexual abuse.* Newbury Park, CA: Sage.

Bradshaw, J. (1988). *Healing the shame that binds you.* Deerfield Beach, FL: Health Communications.

Breuer, J., & Freud, S. (1955). Studies on hysteria. In J. Strachey (Ed. and Trans.), *The standard edition of the complete psychological works of Sigmund Freud* (Vol. 2). London: Hogarth Press. (Original work published 1893-1895)

Briere, J. (1988). Controlling for family variables in abuse effects research: A critique of the "partialling" approach. *Journal of Interpersonal Violence, 3,* 80-89.

Briere, J. (1989). *Therapy for adults molested as children: Beyond survival.* New York: Springer.

Briere, J., & Conte, J. (1993). Self-reported amnesia for abuse in adults molested as children. *Journal of Traumatic Stress, 6,* 21-31.

Briere, J., Evans, D., Runtz, M., & Wall, T. (1988). Symptomatology in men who were molested as children: A comparison study. *American Journal of Orthopsychiatry, 58,* 457-461.

Briere, J., & Runtz, M. (1989). The Trauma Symptom Checklist (TSC-33): Early data on a new scale. *Journal of Interpersonal Violence, 4,* 151-163.

Briere, J., & Smiljanich, K. (1993, August). *Childhood sexual abuse and subsequent sexual aggression against adult women*. Paper presented at the 101st annual convention of the American Psychological Association, Toronto, Ontario.

Browne, A., & Finkelhor, D. (1986). Impact of child sexual abuse: A review of the research. *Psychological Bulletin, 99*, 66-77.

Brownmiller, S. (1975). *Against our will: Men, women and rape*. New York: Simon & Schuster.

Bruckner, D. F., & Johnson, P. E. (1987). Treatment for adult male victims of childhood sexual abuse. *Social Casework: The Journal of Contemporary Social Work, 68*, 81-87.

Burgess, A. W. (Ed.). (1984). *Child pornography and sex rings*. Lexington, MA: Lexington.

Burgess, A. W., Groth, A. N., & McCausland, M. P. (1981). Child sex initiation rings. *American Journal of Orthopsychiatry, 51*, 110-118.

Burgess, A. W., & Holmstrom, L. L. (1974). Rape trauma syndrome. *American Journal of Psychiatry, 131*, 981-986.

Cameron, P., Proctor, K., Coburn, W. J., Forde, N., Larson, H., & Cameron, K. (1986). Child molestation and homosexuality. *Psychological Reports, 58*, 327-337.

Cantwell, H. B. (1988). Child sexual abuse: Very young perpetrators. *Child Abuse & Neglect, 12*, 579-582.

Carlson, S., Dimock, P. T., Driggs, J., & Westly, T. (1987, May). *Relationship of childhood sexual abuse and adult sexual compulsiveness in males*. Workshop presented at the First National Conference on Sexual Compulsivity/Addiction, Minneapolis, MN.

Carmen, E., Rieker, P. P., & Mills, T. (1984). Victims of violence and psychiatric illness. *American Journal of Psychiatry, 141*, 378-383.

Condy, S. R., Templer, D. I., Brown, R., & Veaco, L. (1987). Parameters of sexual contact of boys with women. *Archives of Sexual Behavior, 16*, 379-394.

Constantine, L. L. (1981). Effects of early sexual experiences: A review and synthesis of research. In L. L. Constantine & F. M. Martinson (Eds.), *Children and sex: New findings, new perspectives* (pp. 217-244). Boston: Little, Brown.

Conte, J. R. (1982). Sexual abuse of children: Enduring issues for social work. *Journal of Social Work and Human Sexuality, 1*, 1-19.

Conte, J. R., & Schuerman, J. R. (1987). Factors associated with an increased impact of child sexual abuse. *Child Abuse & Neglect, 11*, 201-211.

Coombs, N. R. (1974). Male prostitution: A psychosocial view of behavior. *American Journal of Orthopsychiatry, 44*, 782-789.

Dahlstrom, W. G., & Welsh, G. S. (1960). *An MMPI (Minnesota Multi-phasic Personality Inventory) handbook: A guide to use in clinical practice and research*. Minneapolis: University of Minnesota Press.

De Francis, V. (1969). *Protecting the child victim of sex crimes committed by adults*. Denver, CO: American Humane Association.

DeJong, A. R., Emmett, G. A., & Hervada, A. R. (1982). Sexual abuse of children: Sex-, race-, and age-dependent variations. *American Journal of Diseases of Children, 136*, 129-134.

Derogatis, L. R., Lipman, R. S., & Covi, L. (1973). The SCL-90: An outpatient rating scale: Preliminary report. *Psychopharmacology Bulletin, 9*, 13-28.

Dimock, P. T. (1988). Adult males sexually abused as children. *Journal of Interpersonal Violence, 3*, 203-221.

Dimock, P. T., Hunter, M., & Struve, J. (1991, November). *The male sexual abuse survivor.* Workshop presented at conference on Treatment of Adult Male Survivors of Childhood Sexual Abuse, Santa Fe, NM.

Dixon, K. N., Arnold, L. E., & Calestro, K. (1978). Father-son incest: Underreported psychiatric problem? *American Journal of Psychiatry, 135*, 835-839.

Donaldson, M. A., & Gardner, R., Jr. (1985). Diagnosis and treatment of traumatic stress among women after childhood incest. In C. R. Figley (Ed.), *Trauma and its wake: The study and treatment of post-traumatic stress disorder* (pp. 356-377). New York: Brunner/Mazel.

Egeland, B., Jacobvitz, D., & Sroufe, L. A. (1988). Breaking the cycle of abuse. *Child Development, 59*, 1080-1088.

Ellerstein, N. S., & Canavan, J. W. (1980). Sexual abuse of boys. *American Journal of Diseases of Children, 134*, 255-257.

Erikson, E. H. (1963). *Childhood and society* (2nd ed.). New York: Norton.

Eth, S., & Pynoos, R. S. (1985). *Post-traumatic stress disorder in children.* Los Angeles: American Psychiatric Association.

Faller, K. C. (1987). Women who sexually abuse children. *Violence and Victims, 2*, 263-276.

Faller, K. C. (1989). Characteristics of a clinical sample of sexually abused children: How boy and girl victims differ. *Child Abuse & Neglect, 13*, 281-291.

Farber, E. D., Showers, J., Johnson, C. F., Joseph, J. A., & Oshins, L. (1984). The sexual abuse of children: A comparison of male and female victims. *Journal of Clinical Child Psychology, 13*, 294-297.

Fehrenbach, P. A., Smith, W., Monastersky, C., & Deisher, R. W. (1986). Adolescent sexual offenders: Offender and offense characteristics. *American Journal of Orthopsychiatry, 56*, 225-233.

Ferenczi, S. (1949). Confusion of tongues between the adult and the child: The language of tenderness and passion. *International Journal of Psychoanalysis, 30*, 225-230.

Finkelhor, D. (1979). *Sexually victimized children.* New York: Free Press.

Finkelhor, D. (1981). The sexual abuse of boys. *Victimology: An International Journal, 6*, 76-84.

Finkelhor, D. (1984). *Child sexual abuse: New theory and research.* New York: Free Press.

Finkelhor, D. (1986). *A sourcebook on child sexual abuse.* Newbury Park, CA: Sage.

Finkelhor, D. (1988). The trauma of child sexual abuse: Two models. In G. E. Wyatt & G. J. Powell (Eds.), *Lasting effects of child sexual abuse* (pp. 61-82). Newbury Park, CA: Sage.

Finkelhor, D. (1990). Early and long-term effects of child sexual abuse: An update. *Professional Psychology: Research and Practice, 21*, 325-330.

Finkelhor, D., & Browne, A. (1985). The traumatic impact of child sexual abuse: A conceptualization. *American Journal of Orthopsychiatry, 55*, 530-541.

Finkelhor, D., & Russell, D. E. H. (1984). Women as perpetrators. In D. Finkelhor (Ed.), *Child sexual abuse: New theory and research* (pp. 171-187). New York: Free Press.

Finkelhor, D., Hotaling, G., Lewis, I. A., & Smith, C. (1990). Sexual abuse in a national survey of adult men and women: Prevalence, characteristics, and risk factors. *Child Abuse & Neglect, 14,* 19-28.

Forward, S. (1978). *Betrayal of innocence: Incest and its devastation.* Middlesex, England: Penguin.

Franklin, C. W., II. (1984). *The changing definition of masculinity.* New York: Plenum.

Freedman, A. M., Kaplan, H. I., & Sadock, B. (Eds.). (1975). *Comprehensive textbook of psychiatry* (2nd ed.). Baltimore: Williams & Wilkins.

Freeman-Longo, R. E. (1986). The impact of sexual victimization on males. *Child Abuse & Neglect, 10,* 411-414.

Freud, S. (1953). Three essays on the theory of sexuality. In J. Strachey (Ed. and Trans.), *The standard edition of the complete psychological works of Sigmund Freud* (Vol. 7, pp. 125-243). London: Hogarth Press. (Original work published 1905)

Freud, S. (1962). The aetiology of hysteria. In J. Strachey (Ed. and Trans.), *The standard edition of the complete psychological works of Sigmund Freud* (Vol. 3, pp. 189-224). London: Hogarth Press. (Original work published 1896)

Friedman, S. (1988). A family systems approach to treatment. In L.E.A. Walker (Ed.), *Handbook on sexual abuse of children* (pp. 326-349). New York: Springer.

Friedrich, W. N. (1990). *Psychotherapy of sexually abused children and their families.* New York: Norton.

Friedrich, W. N., Beilke, R. L., & Urquiza, A. J. (1987). Children from sexually abusive families: A behavioral comparison. *Journal of Interpersonal Violence, 2,* 391-402.

Friedrich, W. N., Beilke, R. L., & Urquiza, A. J. (1988). Behavior problems in young sexually abused boys: A comparison study. *Journal of Interpersonal Violence, 3,* 21-28.

Friedrich, W. N., & Luecke, W. J. (1988). Young school-age sexually aggressive children. *Professional Psychology: Research and Practice, 19,* 155-164.

Friedrich, W. N., Urquiza, A. J., & Beilke, R. L. (1986). Behavior problems in sexually abused young children. *Journal of Pediatric Psychology, 11,* 47-57.

Fritz, G. S., Stoll, K., & Wagner, N. N. (1981). A comparison of males and females who were sexually molested as children. *Journal of Sex and Marital Therapy, 7,* 54-59.

Fromuth, M. E., & Burkhart, B. R. (1987). Childhood sexual victimization among college men: Definitional and methodological issues. *Violence and Victims, 2,* 241-253.

Fromuth, M. E., & Burkhart, B. R. (1989). Long-term psychological correlates of childhood sexual abuse in two samples of college men. *Child Abuse & Neglect, 13,* 533-542.

Froning, M. L., & Mayman, S. B. (1990, November). *Identification and treatment of child and adolescent male victims of sexual abuse.* Workshop presented at the Third National Conference on The Male Survivor, Tucson, AZ.

Gardner, R. A. (1991). *Sex abuse hysteria: Salem witch trials revisited.* Cresskill, NJ: Creative Therapeutics.

Gebhard, P., Gagnon, J., Pomeroy, W., & Christenson, C. (1965). *Sex offenders.* New York: Harper & Row.

Geiser, R. L., & Norberta, M. (1976). Sexual disturbance in young children. *American Journal of Maternal Child Nursing, 1,* 187-194.

Gelinas, D. J. (1983). The persisting negative effects of incest. *Psychiatry, 16,* 312-332.

Gerber, P. N. (1990). Victims becoming offenders: A study of ambiguities. In M. Hunter (Ed.), *The sexually abused male: Vol. 1. Prevalence, impact, and treatment* (pp. 153-176). Lexington, MA: Lexington.

Ginsburg, K. N. (1967). The "meat rack": A study of the male homosexual prostitute. *American Journal of Orthopsychiatry, 21,* 170-185.

Gold-Steinberg, S. E. (1991). *Legal and illegal abortion: Coping with the impact of social policies on women's lives.* Unpublished Doctoral Dissertation, University of Michigan, Ann Arbor.

Gomes-Schwartz, B., Horowitz, J., & Sauzier, M. (1985). Severity of emotional distress among sexually abused preschool, school-age and adolescent children. *Hospital and Community Psychiatry, 30,* 503-508.

Gonsiorek, J. C. (1993, August). *Relationship of sexual abuse of males and sexual orientation confusion.* Paper presented at the 101st annual convention of the American Psychological Association, Toronto, Ontario.

Gonsiorek, J. C., Bera, W. H., & LeTourneau, D. (in press). *Male sexual abuse: A trilogy of intervention strategies.* Newbury Park, CA: Sage.

Grayson, J. (Ed.). (1989, Fall). Sexually victimized boys. *Virginia Child Protection Newsletter, Vol. 29.* Harrisonburg, VA: James Madison University.

Grayson, J. (Ed.). (1990, Summer). Male survivors of childhood sexual abuse. *Virginia Child Protection Newsletter, Vol. 31.* Harrisonburg, VA: James Madison University.

Groth, A. N. (1977). The adolescent sexual offender and his prey. *International Journal of Offender Therapy and Comparative Criminology, 21,* 249-254.

Groth, A. N. (1979a). *Men who rape.* New York: Plenum.

Groth, A. N. (1979b). Sexual trauma in the life histories of rapists and child molesters. *Victimology: An International Journal, 4,* 10-16.

Groth, A. N., & Birnbaum, H. J. (1978). Adult sexual orientation and attraction to underage persons. *Archives of Sexual Behavior, 7,* 175-181.

Groth, A. N., Hobson, W. F., & Gary, T. S. (1982). The child molester: Clinical observations. In J. Conte & D. Shore (Eds.), *Social work and child sexual abuse* (pp. 129-144). New York: Haworth.

Grubman-Black, S. D. (1990). *Broken boys/mending men: Recovery from childhood sexual abuse.* Blue Ridge Summit, PA: Tab Books.

Hamer, D. H., Hu, S., Magnuson, V. L., Hu, N., & Pattatucci, A.M.L. (1993). A linkage between DNA markers on the X chromosome and male sexual orientation. *Science, 261,* 321-327.

Hare-Mustin, R. T., & Maracek, J. (1990). On making a difference. In R. T. Hare-Mustin & J. Maracek (Eds.), *Making a difference: Psychology and the construction of gender* (pp. 1-21). New Haven, CT: Yale University Press.

Hazan, C., & Shaver, P. (1987). Romantic love conceptualized as an attachment process. *Journal of Personality and Social Psychology, 52,* 511-524.

Henderson, J. (1983). Is incest harmful? *Canadian Journal of Psychiatry, 28,* 34-39.

Herman, J. L. (1981). *Father-daughter incest.* Cambridge, MA: Harvard University Press.

Herman, J. L., Russell, D., & Trocki, K. (1986). Long-term effects of incestuous abuse in childhood. *American Journal of Psychiatry, 143,* 1293-1296.

Herman, J. L., & Schatzow, E. (1987). Recovery and verification of memories of childhood sexual trauma. *Psychoanalytic Psychology, 4,* 1-14.

Hoffman, L. (1981). *Foundations of family therapy.* New York: Basic Books.

Holmes, R. M. (1983). *The sex offender and the criminal justice system.* Springfield, IL: Charles C Thomas.

Horton, A. L., Johnson, B. L., Roundy, L. M., & Williams, D. (Eds.). (1990). *The incest perpetrator: A family member no one wants to treat* (pp. 108-125). Newbury Park, CA: Sage.

Howells, K. (1981). Adult sexual interest in children: Considerations relevant to theories of etiology. In M. Cook & K. Howells (Eds.), *Adult sexual interest in children* (pp. 55-94). New York: Academic Press.

Hunter, M. (1987, May). *Membership demographics of the self-help group sex addicts anonymous.* Workshop presented at 1st National Conference on Sexual Compulsivity/Addiction, Minneapolis, MN.

Hunter, M. (1990a). *Abused boys: The neglected victims of sexual abuse.* Lexington, MA: Lexington.

Hunter, M. (Ed.). (1990b). *The sexually abused male: Vol. 1. Prevalence, impact, and treatment.* Lexington, MA: Lexington.

Hunter, M. (1990c). *The sexually abused male: Vol. 2.* Lexington, MA: Lexington.

Hunter, M. (1993, August). *Males who have experienced childhood sexual abuse: Recovery issues.* Paper presented at the 101st annual convention of the American Psychological Association, Toronto, Ontario.

Ingham, M. (1984). *Men: The male myth exposed.* London: Century.

Jacobs, J. L. (1990). Reassessing mother blame in incest. *Signs: Journal of Women in Culture and Society, 15,* 500-514.

Jaffe, A. C., Dynneson, L., & Ten Bensel, R. (1975). Sexual abuse: An epidemiological study. *American Journal of Diseases of Children, 129,* 689-692.

Janoff-Bulman, R. (1985). The aftermath of victimization: Rebuilding shattered assumptions. In C. R. Figley (Ed.), *Trauma and its wake: The study and treatment of post-traumatic stress disorder* (pp. 15-35). New York: Brunner/Mazel.

Janoff-Bulman, R. (1989). Assumptive worlds and the stress of traumatic events: Applications of the schema construct. In Stress, coping, and social cognition [Special issue], *Social Cognition, 7,* 113-136.

Janus, M.-D., Scanlon, B., & Price, V. (1984). Youth prostitution. In A. W. Burgess (Ed.), *Child pornography and sex rings* (pp. 127-146). Lexington, MA: Lexington.

Johnson, R. L., & Shrier, D. K. (1985). Sexual victimization of boys: Experience at an adolescent medicine clinic. *Journal of Adolescent Health Care, 6,* 372-376.

Johnson, R. L., & Shrier, D. K. (1987). Past sexual victimization by females of male patients in an adolescent medicine clinic population. *American Journal of Psychiatry, 144,* 650-652.

Johnson, T. C. (1988). Child perpetrators—Children who molest other children: Preliminary findings. *Child Abuse & Neglect, 12,* 219-229.

Justice, B., & Justice, R. (1979). *The broken taboo: Sex in the family.* New York: Human Sciences Press.

Karen, R. (1992). Shame. *The Atlantic, 269*(2), 40-70.

Kasl, C. D. (1990). Female perpetrators of sexual abuse: A feminist view. In M. Hunter (Ed.), *The sexually abused male: Vol. 1. Prevalence, impact, and treatment* (pp. 259-274). Lexington, MA: Lexington.

Kaufman, G. (1989). *The psychology of shame: Theory and treatment of shame-based syndromes.* New York: Springer.

Kaufman, J., & Zigler, E. (1987). Do abused children become abusive parents? *American Journal of Orthopsychiatry, 57,* 186-192.

Kelly, R. J., & Gonzalez, L. S. (1990, November). *Psychological symptoms reported by sexually abused men.* Workshop presented at the Third National Conference on The Male Survivor, Tucson, AZ.

Kempe, C. H., Silverman, F. N., Steele, B. F., Droegemiller, W., & Silver, H. K. (1962). The battered child syndrome. *Journal of the American Medical Association, 181,* 17-24.

Kempe, C. H., & Helfer, R. E. (1980). *The battered child* (3rd ed.). Chicago: University of Chicago Press.

Kempe, R. S., & Kempe, C. H. (1978). *Child abuse.* Cambridge, MA: Harvard University Press.

Kercher, G., & McShane, M. (1984). The prevalence of child sexual abuse victimization in an adult sample of Texas residents. *Child Abuse & Neglect, 8,* 485-502.

Keyser, L. (1975). Sex in the contemporary European film. In T. R. Atkins (Ed.), *Sexuality in the movies* (pp. 172-190). Bloomington: Indiana University Press.

Knopp, F. H. (1986). Introduction. In E. Porter, *Treating the young male victim of sexual assault: Issues and intervention strategies.* Syracuse, NY: Safer Society Press.

Kohan, M. J., Pothier, P., & Norbeck, J. S. (1987). Hospitalized children with history of sexual abuse: Incidence and care issues. *American Journal of Orthopsychiatry, 57,* 258-264.

Koss, M. P., & Dinero, T. E. (1988). Predictors of sexual aggression among a sample of male college students. *Annals of the New York Academy of Sciences, 528,* 133-147.

Koss, M. P., & Oros, C. J. (1982). Sexual experiences survey: A research instrument investigating sexual aggression and victimization. *Journal of Consulting and Clinical Psychology, 50,* 455-457.

Krug, R. S. (1989). Adult male report of childhood sexual abuse by mothers: Case descriptions, motivations and long-term consequences. *Child Abuse & Neglect, 13,* 111-119.

Landis, J. (1956). Experiences of 500 children with adult sexual deviants. *Psychiatric Quarterly Supplement, 30,* 91-109.

Langsley, D. G., Schwartz, M. N., & Fairbairn, R. H. (1968). Father-son incest. *Comprehensive Psychiatry, 9,* 218-226.

LeVay, S. (1991). A difference in hypothalamic structure between heterosexual and homosexual men. *Science, 253,* 1034-1037.

Lew, M. (1990a, January). *Victims no longer: Assessment and treatment of men recovering from incest and other childhood sexual abuse.* Workshop, Ann Arbor, MI.

Lew, M. (1990b). *Victims no longer: Men recovering from incest and other sexual child abuse* (2nd ed.). New York: Harper & Row.

Limbacher, J. L. (1983). *Sexuality in world cinema.* Metuchen, NJ: Scarecrow Press.

Lindberg, F. H., & Distad, L. H. (1985). Post-traumatic stress disorder in women who experienced childhood incest. *Child Abuse & Neglect, 9,* 329-334.

Loftus, E. F. (1993). The reality of repressed memories. *American Psychologist, 48,* 518-537.

Love, P. (1990). *The emotional incest syndrome: What to do when a parent's love rules your life.* New York: Bantam Books.

Maccoby, E. E., & Jacklin, C. N. (1974). *The psychology of sex differences.* Palo Alto, CA: Stanford University Press.

MacFarlane, K. (1978). Sexual abuse of children. In J. R. Chapman & M. Gates (Eds.), *The victimization of women* (pp. 81-109). Beverly Hills, CA: Sage.

Masson, J. M. (1984). *The assault on truth: Freud's suppression of the seduction theory.* New York: Farrar, Straus & Giroux.

Masters, W. H., Johnson, V. E., & Kolodny, R. C. (1985). *Human sexuality* (2nd ed.). Boston: Little, Brown.

Mathews, R. (1987, May). *Female sexual offenders.* Workshop presented to the Third National Adolescent Perpetrator Network Meeting, Keystone, CO.

Mathews, R., Matthews, J., & Speltz, K. (1990). Female sexual offenders. In M. Hunter (Ed.), *The sexually abused male: Vol. 1. Prevalence, impact, and treatment* (pp. 275-293). Lexington, MA: Lexington.

McCarty, L. M. (1986). Mother-child incest: Characteristics of the offender. *Child Welfare, 65,* 447-458.

McCormack, A., Burgess, A. W., & Janus, M. D. (1986). Runaway youths and sexual victimization: Gender differences in an adolescent runaway population. *Child Abuse & Neglect, 10,* 387-395.

McCurdy, K., & Daro, D. (1993). *Current trends in child abuse reporting and fatalities: The results of the 1992 annual fifty state survey.* Chicago: National Committee for the Prevention of Child Abuse.

Meiselman, K. (1979). *Incest: A psychological study of causes and effects with treatment recommendations.* San Francisco: Jossey-Bass.

Miller, A. (1984). Thou shalt not be aware: Society's betrayal of the child (H. Hannum and H. Hannum, Trans.). New York: Farrar, Straus & Giroux. (Original work, in German, published 1980)

Millett, K. (1969). *Sexual politics.* Garden City, NY: Doubleday.

Minuchin, S. (1967). *Families of the slums: An exploration of their structure and treatment.* New York: Basic Books.

Murphy, J. E. (1987, July). *Prevalence of child sexual abuse and consequent victimization in the general population.* Paper presented at the Third National Family Violence Research Conference, Durham, NH.

Murphy, J. E. (1989, January). *Telephone surveys and family violence: Data from Minnesota.* Paper presented at the Responses to Family Violence Conference, West Lafayette, IN.

Myers, M. F. (1989). Men sexually assaulted as adults and sexually abused as boys. *Archives of Sexual Behavior, 18,* 203-215.

Nasjleti, M. (1980). Suffering in silence: The male incest victim. *Child Welfare, 59,* 269-275.

National Center on Child Abuse and Neglect. (1988). *Study findings: Study of national incidence and prevalence of child abuse and neglect.* Washington, DC: U.S. Department of Health and Human Services.

Neilsen, T. (1983). Sexual abuse of boys: Current perspectives. *Personnel and Guidance Journal, 62,* 139-142.

Olson, P. E. (1990). The sexual abuse of boys: A study of the long-term psychological effects. In M. Hunter (Ed.), *The sexually abused male: Vol. 1. Prevalence, impact, and treatment* (pp. 137-152). Lexington, MA: Lexington.

Payne, A. B., & Zuber, B. (1991). *Treatment of incest survivors and adult children of alcoholics: A comparison.* Paper presented at the ACPA Conference, Atlanta, GA.

Peters, S., Wyatt, G., & Finkelhor, D. (1986). Prevalence. In D. Finkelhor and Associates, *A sourcebook on child sexual abuse.* Newbury Park, CA: Sage.

Petrovich, M., & Templer, D. I. (1984). Heterosexual molestation of children who later became rapists. *Psychological Reports, 54,* 810-811.

Pierce, R., & Pierce, L. H. (1985). The sexually abused child: A comparison of male and female victims. *Child Abuse & Neglect, 9,* 191-199.

Pleck, J. H. (1981). *The myth of masculinity.* Cambridge: MIT Press.

Plummer, K. (1981). Pedophilia: Constructing a sociological baseline. In M. Cook & K. Howells (Eds.), *Adult sexual interest in children* (pp. 221-250). New York: Academic Press.

Porter, E. (1986). *Treating the young male victim of sexual assault: Issues and intervention strategies.* Syracuse, NY: Safer Society Press.

Ramey, J. (1979). Dealing with the last taboo. *SIECUS Report, 7,* 1-7.

Ramsey-Klawsnik, H. (1990a, April). *Sexual abuse by female perpetrators: Impact on children.* Paper presented at the National Symposium on Child Victimization, Atlanta, GA.

Ramsey-Klawsnik, H. (1990b, November). *Sexually abused boys: Indicators, abusers and impact of trauma.* Paper presented at the Third National Conference on The Male Survivor, Tucson, AZ.

Rascovsky, M., & Rascovsky, A. (1950). On consummated incest. *International Journal of Psychoanalysis, 31,* 42-47.

Reinhart, M. A. (1987). Sexually abused boys. *Child Abuse & Neglect, 11,* 229-235.

Reynolds, C. F. I., Frank, E., Thase, M. E., Houck, P. R., Jennings, J. R., Howell, J. R., Lilienfeld, S. O., & Kupfer, D. J. (1988). Assessment of sexual function in depressed, impotent, and healthy men: Factor analysis of a brief sexual function questionnaire for men. *Psychiatry Research, 24,* 231-250.

Risin, L. I., & Koss, M. P. (1987). The sexual abuse of boys: Prevalence and descriptive characteristics of childhood victimizations. *Journal of Interpersonal Violence, 2,* 309-323.

Robinson, R. K. (1991, October 25). Abuse: Lesbian battering real. *State News, 86*(147), p. 1.

Rogers, C. M., & Terry, T. (1984). Clinical interventions with boy victims of sexual abuse. In I. Stewart & J. Greer (Eds.), *Victims of sexual aggression* (pp. 91-104). New York: Van Nostrand Reinhold.

Runtz, M. (1987). *The psychosocial adjustment of women who were sexually and physically abused during childhood and early adulthood: A focus on revictimization.* Unpublished master's thesis, University of Manitoba.

Rush, F. (1980). *The best kept secret: Sexual abuse of children.* New York: McGraw-Hill.

Russell, D. E. H. (1983). The incidence and prevalence of intrafamilial and extrafamilial sexual abuse of female children. *Child Abuse & Neglect, 7,* 133-146.

Russell, D. E. H. (1986). *The secret trauma: Incest in the lives of girls and women.* New York: Basic Books.

Russell, D. E. H., & Finkelhor, D. (1984). The gender gap among perpetrators of sexual abuse. In D.E.H. Russell (Ed.), *Sexual exploitation: Rape, child sexual abuse and workplace harassment* (pp. 215-231). Beverly Hills, CA: Sage.

Sanders, T. (1991). *Male survivors.* Freedom, CA: The Crossing Press.

Sarrel, P. M., & Masters, W. H. (1982). Sexual molestation of men by women. *Archives of Sexual Behavior, 11,* 117-131.

Schultz, L. G. (Ed.). (1979). *The sexual victimology of youth.* Springfield, IL: Charles C Thomas.

Sebold, J. (1987). Indicators of child sexual abuse in males. *Social Casework: The Journal of Contemporary Social Work, 68,* 75-80.

Seidner, A. L., & Calhoun, K. S. (1984, August). *Childhood sexual abuse: Factors related to differential adult adjustment.* Paper presented at the Second National Conference for Family Violence Researchers, Durham, NH.

Sepler, F. (1990). Victim advocacy and young male victims of sexual abuse: An evolutionary model. In M. Hunter (Ed.), *The sexually abused male: Vol. 1. Prevalence, impact, and treatment* (pp. 73-85). Lexington, MA: Lexington.

Serrill, M. S. (1974, November-December). Treating sex offenders in New Jersey. *Corrections Magazine,* pp. 13-24.

Sgroi, S. M. (1975). Child sexual molestation: The last frontier in child abuse. *Children Today, 44,* 18-21.

Shengold, L. (1980). Some reflections on a case of mother/adolescent son incest. *International Journal of Psychoanalysis, 61,* 461-475.

Showers, J., Farber, E. D., Joseph, J. A., Oshins, L., & Johnson, C. F. (1983). The sexual victimization of boys: A three-year survey. *Health Values, 7,* 15-18.

Shrier, D. K., & Johnson, R. L. (1988). Sexual victimization of boys: An ongoing study of an adolescent medicine clinic population. *Journal of the National Medical Association, 80,* 1189-1193.

Simari, C. G., & Baskin, D. (1982). Incestuous experiences within homosexual populations: A preliminary study. *Archives of Sexual Behavior, 11,* 329-344.

Spencer, M. J., & Dunklee, P. (1986). Sexual abuse of boys. *Pediatrics, 78,* 133-137.

Steele, B., & Alexander, H. (1981). Long-term effects of sexual abuse in childhood. In P. B. Mrazek & C. H. Kempe (Eds.), *Sexually abused children and their families* (pp. 223-234). Oxford: Pergamon.

Stein, J. A., Golding, J. M., Siegel, J. M., Burnam, M. A., & Sorenson, S. B. (1988). Long-term psychological sequelae of child sexual abuse: The Los Angeles Epidemiologic Catchment Area Study. In G. E. Wyatt & G. J. Powell (Eds.), *Lasting effects of child sexual abuse* (pp. 135-154). Newbury Park, CA: Sage.

Struve, J. (1990). Dancing with the patriarchy: The politics of sexual abuse. In M. Hunter (Ed.), *The sexually abused male: Vol. 1. Prevalence, impact, and treatment* (pp. 3-46). Lexington, MA: Lexington.

Swift, C. (1979). Sexual victimization of children: An urban mental health survey. In L. Schultz (Ed.), *The sexual victimology of youth* (pp. 18-24). Springfield, IL: Charles C Thomas.

Summit, R. (1983). The child sexual abuse accommodation syndrome. *Child Abuse & Neglect, 7,* 177-193.

Swaab, D. F., & Hofman, M. A. (1990). An enlarged suprachiasmatic nucleus in homosexual men. *Brain Research, 537,* 141-148.

Swett, C., Jr., Surrey, J., & Cohen, C. (1990). Sexual and physical abuse histories and psychiatric symptoms among male psychiatric outpatients. *American Journal of Psychiatry, 147,* 632-636.

Symonds, C. L., Mendoza, M. J., & Harrell, W. C. (1980). Forbidden sexual behavior among kin: A study of self-selected respondents. In L. L. Constantine & F. M.

Martinson (Eds.), *Children and sex: New findings, new perspectives* (pp. 217-244). Boston: Little, Brown.

Thomas, T. (1989). *Men surviving incest.* Walnut Creek, CA: Launch Press.

Tobias, J. L., & Gordon, T. (1977). *Special projects: Operation LURE,* pp. 3-4. Oakland, CA: Oakland County Homicide Task Force.

Trivelpiece, J. W. (1990). Adjusting the frame: Cinematic treatment of sexual abuse and rape of men and boys. In M. Hunter (Ed.), *The sexually abused male: Vol. 1. Prevalence, impact, and treatment* (pp. 47-72). Lexington, MA: Lexington.

Tsai, M., Feldman-Summers, S., & Edgar, M. (1979). Childhood molestation: Variables related to differential functioning in adult women. *Journal of Abnormal Psychology, 88,* 407-417.

Tufts' New England Medical Center, Division of Child Psychiatry. (1984). *Sexually exploited children: Service and research project: Final report.* Washington, DC: U.S. Department of Justice, Office of Juvenile Justice and Delinquency Prevention.

Urquiza, A. J. (1988). *The effects of childhood sexual abuse in an adult male population.* Unpublished doctoral dissertation, Washington University, Seattle.

Urquiza, A. J. (1993, August). *Adult male survivors of child sexual abuse: Issues in intimacy.* Paper presented at the 101st annual convention of the American Psychological Association, Toronto, Ontario.

Urquiza, A. J., & Capra, M. (1990). The impact of sexual abuse: Initial and long-term effects. In M. Hunter (Ed.), *The sexually abused male: Vol. 1. Prevalence, impact, and treatment* (pp. 105-136). Lexington, MA: Lexington.

Urquiza, A. J., & Crowley, C. (1986, May). *Sex differences in the long-term adjustment of child sexual abuse victims.* Paper presented at the Third National Conference on the Sexual Victimization of Children, New Orleans, LA.

Urquiza, A. J., & Keating, L. M. (1990). The prevalence of sexual victimization of males. In M. Hunter (Ed.), *The sexually abused male: Vol. 1. Prevalence, impact, and treatment* (pp. 89-104). Lexington, MA: Lexington.

Vander Mey, B. J. (1988). The sexual victimization of male children: A review of previous research. *Child Abuse & Neglect, 12,* 61-72.

Vander Mey, B. J. (1990, November). *Comparing boy and girl sexual abuse victims: Before and after the revolution.* Workshop presented at the Third National Conference on The Male Survivor, Tucson, AZ.

Vander Mey, B. J., & Neff, R. L. (1982). Adult-child incest: A review of research and treatment. *Adolescence, 17,* 717-735.

Violato, C., & Genuis, M. (1993). Problems of research in male child sexual abuse: A review. *Journal of Child Sexual Abuse, 2,* 33-54.

Weinberg, S. K. (1955). *Incest behavior.* New York: Citadel.

Whitfield, C. L. (1987). *Healing the child within: Discovery and recovery for adult children of dysfunctional families.* Pompano Beach, FL: Health Communications.

Williams, L. (1992, Summer). Adult memories of childhood abuse: Preliminary findings from a longitudinal study. *The Advisor* [American Professional Society on the Abuse of Children], pp. 19-21.

Williams, M. B. (1991). Post-traumatic stress disorder and child sexual abuse: The enduring effects (Doctoral dissertation, Fielding Institute, Santa Barbara, CA). *Dissertation Abstracts International, 52*(4-B), 2320.

Wolfe, F. A. (1987, March). *Twelve female sexual offenders.* Paper presented at Next Steps in Research on the Assessment and Treatment of Sexually Aggressive Persons (Paraphiliacs) Conference, St. Louis, MO.

Wood, B. (1987). *Children of alcoholism.* New York: New York University Press.

Woods, S. C., & Dean, K. S. (1984). *Final report: Sexual abuse of males research project* (90 CA/812). Washington, DC: National Center on Child Abuse & Neglect.

Wyatt, G. (1985). The sexual abuse of Afro-American and white American women in childhood. *Child Abuse & Neglect, 9,* 231-240.

Wyatt, G. E., & Peters, S. D. (1986a). Methodological considerations in research on the prevalence of child sexual abuse. *Child Abuse & Neglect, 10,* 241-251.

Wyatt, G. E., & Peters, S. D. (1986b). Issues in the definition of child sexual abuse in prevalence research. *Child Abuse & Neglect, 10,* 231-240.

Yeary, J. (1982). Incest and chemical dependency. *Journal of Psychoactive Drugs, 14,* 133-135.

Zaphiris, A. (1986). The sexually abused boy. *Preventing Sexual Abuse, 1,* 1-4.

Index

231

About the Author

NATIONAL UNIVERSITY
LIBRARY

Matthew Parynik Mendel, Ph.D., is a clinical psychologist specializing in work with children and families. He received his advanced baccalaureate degree from Princeton University in 1984 and his doctorate in Clinical Psychology from the University of Michigan in 1992. He now works with Psychological Health Systems, P.C., and has a private practice in Lansing, MI. He is a Visiting Assistant Professor at Michigan State University, where he supervises the clinical work of child and family track clinical psychology doctoral students.

Dr. Mendel has a primary focus in work with individuals and families who have undergone trauma or extreme stress. He has worked with groups of children whose parents have divorced and with groups of children who have lost a parent, and has published in each of those areas. He has also worked extensively with victims and survivors of child abuse. He facilitated a self-help group for adult male survivors of childhood sexual abuse. He was the psychologist at the Family Assessment Clinic, an interdisciplinary team at the University of Michigan that provided assessments of families in which allegations of child abuse or neglect had been made. He was a member of the Interdisciplinary Project on Child Abuse and Neglect at the University of Michigan.